CORRESPONDENCE

BETWEEN

THE DEPARTMENT OF STATE

AND

THE UNITED STATES MINISTER AT MADRID,

AND THE

CONSULAR REPRESENTATIVES OF THE UNITED STATES IN THE ISLAND OF CUBA,

AND

OTHER PAPERS RELATING TO CUBAN AFFAIRS,

TRANSMITTED TO

THE HOUSE OF REPRESENTATIVES IN OBEDIENCE TO A RESOLUTION.

WASHINGTON
GOVERNMENT PRINTING OFFICE.
1870.

41st Congress, 2d Session. } HOUSE OF REPRESENTATIVES. { Ex. Doc. No. 160.

STRUGGLE FOR INDEPENDENCE IN THE ISLAND OF CUBA.

MESSAGE

FROM THE

PRESIDENT OF THE UNITED STATES

IN ANSWER TO

A resolution of the House of 7th instant, transmitting correspondence relative to the struggle for freedom in the Island of Cuba.

February 22, 1870.—Referred to the Committee on Foreign Affairs and ordered to be printed.

To the House of Representatives:

I transmit to the House of Representatives, in answer to their resolution of the 7th instant, a report from the Secretary of State, with accompanying documents.

U. S. GRANT.

Washington, *February* 21, 1870.

Department of State,
Washington, February 21, 1870.

The Secretary of State, to whom was referred the resolution of the House of Representatives of the 7th instant, requesting the President, "if not incompatible with the public interest, to communicate to this House so much of the correspondence between our government and the government of Spain, and between the United States legation at Madrid and the Department of State, as relates to affairs connected with the island of Cuba; and also [under like reservation] such information as may be in his possession in reference to the present struggle for independence in that island," has the honor to lay before the President the following papers, numbered and specified as in the accompanying synoptical list, viz:

I. Extracts from late correspondence between this department and the legation of the United States at Madrid, contained in numbers 1 to 46 inclusive.

II. Printed extracts from late correspondence between this department and the Spanish minister accredited to this government, (Mr. Lopez Roberts,) and between this department and several diplomatic and consular representatives of the United States, and other printed papers, which were transmitted to the Senate by the President on the 20th of

December last, in answer to their resolution of the 8th of December, and which are numbered in the synoptical list numbers 47 to 121 inclusive.

III. Extracts from the correspondence between this department and the following consular representatives of the United States:

Mr. La Reintrie, who performed consular duties at Havana until March 4, 1869.

Mr. Hall, consul at Matanzas, transferred temporarily to Havana, December 1, 1869.

Mr. Phillips, acting vice-consul at Santiago de Cuba.

These several extracts are numbered from 122 to 129 inclusive, in the synoptical list.

Respectfully submitted.

HAMILTON FISH.

The PRESIDENT.

SYNOPTICAL LIST OF PAPERS.

I.—EXTRACTS FROM THE CORRESPONDENCE BETWEEN THE DEPARTMENT OF STATE AND THE LEGATION OF THE UNITED STATES AT MADRID.

No.	From whom and to whom.	Date.	Subject.	Page.
1	Mr. Fish to Gen. Sickles.	June 19, 1869, No. 2.	The insurrection in Cuba is causing great devastation, and will result, if continued, in the destruction of the productive capacity of the island. Reasons why the United States have a peculiar interest in the fortunes and prosperity of the island. Contest one for self-government and freedom. Self-government for every part of the American hemisphere and freedom from transatlantic rule a growing sentiment in the United States. This has been recognized by other powers. Spain may, with honor, recognize it, and treat for the surrender of her rights in Cuba. General Sickles instructed to offer good offices of United States to terminate civil war on the basis of independence; the payment of an equivalent to Spain by Cuba; abolition of slavery, and armistice pending negotiations; negotiations to be conducted at Washington. This dispatch to be read, at earliest opportunity, to minister, and copy left with him.	13
2	......do	June 19, 1869, No. 3.	If, in tendering good offices under previous instructions, the use of the term "civil war" be objected to, say that it has been used advisedly. Should the offer be refused, and should the condition of parties not be changed, the United States may be forced to recognize a condition of belligerency. Cautioned to observe delicacy on this point, so as not to wound sensibilities of government, ministers, or people of Spain. May receive propositions concerning Porto Rico, if Spain makes them. Mr. Paul Forbes will meet General Sickles in Madrid and advise with him in these negotiations.	16
3	Gen. Sickles to Mr. Davis.	July 27, 1869, Telegram.	His arrival and presentation. Favorable appearance of things.	17
4	Mr. Fish to Gen. Sickles.	July 29, 1869, Telegram.	Early decision important. No protection of life of our citizens in Cuba. Do not connect Cuba and Porto Rico in negotiations.	18
5	Gen. Sickles to Mr. Fish.	July 31, 1869, Telegram.	Good offices offered. Discussion limited by minister to overture. See Prim to-morrow.	18
6	......do	Aug. 1, 1869, Telegram.	Basis communicated to Prim. He asked how much Cuba and Porto Rico would give. Answered, no instructions; suggested $125,000,000. Prim said preliminaries might be arranged after cessation of hostilities.	18
7	......do	Aug. 6, 1869	Illness of secretary of state has delayed answer	18
8	......do	Aug. 12, 1869	Interview with Mr. Silvela, July 31. (See No. 5, above.) Informal offer of good offices. Minister replies, acknowledging fidelity of United States in fulfilling their international obligations. Spain grateful therefor. When pro-slavery party in power there was danger of trouble from recklessness of filibusters. Since victory of national cause the liberal people of Spain regard United States as their national friend. The Spanish liberals, who executed the Spanish revolution, desire to give liberal institutions to Cuba, but the fatality of the situation makes it impossible while the insurrection continues. Would be gratified at a settlement that would not infringe upon the honor of Spain. Will report conversation to his colleagues.	19
9	......do	Aug. 12, 1869	Interview with General Prim. (See No. 6, above.) Propositions of the United States already communicated to General Prim by Mr. Forbes. General Prim answered, that armistice would not be granted, nor would Spain consider question of independence while insurgents were in arms; full amnesty will be granted when insurgents lay down arms. Question of emancipation would be left to Cubans. Conference at Washington not favored. Cuba would be heard through her deputies in the Cortes. Spain would treat only with United States. Subject would be brought before council.	21
10	......do	Aug. 13, 1869, Telegram.	General Prim authorizes General Sickles to say that good offices are accepted. Spain suggests for basis—1. Arms to be laid down by insurgents. 2. Simultaneous amnesty. 3. Popular vote in Cuba on independence. 4. Independence granted by Spain through Cortes on receipt of indemnity guaranteed by United States.	22

Synoptical list of papers—Continued.

No.	From whom and to whom.	Date.	Subject.	Page.
11	Gen. Sickles to Mr. Fish.	Aug. 14, 1869, No. 6.	Transmits an account of an interview with Mr. Silvela, and a copy of article 108 of the Spanish constitution. Mr. Silvela regards the proposition of the United States as conflicting with article 108. He expresses the views of the administration. General Sickles expresses his regret, and fears that the complications will soon be beyond control. General Prim is in advance of his colleagues.	22
12	Mr. Fish to Gen. Sickles.	Aug. 16, 1869, Telegram.	Spanish propositions to insurgents to lay down arms, and to Cubans to vote, impracticable. Urge acceptance of United States propositions.	25
13	Gen. Sickles to Mr. Fish.	Aug. 16, 1869, No. 8.	Details of interview with General Prim. (See No. 10, above.) General Prim says his colleagues do not realize difficulty of carrying on war in America. He would say to Cuba, "Make good the treasure you have cost and go." Defiant attitude of insurgents the great difficulty. No power can obtain concessions from Spanish people while the rebellion maintains its footing. General Sickles combats these views. The telegram of the 13th submitted to the council and approved by them.	25
14	......do...	Aug. 20, 1869, No. 9.	Interview with General Prim. Communicates views in Mr. Fish's telegram. (See No. 12, above.) General Prim says cessation of hostilities not a preliminary to negotiations with United States, but no treaty can be made while insurgents in arms. He recognizes inevitable termination of colonial relations in America, but Spain cannot be reconciled to that till hostilities cease. General Sickles replies that Spain is not asked to treat with insurgents, but with a friendly power and old ally. Prim replies that United States may be assured of good faith of Spain, but that insurrection has not assumed proportions which can require a government to treat during hostilities. The insurgents hold no port or ships, and have no army that offers or accepts battle. General Sickles thinks that General Prim wishes to come to an agreement with United States, and will not object to independence of Cuba.	27
15	......do.........	Aug. 20, 1869, Telegram.	Account of same interview. Armistice impossible. Emancipation cannot be separated from other questions. Communication with insurgents will be permitted after agreement with United States.	28
16	......do.........	Aug. 21, 1869, No. 10.	A further account of the same interview. General Prim's views stated more at length. He proposes—1. Settlement of basis of agreement. 2. United States to counsel its acceptance by Cubans. 3. Cessation of hostilities and amnesty. 4. Election of deputies. 5. Action of the Cortes. 6. Plebiscit and independence. General Sickles thinks that the Spanish cabinet are sincere in their desire to make an arrangement with the United States.	29
17	Mr. Fish to Gen. Sickles.	Aug. 24, 1869, Telegram.	Propositions of Spain are impracticable. Representatives of the insurgent government are necessary parties to negotiation. If insurgents are disarmed, volunteers should be disarmed and disbanded. An armistice will prevent destruction of life, property, and outrages upon American citizens, and make opportunity to settle terms of compensation to be made to Spain by Cuba. Spain may, in honor, grant armistice, which is indispensable to success of negotiation.	31
18	Gen. Sickles to Mr. Fish.	Aug. 24, 1869, No. 12.	Spanish journals speak of insurrection as likely to be successful. Discussion stimulated by agents of Americans who have undertaken to purchase Cuba as a private enterprise. Minister of finance well disposed to separation. Less susceptibility to a transfer to the United States than to independence.	31
19	Mr. Fish to Gen. Sickles.	Sept. 1, 1869, Telegram.	United States propose for basis—1. Armistice. 2. Payment by Cuba for public property taken. No guarantee by United States without approval by Congress. 3. Persons and property of Spaniards in Cuba to be protected. Offers to be withdrawn if not accepted before October 1.	32
20	Gen. Sickles to Mr. Fish.	Sept. 4, 1869, Telegram.	Has communicated formally propositions and asked for early and decisive answer. Spanish government solicitous as to gunboats.	32
21	......do.........	Sept. 5, 1869, No. 14.	Transmits copy of General Sickles's formal note to Mr. Becerra with the propositions of the United States. Mr. Becerra remonstrates against detention of gunboats. General Sickles replies that he has no instructions on the subject. Mr. Becerra agrees with General Prim as to the future of Cuba, but Spain cannot with honor treat with insurgents with arms in their hands. General Sickles's note to Mr. Becerra, dated September 3, recapitulates previous negotiations, presents the considerations contained in Mr. Fish's instructions, (See No. 1;) also the propositions of the United States; says that the time is approach-	33

Synoptical list of papers—Continued.

No.	From whom and to whom.	Date.	Subject.	Page.
21	Gen. Sickles to Mr. Fish—Con.	Sept. 5, 1869, No. 14.	ing when the recognition of the parties as belligerents cannot be delayed, and asks to be informed as soon as possible of the decision of the Spanish government.	
22	Gen. Sickles to Mr. Fish.	Sept. 8, 1869, No. 15.	Incloses his note to Mr. Becerra in relation to Charles Speakman and Albert Wyeth, executed at Santiago de Cuba. A protest against such deplorable excesses. Spanish government having allowed the purport of Mr. Sickles's note tendering good offices to get out, it has been accepted as indicating the purpose of United States to recognize the Cubans as belligerents if the mediation of the United States be refused. Excitement resulting from this announcement and its effect on public opinion. Communication by letter with General Prim in regard to the urgency of the subject. Political situation and reason for unfriendly tone of monarchical journals in Spain; this tone not shared by republicans.	36
23	Mr. Fish to Gen. Sickles.	Sept. 11, 1869, Telegram.	Hopes there is no truth in rumor that Spain is about to send more troops to Cuba.	37
24	Gen. Sickles to Mr. Fish.	Sept. 14, 1869, Telegram.	Additional troops will go. Great excitement. General belief that United States will soon acknowledge state of belligerency.	37
25	......do	Sept. 14, 1869, No. 17.	Interview with Mr. Becerra. He denies that Spain has opened negotiations with European powers on the subject of Mr. Sickles's note of 3d September. Says government cannot act on it before the meeting of the Cortes. States in reply to expression of regret, that Spain sends more troops to Cuba. That Cuban question is a domestic one, and that Spain must restore order in Cuba by force of arms. She will also extend to the island the reforms enjoyed in the peninsula; an amnesty will be granted, preparations made for election of deputies in Cuba, whose advice will be sought in future reforms, including abolition of slavery. Spain accepts good offices but not the bases proposed by United States. Mediation incompatible with the honor of Spain. Permanent committee of Cortes voted unanimously that independence of Cuba was inadmissible as a basis of negotiation. Any alienation of Spanish territory, without consent of Cortes, would be unconstitutional. Withdrawal of Mr. Sickles's note of 3d of September, is requested. Difficulties in the way of an armistice. Captain General has been requested to report in relation to execution of Speakman and Wyeth, and if facts proved as alleged, reparation will be made and such cruelty in future prevented. These are believed to be the views of the Spanish cabinet.	38
26	Mr. Fish to Gen. Sickles.	Sept. 15, 1869, Telegram.	If negotiation on basis of six successive steps, omitting plebiscit, were opened, can United States be assured that if insurgents lay down arms and elect deputies, Cortes will recognize independence of Cuba? Doubtful whether fair vote can be obtained in island or whether insurgents will lay down arms unless independence be assured.	41
27	Gen. Sickles to Mr. Fish.	Sept. 16, 1869, Telegram.	Account of same interview described in No. 25, above	41
28	......do	Sept. 17, 1869, Telegram.	Mr. Fish's dispatch of 15th received. General Prim expected soon. Asks further information as to gunboats and recognition of belligerency.	42
29	......do	Sept. 19, 1869, No. 19.	Spanish temper such that General Sickles has not thought wise to say that he was authorized to withdraw offers of good offices, nor to make new suggestions. Incloses plans for reforms in Porto Rico, including abolition of slavery. Cruel manner in which war is carried on is denounced by president of Cortes and by General Concha.	42
30	Mr. Fish to Gen. Sickles.	Sept. 23, 1869, Telegram.	May withdraw offer of good offices, if not acceptable to Spain. Gunboats detained at request of Peru. No steps yet taken toward recognition of belligerency. Will be recognized when necessities of the case and complications of controversy force it upon us.	46
31	Gen. Sickles to Mr. Fish.	Sept. 25, 1869, No. 21.	The reasons for his course in addressing a formal offer of good offices to the Spanish goverment.	47
32	......do	Sept. 25, 1869, No. 22.	Interviews with Mr. Silvela on the 23d, and with General Prim. Mr. Silvela spoke of an expedition from Cedar Keys. General Sickles claimed that the United States had done their whole duty as neutrals. Mr. Silvela admitted that they had, notwithstanding the escape of the expedition. Mr. Silvela complains of the detention of the gunboats. General Sickles has no instructions on the subject. General Prim thinks that the excitement has advanced public opinion upon the subject of Cuba. Reiterates the necessity of settling the question in harmony with Spanish constitution. Orders have been given Captain General to disarm volunteers, and to stop scandalous executions.	48

Synoptical list of papers—Continued.

No.	From whom and to whom.	Date.	Subject.	Page.
32	Gen. Sickles to Mr. Fish—Con.	Sept. 25, 1869. No. 22.	He reiterates assurances that liberal reforms shall be granted. He complains of detention of gunboats. General Sickles explains that it is done at request of Peru. General Prim says Spain is not at war with Peru. General Sickles says he is authorized to withdraw the offer of good offices; before doing so, wishes to know if any modification that can be made by United States will be acceptable to Spain. General Prim thinks not; prefers the withdrawal; thinks the time will soon come when Spain will desire good offices of United States, and will then indicate bases. General Sickles said he should withdraw the offer.	
33	Gen. Sickles to Mr. Fish.	Sept. 29, 1869, No. 23.	Transmitting copies of telegrams relating to foregoing interviews.	52
34	Mr. Fish to Gen. Sickles.	Oct. 12, 1869 No. 10,	Reasons for the detention of the Spanish gunboats..........	53
35	Gen. Sickles to Mr. Fish.	Oct. 16, 1869, No. 26.	Transmitting a copy of General Sickles's official note withdrawing the offer of the good offices of the United States; and also a copy of Mr. Silvela's reply to that note.	56
36	......do	Oct. 16, 1869, No. 27.	Same subject. Mr. Silvela's original reply to General Sickles's note withdrawing the offer of good offices regarded the note itself as withdrawn. General Sickles refused to receive such a note, and the reply was so modified as to state that the offer of good offices was withdrawn.	58
37	......do	Nov. 3, 1869, No. 31.	Ministerial changes. Spanish politics. Commission for reforms in Porto Rico dissolved. Reasons given therefor. Cuban question not mentioned in Cortes. Troops continue to be sent to Havana.	59
38	......do	Nov. 14, 1869, No. 33.	Reforms in Porto Rico	60
39	......do	Nov. 17, 1869, No. 34.	General Sickles dines with the president of the Cortes. Meets secretaries of state and of the colonies, Mr. Silvela, and others. Mr. Martos, Mr. Becerra, and Mr. Rivos, each said the remarks to General Sickles were to be considered official as well as personal. He therefore reports them. It was said that Spain desired intimate relations with United States; would extend free institutions to Cuba; that Cubans were prepared for free institutions; that the government had been asked to order immediate elections for Cortes in Cuba, but had refused because the native population could not participate; that the Cuban question could not be considered in Cortes while Cuba was in rebellion; but that the government were prepared to recommend the largest liberties. General Sickles urged the immediate promulgation of their plan as the best way to terminate hostilities. In reply, they said the war would soon be ended. The propriety of an armistice was discussed; it was regarded as impracticable. They stated that the Cuban question will be settled when war is ended on bases of self-government and commercial reciprocity, and that slavery will be gradually abolished. The native Cubans were a majority of the inhabitants, and their wishes ought to be respected in the determination which the government should make. They desire the President to know that Spain is no longer governed by reactionary and antiquated ideas of the Bourbons.	61
40	......do	Dec. 3, 1869, No. 37.	Inclosing telegrams concerning reforms in Porto Rico, and concerning gunboats.	63
41	......do	Dec. 5, 1869, No. 38.	Total number of Spanish troops in Cuba..........................	64
42	......do	Dec. 29, 1869, No. 46.	Transmitting further statements as to the "army of Cuba." Anxiety in Spain as to the course of the United States. Winter campaign regarded as a failure. Despondency apparent in all except official circles. Views of the press. British minister instructed to second General Sickles's efforts to secure abolition of slavery. He replies that what he had said was unofficial and so understood by the cabinet. Changes in Porto Rico to include abolition of slavery. This may decrease in Cuba the resistance to independence.	66
43	Mr. Fish to Gen. Sickles.	Dec. 30, 1869, No. 20.	Satisfaction at news of reforms in Spanish colonial policy contained in General Sickles's No. 36. (See No. 39, above.)	68
44	......do	Jan. 7, 1870, No. 22.	It is stated by Mr. Lopez Roberts that only persons imprisoned for political offenses are enlisted for service in Cuba. No ordinary criminals are so enlisted.	68
45	Gen. Sickles to Mr. Fish.	Jan. 9, 1870, Telegram.	Sees no objection to the publication of all his correspondence. Prefers it should all be communicated.	69
46	Mr. Fish to Gen. Sickles.	Jan. 26, 1870, No. 26.	Public interest in Cuban affairs decreased since flagrant violations of law by insurgents. Instructed to report opinion at Madrid as to campaign in Cuba. This government has maintained its freedom of action against great pressure. Its action will be governed by facts as they	69

Synoptical list of papers—Continued.

No.	From whom and to whom.	Date.	Subject.	Page.
46	Mr. Fish to Gen. Sickles—Con.	Jan. 26, 1870, No. 26.	occur. President reserves complete liberty of action in case Spain fails to restore peace. This department insists upon the abolition of slavery. It regards the government of Madrid as committed to that.	

II.—CORRESPONDENCE AND PAPERS TRANSMITTED TO THE SENATE DECEMBER 20, 1869.

No.	From whom and to whom.	Date.	Subject.	Page.
47	Mr. Hall to Mr. Seward.	Nov. 18, 1868, No. 82.	Quotes the views of a conservative Cuban, viz: News of Spanish revolution enthusiastically received in Cuba. Views of Cubans as to slavery are diverse—some desire immediate abolition of it; some gradual; some its continuance. The insurrection in the eastern and central departments is formidable. Mr. Hall adds that good order prevails in his department.	70
48	......do	Dec. 17, 1868, No. 83.	Insurrection gaining strength. Condition at Matanzas. General distrust and paralysis.	72
49	......do	Feb. 25, 1869, No. 89.	Transmitting letter from consular agent at Sagua la Grande. State of things there much exaggerated. Details of movements.	73
50	Mr. Hall to Mr. Washburne.	Mar. 11, 1869, No. 4.	Transmitting what purports to be a decree of the insurgents' assembly abolishing slavery.	74
51	Mr. Hall to Mr. Hunter.	Mar. 27, 1869, No. 17.	Transmitting decree of Captain General authorizing capture on the high seas of vessels carrying men, arms, munitions, or effects in aid of insurgents, and directing execution as pirates of persons so captured.	74
52	Mr. Fish to Mr. Lopez Roberts.	Apr. 3, 1869	Calling attention to Captain General's decree of March 24, and informing him that United States citizens have the right to carry on the high seas articles destined for the enemies of Spain, subject to seizure of such as may be contraband of war, or to capture for violation of a lawfully established blockade. Persistence in the decree will endanger friendly relations.	75
53	Mr. Hall to Mr. Fish.	Apr. 2, 1869, No. 22.	Transmitting letter from Remedios, and saying that majority of American merchants agree with the writer, who states that American-born citizens are well treated by the Spanish authorities, do not favor the insurrection, and think it cannot succeed.	76
54	Mr. Lopez Roberts to Mr. Fish.	Apr. 5, 1869	Attempts are made by false and exaggerated statements and public meetings to create sentiment in favor of Cuba. Persons in New York style themselves "the independent government of Cuba," and dispatch expeditions and arms in aid of the insurgents. He asks for a proclamation similar to that issued by Mr. Fillmore April 5, 1851.	76
55	Mr. Fish to Mr. Lopez Roberts.	Apr. 17, 1869	Does not perceive the necessity or propriety of issuing such proclamation. When Mr. Fillmore's proclamation was issued peace prevailed in Cuba, but an armed invasion was threatened from the United States. Now a portion of the people of Cuba are in insurrection to redress alleged wrongs, and no expeditions are leaving the United States. Mr. Roberts admits that whenever called upon the officers of the United States have interfered effectively to prevent violation of law. United States still suffering from effects of precipitate recognition of belligerent rights, and will not depart from their traditional policy. The sympathy of the United States is with people striving to secure right of self-government, and with all efforts to free this continent from transatlantic control, but they desire to maintain friendly relations with governments still claiming control over neighboring possessions. They will not abridge the right of free discussion, but will limit their interference to preventing unlawful acts in infraction of their obligations to Spain and other friendly powers.	79
56	Mr. Hall to Mr. Fish.	Apr. 22, 1869, No. 33.	Transmitting decree of April 1, 1869, prohibiting alienation of property except with the assent of the government.	81
57	Mr. Fish to Mr. Lopez Roberts.	Apr. 30. 1869	The President has seen with regret the decree of April 1, forbidding alienation of property in Cuba. Hopes it may be modified so as not to be applicable to property of citizens of the United States.	82
58	Mr. Hall to Mr. Fish.	Apr. 30, 1869, No. 37.	Transmitting Count Valmaseda's proclamation of April 4, that every man over fifteen years of age found away from home may be shot; that every unoccupied house and every house not flying a white flag may be burned; and that women not living at home or with their relatives may be carried forcibly to Jiguani or Bayamo; also informing the department that Count Valmaseda was moving his forces into the country.	84

Synoptical list of papers—Continued.

Synoptical list of papers—Continued.

No.	From whom and to whom.	Date.	Subject.	Page.
77	Mr. Fish to Mr. Lopez Roberts.—Continued.	July 16, 1869	States. Mr. Fish asks whether Spain recognizes a state of war as existing, and states that a continuance of the decree or any attempt to enforce it will be regarded as a recognition by Spain of a state of war with Cuba.	
78	Mr. Plumb to Mr. Fish.	July 21, 1869, No. 83.	Transmitting modifications of Captain General's decree of July 7, as to search of vessels on the high seas.	116
79	......do	July 13, 1869, No. 75.	Transmitting general order of the Captain General for conduct of the war with more humanity.	117
80	Gen. Sickles to Mr. Fish.	Aug. 12, 1869, No. 4.	Conversation with Spanish minister, in which he states the wish of the liberal party in Spain to confer upon Cuba free institutions; the insurrection, unfortunately, prevented it.	118
81	Mr. Plumb to Mr. Davis.	Aug. 18, 1869, No. 115.	The accounts in the United States favorable to the insurrection are exaggerated.	119
82	Gen. Sickles to Mr. Fish.	Aug. 14, 1869, No. 6.	Incloses article 108 of Spanish constitution about Cuba. Mr. Silvela regards it as preventing action upon Cuba till Cuban deputies arrive at the Cortes.	119
83	......do	Aug. 20, 1869, No. 9.	General Prim states to Mr. Sickles that Cuban insurgents hold no city or fortress, port or ships, and have no army that offers battle.	120
84	......do	Aug. 21, 1869, No. 10.	Reasons why General Prim thinks the Cuban insurgents are not in a condition to negotiate.	120
85	......de	Aug. 24, 1869, No. 12.	Spain more willing to transfer Cuba to the United States than to concede independence.	121
86	Mr. Plumb to Mr. Davis.	Aug. 21, 1869, No. 119.	Transmitting information about the murder of twenty prominent citizens of Santiago de Cuba at Jiguani.	121
87	......do	Aug. 24, 1869, No. 123.	Same subject..	123
88	......do	Aug. 26, 1869, No. 127.	With abstracts of the several decrees for the embargo of property.	124
89	......do	Aug. 27, 1869, No. 129.	The insurgents have resolved upon a general destruction of property, and especially the destruction of sugar estates. This will entail great loss on citizens of the United States.	126
90	......do	Aug. 31, 1869, No. 135.	Transmitting a decree said to have been issued by the insurgents on the 4th May, 1869, for the conduct of the war.	127
91	......do	Sept. 1, 1869, No. 139.	Transmitting communication from consular agent at Manzanillo as to affairs in that quarter, and murders at Santiago de Cuba.	129
92	Mr. Roberts to Mr. Fish.	Sept. 18, 1869,	Belligerent rights to the Cubans. The United States are apparently on the eve of granting them. The doctrine as always held by the United States, and set forth by Mr. C. F. Adams and Mr. Sumner, stated. Mr. R. H. Dana quoted. Cubans have no ships, ports, or prize courts. Their army a band roaming in the eastern department. Policy of Spain in 1861 compared with what Mr. Roberts imagines to be the contemplated policy of the United States. Mr. Perry and Mr. Schurz cited. Malcontent Cubans in the United States have organized attacks on Spain; have enlisted men, emigrants even. Expeditions have openly left New York without interference, and Mr. Roberts has been obliged, by apathy of authorities, to initiate proceedings. Extravagant demonstrations in the country echoed by the press. Cuban emissaries have boasted of private official information. In this connection Mr. Roberts quotes from Mr. Dallas. Why do Cuban agents ask recognition? Because they need aid of the United States. Quotes again from Mr. Adams.	130
93	Mr. Fish to Mr. Lopez Roberts.	Oct. 13, 1869	Mr. Roberts's letter of September 18 not received till September 25, on which day Mr. Fish left Washington on temporary absence. Might be sufficient answer to say that no intention to grant belligerent rights has been announced. More perfect answer to say that no such intention has been reached by the United States. Mr. Fish pleased that Mr. Roberts draws his authorities from the history and statesmen of the United States. Mr. Roberts has contrasted the course of Spain in 1861 with that of the United States, and says that Spain could not do otherwise than she did by reason of her geographical position. Spain conceded belligerency to the South sixty-six days after assault on Sumter—a bloodless combat. Mr. Fish admits the weight of the argument from geographical position. The geographical position of Cuba considered, also the prolongation of the contest, the number of combats, the number of the killed, position of parties in Cuba as compared with parties in the United States in 1861. Riquelme quoted to prove that foreign intervention may be made in interest of humanity. The United States have frequently remonstrated in this interest against the manner in which this contest is waged. The United States have hitherto acted on their well-established policy. The present state cannot be in-	135

Synoptical list of papers—Continued.

No.	From whom and to whom.	Date.	Subject.	Page.
93	Mr. Fisk to Mr. Lopez Roberts. —Continued.	Oct. 13, 1869	definitely prolonged. The United States reserve right of future action. Many of Mr. Roberts's complaints are founded upon misapprehension of spirit of our institutions. The United States offer an asylum to the oppressed, and give freedom of speech and of action, restricted only by observance of the rights of others and maintenance of public peace; within those bounds all may assemble—malcontent Cubans and subjects of Spain. Unlawful expeditions have been planned, and, in one case, did succeed without attracting notice; but the United States have always been ready (as Mr. Roberts was informed) to act on information furnished by him, and have acted on such information, even when it has proved erroneons.	
94	Gen. Sickles to Mr. Fish.	Sept. 19, 1869, No. 19.	Inclosing a decree for organization of commission for reforms in Porto Rico, including abolition of slavery. The cruel mode of warfare in Cuba will be early considered in the Cortes.	138
95	Mr. Plumb to Mr. Fish.	Sept. 16, 1869	Incloses a copy of the constitution of the Cuban republic....	142
96	......do	Sept. 20, 1869, No. 156.	Formation of the volunteer reserve corps. Time come for all to define positions.	143
97	Mr. Plumb to Mr. Fish.	Sept. 21, 1869, No. 159.	People of Havana begin to read newspapers and think upon current events. Ten thousand young men enrolled as volunteers in Havana, and daily read the papers. A sketch of the kind of reading thus furnished.	144
98	Gen. Sickles to Mr. Fish.	Sept. 25, 1869, No. 52.	General Prim does not intend to have re-enacted the scenes that took place under General Dulce. Orders given to prevent repetition of barbarities. General Sickles recommended cartels. General Prim said it was necessary to move cautiously.	145
99	......do	Sept. 25, 1869, Telegram.	Volunteers to be disbanded when hostilities cease. Scandalous executions to be stopped; slavery to be gradually abolished; liberal reforms to be granted without waiting for termination of war.	145
100	Mr. Davis to Mr. Plumb.	Sept. 28, 1869, No. 46.	Transmits substance of General Sickles's telegram, (*ante* 99,) and instructs him to inquire and report upon same.	146
101	Mr. Plumb to Mr. Davis.	Oct. 21, 1869, No. 193.	Does not think disarmament of volunteers practicable. Reasons why it is not. Sees no evidence of intention to cease hostilities before insurrection is suppressed. The rulers in Cuba wish well to island and desire to stop effusion of blood. General opinion that abolition should be gradual; none think it should be deferred over five years.	146
102	Mr. Plumb to Mr. Fish.	Sept. 27, 1869, No. 167.	Transmitting an account from Mr. Hall of the violent and illegal conduct of the volunteers at Matanzas, and a copy of a decree of the governor relating thereto.	149
103	Mr. Plumb to Mr. Davis.	Oct. 15, 1869, No. 181.	Transmitting copy of a decree of Captain General, dated September 28, 1869, concerning passenger vessels and passengers. Mr. Plumb objected to it and secured the modifications published October 13, of which copies are inclosed.	152
104	Mr. Fish to Mr. Plumb.	Oct. 25, 1869, No. 63.	Mr. Plumb instructed to protest against the decree and rules for enforcing same, contained in his number 181, (*ante*,) so far as concerns passenger vessels of the United States.	153
105	Mr. Plumb to Mr. Fish.	Nov. 17, 1869, No. 225.	The decree, (see *ante* 103 and 104,) not intended to refer to passengers in transit, will be modified.	154
106	......do	Nov. 20, 1869, No. 230.	Inclosing modification of decree as to passenger vessels. (*Ante* 105.)	155
107	Gen. Sickles to Mr. Fish.	Oct. 16, 1869, No. 26.	Transmitting copy of decree giving liberty of worship in Cuba. Also a copy of Mr. Silvela's note desiring the President to use his influence with Cuban refugees to secure less savage character to the war, and to release the Spanish gunboats, which are neither intended to operate against Peru or Cuba, but to defend the coast against the aggressions of filibusters and pirates.	155
108	Mr. Plumb to Mr. Davis.	Oct. 26, 1869, No. 195.	Inclosing copy of decree for freedom of worship.	156
109	......do	Oct. 26, 1869, No. 196.	A decree has been promulgated removing restrictions of formation of joint-stock companies.	158
110	Mr. Plumb to Mr. Fish.	Oct. 15, 1869, No. 183.	Sibamcá and Guaimaro—the former a hamlet, the latter a place of five hundred inhabitants—the only places occupied by the insurgents.	158
111	Mr. Plumb to Mr. Davis.	Nov. 2, 1869, No. 207.	Sibamcá and Guaimaro are both destroyed	158
112	......do	Nov. 2, 1869, No. 208.	Inclosing a circular inciting the negroes to burn the estates, forwarded by the consul at Matanzas, and said by him to have been "probably printed in New York."	159
113	......do	Nov. 4, 1869, No. 211.	As to the orders given by the insurgents for the burning of estates and cane-fields.	160
114	Gen. Sickles to Mr. Fish.	Nov. 3, 1869, No. 31.	Commission on reforms in Porto Rico has been dissolved....	160

Synoptical list of papers—Continued.

No.	From whom and to whom.	Date.	Subject.	Page.
115	Gen. Sickles to Mr. Fish.	Nov. 14, 1869, No. 33.	No reform for Cuba to be brought forward till hostile bands are dispersed. Incloses copies of speeches of the colonial minister on the 6th October and the 9th November.	161
116	......do	Nov. 25, 1869, No. 35.	Transmitting project of reforms for Porto Rico	162
117	......do	Nov. 28, 1869, Telegram.	Government programme for Porto Rico to include local self-government, free press, impartial suffrage, speedy abolition of slavery, equal civil and political rights without distinction of color, &c., to be extended to Cuba when hostilities cease.	163
118	......do	Dec. 3, 1869, Telegram.	Spain desires friendly relations with South American republics, and will begin liberal colonial reforms at once.	164
119	Mr. Lowrie to Mr. Fish.	Dec. 15, 1869	Had called upon the Attorney General in company with Mr. Evarts, and they had submitted affidavits; but the Attorney General had informed him they would be disregarded, as not furnishing good evidence, and had clearly stated the purpose of the government. He incloses the affidavits.	164
120	The Attorney General to Mr. Fish.	Dec. 16, 1869	The Attorney General thinks that it is not proper for the United States to cause a libel to be filed, under the third section of the statute of 1818, against the Spanish gun-boats, on the ground that they are procured to be fitted out and armed with intent that they shall be employed in the service of Spain, a foreign state, with intent to cruise or commit hostilities against the subjects, citizens, or property of a colony, district, or people with whom the United States are at peace—namely, a colony, district, or people claiming to be the republic of Cuba. He has so advised, and the government has acted on his advice.	164
121	....	....	The affidavits of Miguel de Aldama, J. M. Mestre, Emálo F. Cavado, William Clarence Tinker, Francis Coppinger, Enrique Leinaz, and Francis Xavier Cisneroś, submitted to the Attorney General by Mr. Grosvenor P. Lowrie and Mr. William M. Evarts, counsel for the Cubans, to establish the existence of a state of war and of an independent government in Cuba.	167

III.—CORRESPONDENCE BETWEEN THE DEPARTMENT OF STATE AND CONSULAR REPRESENTATIVES IN CUBA.

No.	From whom and to whom.	Date.	Subject.	Page.
122	Mr. La Reintrie to Mr. Seward.	Oct. 17, 1868, No. 105.	Rumors that the telegraphic wires beyond Puerto Principe have been cut, and that the insurgents are rising in various parts of the island. Movements on foot to proclaim independence. Slavery. Political situation of Spain a cause of discontent among Cubans. Fortifications being strengthened. Houses of persons suspected of republican proclivities searched. Recommends that a United States squadron be stationed in Cuban waters.	181
123	......do	Oct. 24, 1868, No. 107.	Excitement continues to increase. National guard called out. Strength of revolutionary forces. Interview with General Lersundi. The general desired to know if filibuster expeditions were likely to come from the United States. Rumors of an intended rising of republicans and negroes in the city. Commercial transactions affected by excitement. Requests presence of naval force. Political views of the two parties contending for political supremacy. Asks instructions for his guidance in case independence is declared.	182
124	......do	Dec. 14, 1868, No. 119.	Incloses communication from United States commercial agent at Nuevitas relative to events in that quarter. Reasons for the presence of a United States squadron in Cuban waters. Encounter between insurgents and volunteers. Two young men, insurgents, shot at Principe. Incidents attending the march to, and occupation of, San Miguel by Count Valmaseda. Feeling between Spaniards and Cubans. Progress of the insurgents.	183
125	......do	Jan. 29, 1869, No. 130.	Refers to murder of Mr. Samuel Alexander Cohner, a United States citizen. The assassin thought to be a volunteer. Dissatisfaction of volunteers at new system inaugurated by General Dulce. They roam about the city at will and utter threats of vengeance against all Cubans and foreigners who do not agree with them in political opinions. They surround a theater and fire upon the assembled audience. Their conduct severely condemned by the Captain General. Further violent demonstrations. The mansion of Mr. Delmonte y Aldama entered and ransacked. A protest addressed to him by United States	184

Synoptical list of papers—Continued.

No.	From whom and to whom.	Date.	Subject.	Page.
125	Mr. La Reintrie to Mr. Seward—Continued.	Jan. 29, 1869, No. 130.	citizens setting forth their complaints. Correspondence with the Captain General relative to the murder of Mr. Cohner unsatisfactory. Further appeal for a naval force. Threatened forcible removal of General Dulce from office. Requests instructions as to how far he can extend protection of United States in the case of Mr. Aldama.	
126	Mr. Phillips to Mr. Fish.	Jan. 3, 1870	Political state of affairs in his consular district in a deplorable condition. The assassination at Bayamo of the citizens sent from Santiago de Cuba by order of Count Valmaseda was nothing more than what is daily perpetrated. Count Valmaseda aspires to the position of Captain General. To increase his popularity among the Catalans he gives imperative orders to make the war one of extermination. Assassination of peaceful citizens residing in the country by Spanish troops daily reported. Orders probably carried to an extreme. Reasons for the same. The insurrection, notwithstanding the reports of the Spanish press to the contrary, remains in full force. Cubans, better armed and disciplined than formerly, in many cases take the offensive, and, with ranks increased by desertion from the enemy, are becoming bold and fight well. Sickness among the newly arrived Spanish troops. The insurrection likely to continue for a long time. Liberal-minded Spanish officers think it cannot be suppressed. Only inducement offered for its continuance is that the commanding officers are enabled to fill their pockets at the expense of the country.	187
127	Mr. Hall to Mr. Davis.	Jan. 31, 1870, No. 43.	The statement which appeared in the New York Sun, of October 5, relative to the murder of Robert Wells at Cienfuegos, proves to be untrue.	188
128	......do	Feb. 5, 1870, No. 47.	Effect produced by the news of the assassination, at Key West, of Don Gonzalo Castañon. Don Vicente Dawney, or Dauni, shot in an affray with Spanish volunteers. In the opinion of Mr. Hall, the lives of American citizens are as well protected as those of any other class.	189
129	......do	Feb. 9, 1870, No. 52.	News of the retreat of General Puello from Guaimaro followed by cable telegram announcing assassination of Don Gonzalo Castañon at Key West. Its effect. Authorities unconciously caused an excitement that they are unable to control. Their inability to protect the lives of peaceable inhabitants, or to punish atrocities that are being daily committed, is evident. Absence of United States vessels of war in Cuban ports. They may be needed for the purpose of offering refuge to United States citizens in the event of popular outbreaks.	190
130	......do	Feb. 11, 1870, No. 53.	Inclosing copy of communication addressed to him from Matanzas, narrating recent occurrences at that place upon the receipt of the news of the assassination of Don Gonzalo Castañon. Violent demonstrations of Spanish volunteers. They assemble in front of the palace and demand from the governor certain Cuban prisoners confined in jail under charge of having concealed weapons on their estates, that they may be put to death in revenge for the murder of Castañon. Their demand refused by the governor. Other attempts to obtain the prisoners unsuccessful. Efforts of the officers to restore order finally prove successful. The ringleaders of the riot arrested and placed in prison. They are finally conveyed to Havana, and are said to have been shipped to Spain. Indignation of volunteers against the governor and officers of police who executed his orders. Rumors of another demonstration. Precautionary measures of the governor. Great excitement among volunteers. They finally demand resignation of chief of police, which is complied with.	191

CORRESPONDENCE.

I.—EXTRACTS FROM LATE CORRESPONDENCE BETWEEN THE DEPARTMENT OF STATE AND THE LEGATION OF THE UNITED STATES AT MADRID.

No. 1.

Mr. Fish to General Sickles.

No. 2.] WASHINGTON, *June* 29, 1869.

The condition of the Island of Cuba excites the most serious concern. For more than nine months a civil conflict has been raging there that gives as yet no promise of a speedy termination; a conflict marked with a degree of fierceness and excess on either side rarely witnessed in later ages, and threatening, if continued, to work the desolation and destruction of the wealth and the resources of the island.

This government has felt itself constrained to remonstrate against a certain proclamation that was issued by the Captain General of Cuba in the course of this conflict, and which it appeared to the President would, if carried into effect, infringe upon the rights of our people, in the pursuit of lawful commerce, and under the protection of the recognized law of nations, freely to navigate the high seas. We also felt ourselves called upon to remonstrate against another proclamation that threatened a mode of warfare that varied with the recognized customs of civilized nations. Assurances have been received orally from the representative of Spain at Washington that the former of these proclamations has been revoked. We therefore have good reason to think that no further cause of complaint will arise therefrom. It is true that one of our vessels was illegally and violently arrested on the high seas, and two passengers forcibly taken therefrom, for which we have demanded atonement. The passengers were, however, returned to the consul, and the Spanish minister here has assured me that the passengers will be indemnified, and that a suitable apology will be made to the government for the affront to its flag. It is hoped that a satisfactory adjustment of this very unjustifiable outrage may be effected through the representative of Spain to this government, without the necessity of your intervention at the court of Madrid.

The proximity of the Island of Cuba, the constant intercourse between its inhabitants and our citizens, and its extended and increasing commerce with this country, all tend to awaken an earnest interest in our people in what concerns its inhabitants. Many citizens of the United States are largely interested in property there, many reside there, and many visit the island more or less frequently either on business, or to enjoy the benefit of the climate. Even more numerous, possibly, are the Cubans who own property, or who visit, or who reside, in the United States; and thus there have grown up close personal relations, both business and social, between the inhabitants of Cuba and of the United States. A strong political sympathy also exists, and the civil strife now raging in the island thus appeals with unusual power to the sympathy which Americans feel for all peoples striving to secure for themselves more liberal institutions, and that inestimable right of self-government which we prize as the foundation of all progress and achievement.

During the nine months that the insurrection in Cuba has existed this government has, in the utmost good faith, and with great success, exerted its powers to perform all its duties and obligations toward Spain, and to maintain its friendly relations with that power. It has been no easy task to restrain our citizens within the bounds prescribed by the obligations of one friendly power to another, and to repress the spirit of adventure and enterprise from entering the field of an extended and prolonged contest, where the cry was in favor of liberty, emancipation, and self-government, especially when all the claims of neighborhood, of personal intimacies, and of political sympathies were tending in the direction of material aid to the insurrection, and when these tendencies were warmed into life by the personal presence and the appeals of the Cubans who were either resident among us, or whom the desolation of their country had brought to our shores. But this government claims that it has faithfully discharged all these duties.

The strife still continues in Cuba. It has already marked its track by devastation and ruin—towns sacked, houses burned, plantations destroyed, and lives lost. On either side the war has been one of desolation, and, if continued, must result in the entire destruction of a large part of the productive capacity of the island as well as of an immense amount of property and of human life.

It is not impossible that the Cubans may be conquered, if Spain devotes her whole energies to the work; but they can never again be contented, happy, faithful, or quiet subjects of that power. Assuming that Spain may eventually subdue the present insurrection, she will find herself in possession of a devastated and ruined territory, inhabited by a discontented people. The enlightened statesmen of Spain cannot fail to appreciate that the feelings and the affections of the entire native population of the island are not only estranged, but that they are deeply hostile to the continuance of Spanish rule. Nor can they fail to recognize the advancing growth of that sentiment which claims for every part of the American hemisphere the right of self-government and freedom from transatlantic dependence.

England, bound as she has been to the traditions of the past, tenacious as she has been of her possessions, and conservative of all her rights and interests, has recognized the force of this feeling, and has anticipated events by granting self-government to her North American provinces. Denmark, approving the policy of the separation of colonies from the parent state, is endeavoring to part with her insular possessions. Russia has set a recent example of parting with her possessions in America. Nor are these the only governments in the Old World that are preparing their colonies for independence and self-government. It can no longer be a question of national dignity, nor can the proper pride or the just susceptibilities of a great power refuse to consider the question of a voluntary severance of past relations between itself and distant possessions. Spain herself was one of the first of the great European powers to cede voluntarily its distant colonial possessions, for she transferred Louisiana to France, and subsequently ceded Florida to the United States. France, engaged in war, and finding Louisiana liable to military attack, replenished her treasury by its sale, while relieving herself of the burden of the defense of a distant possession.

We hope that, with these examples, Spain will now be prepared to consider and to adopt, with respect to Cuba, a like course of wise foresight and enlightened statesmanship. In the name of humanity she can afford to arrest this war; and were it not for her traditional pride, and her recognized disregard of all considerations of mere interest where her honor is involved, we might appeal to considerations of interest, (which, after all, must be regarded by those who would wisely and prudently conduct the affairs of a nation,) to induce her to surrender her rights in the Island of Cuba, on receiving an equivalent for her property and her right of domain.

After much consideration and a careful survey of the question in all its relations, this government has arrived at the conclusion that it is its duty to exert its friendly influence to bring this unhappy strife to a close. Duty to its own citizens and to their large property interests, jeoparded by the continuance of the war—the necessity of mantaining quiet within its borders now seriously disturbed by the continued strife carried on so near its borders—our friendship for Spain, one of the earliest and oldest of our allies, with whom no interruption of friendly relations has occurred since our entrance into the family of nations—our sympathy for the Cubans, who are our neighbors—all alike impel the government to this course.

The President therefore directs you to offer to the cabinet at Madrid the good offices of the United States for the purpose of bringing to a close the civil war now ravaging the Island of Cuba, on the following bases:

1. The independence of Cuba to be acknowledged by Spain.

2. Cuba to pay to Spain a sum, within a time and in a manner to be agreed upon by them, as an equivalent for the entire and definite relinquishment by Spain of all her rights in that island, including the public property of every description. If Cuba should not be able to pay the whole sum at once in cash, the future payments, by installments, are to be adequately secured by a pledge of the export and import customs duties under an arrangement to be agreed upon for their collection, in trust, for the purpose of securing both the principal and interest of those installments until their final discharge.

3. The abolition of slavery in the Island of Cuba.

4. An armistice pending the negotiations, for the settlement above referred to.

In case the good offices of the United States are accepted by Spain, you will request that such steps may be immediately taken as will arrest the progress of the fight, and you will communicate at once by telegraph with the department, using the cipher when necessary. Authority should also be asked in that case for the representatives of the revolutionary party, now in the United States, to communicate through the Spanish lines with those in command of the revolutiontary party in Cuba, in order that all further destruction of life and property may be arrested at the earliest possible moment.

It is proposed that the negotiations for the settlement of the several questions to be adjusted between the contending parties shall be conducted here. You will therefore, in the event of our good offices being accepted, propose that a conference be held in the city of Washington, at an early day to be agreed upon between yourself and the cabinet of Madrid, between properly authorized representatives of the two parties, the representative of each party to be clothed with full powers to agree to and to enter into a convention for a settlement on the bases above indicated, and to arrange, settle, and sign all necessary details and other agreements that may be thought proper on both sides.

The President of the United States will, if desired by the representatives of the two parties, designate some person to attend, or to attend and preside in such conference, and to use his good offices in the form of information and advice in facilitating the objects thereof; but such person will have no other power therein, and shall not assume any obligation on the part of the United States, unless upon the joint request of the representatives of both parties, and with the assent of the President of the United States, which cannot be given until after consideration by him of such joint request.

The President of the United States will undertake to decide all questions which shall be referred to him by the conference. His decision shall be made upon protocols and other documents and proceedings of the conference, which may be so referred, and shall be conclusive and binding upon the parties.

The expenses of each representative attending the conference will be defrayed by the state or party by which he is appointed. The conference will have accommodations (as to a place for transacting its business) furnished by the President of the United States.

An armistice shall take place as soon as the government of the United States shall receive official information of the acceptance by Spain and Cuba of these propositions, and shall continue until the termination of the conference.

You will take the earliest opportunity after your arrival to read these instructions to the Spanish minister for foreign affairs, and will also leave with him the office copy thereof herewith inclosed.

No. 2.

Mr. Fish to General Sickles.

No. 3.] WASHINGTON, *June* 29, 1869.

Your instruction No. 2, of even date, contains certain general views upon the Cuban question, which you are therein instructed to place before the cabinet at Madrid in the form transmitted to you. I now desire to add certain other considerations, which you may or may not, at your discretion, put before the Spanish minister in your conversations and correspondence with him.

You will notice that the proposal contained in your instruction No. 2 is expressed to be for the purpose of bringing to a close the civil war now ravaging the island. While this expression is not designed to grant any public recognition of belligerent rights to the insurgents, it is nevertheless used advisedly, and in recognition of a state and condition of the contest which may not justify a much longer withholding of the concession to the revolutionary party of the recognized rights of belligerents. Should the expression therefore be commented upon, you will admit what is above stated with reference to it, and may add, in case of a protracted discussion, or the prospect of a refusal by Spain to accept the proposed offer of the United States, that an early recognition of belligerent rights is the logical deduction from the present proposal, and will probably be deemed a necessity on the part of the United States, unless the condition of the parties to the contest shall have changed very materially. I need not caution you of the delicacy to be observed on this point, (as well as on all others,) so as not to arouse or excite any just susceptibilities of the government, of the minister, or of the people of Spain.

It may also be made a *sine qua non* by the Spanish cabinet that the United States should guarantee the payment of the sum proposed to be paid by Cuba to Spain. While it is desirable, if possible, to avoid such a complication, yet a state of things may arise in the course of the negotiations at Washington that would induce the President to recommend Congress to authorize that to be done. In the event, therefore, of the point being raised and insisted upon, you will say that the President understands that a state of things may arise in which he will not object to the assumption of such a liability on the part of the United States, should Congress assent to it.

The President, being also desirous of removing all possible future sources of trouble in the Antilles, is willing, should the propositions of the United States be accepted, and should the subject of Porto Rico and its future political condition be mentioned by the Spanish minister, that you should inquire whether the cabinet at Madrid desire to make any suggestions as to that condition, and should they manifest a disposition to also sever their political relations with that island, you may receive and transmit to the department, for the consideration of the President, any suggestions or proposals which may be made with respect thereto. The same causes which have produced the present convulsion in Cuba exist latent in Porto Rico, and may be fanned into flames hereafter should free government and a system of free labor be brought in immediate contact with that island by establishing them in Cuba. It is not improbable, therefore, that the cabinet of Madrid may think it wise to determine the political condition of both islands at the same time. While, therefore, you will not obtrude this subject into any conference that may take place between you and the minister for foreign affairs, you will, should the question be brought forward by him, meet it as above directed.

You have already been advised in your personal interview with me of the nature of a confidential conversation between General Prim and Mr. Paul S. Forbes, a citizen of the United States, whose personal relations with General Prim, the president of the council, and with other leading personages in the Spanish capital, have led the President to name him as a special and confidential agent of this government, to proceed to Madrid for the purpose of there conferring with the Spanish authorities with a view to secure the termination of hostilities and the independence of the island. Mr. Forbes' powers are advisory only. You will avail yourself of Mr. Forbes's assistance in the delicate but very important negotiations on this subject. Should he have arrived in Madrid before you reach there, he may have notified the cabinet informally of the nature of the proposition which, under the instructions contained in my No. 2, you are directed to present. In that event you will be able to govern yourself in their formal and official presentation somewhat by his report and advice. Every consideration of humanity as well as of interest will call upon you so to shape this negotiation within the line of yo instructions as to bring it to a successful result if possible.

No. 3.

General Sickles to Mr. Davis.

[Telegram.]

JULY 27, 1869.

Arrived last Wednesday. Regent at Granja. Will be presented Thursday. Shall ask formal interview with minister immediately after presentation and report promptly. Disposition good. Enforcing neutrality laws and withholding belligerent rights have conciliated Spanish government, people, and press.

No. 4.

Mr. Fish to General Sickles.

[Telegram.]

WASHINGTON, *July* 29, 1869.

An early decision on the proposition to mediate is extremely important. Hasten it. Spanish authorities in Cuba are impotent for protection of the lives of our citizens. Cuba and Porto Rico should not be connected in the submission or negotiation.

No. 5.

General Sickles to Mr. Fish.

[Telegram.]

JULY 31, 1869.

Offered good offices of President. Secretary of state replied he would consult his colleagues, and see me Monday. Interview cordial. Discussion to-day limited by minister to overture. Prim receives me to-morrow by appointment. Will report result immediately.

No. 6.

General Sickles to Mr. Fish.

[Telegram.]

AUGUST 1, 1869.

Communicated to Prim informally basis of convention. He pressed me to say how much Cuba and Porto Rico would give. I said I had no instructions, and suggested one hundred and twenty-five millions as probable. Prim said Spain might arrange preliminaries with United States and concede autonomy of Cuba and Porto Rico for satisfactory equivalent as soon as hostilities ceased. He promised to bring the whole subject before the council to-night.

No. 7.

General Sickles to Mr. Fish.

[Telegram.]

AUGUST 6, 1869.

Prim says sudden illness of secretary of state has delayed reply.

No. 8.

General Sickles to Mr. Fish.

No. 4.] MADRID, *August* 12, 1869.

On my arrival Mr. Forbes reported to me that he had not presented his letter to the minister of state; that Marshal Prim, to whom Mr. Forbes had intimated the purport of the propositions contained in his instructions, did not receive them with favor, and as the president of the council was understood to be more inclined to our views than his colleagues, Mr. Forbes determined to await my arrival before making any communication to the minister of state.

In view of his report and advice, I deemed it prudent, in compliance with your instructions, to postpone, for the present, the formal communication of your dispatch No. 2, and accordingly in my interview with Señor Silvela, on the 31st ultimo, you will observe that I confined myself to the general views I was instructed to express.

The conversation began by a reference, on my part, to the kindness and consideration with which I had been received by the regent at La Granja, to which the minister courteously replied that the regent was glad of an occasion to show not only his regard for myself, but the value which the Spanish nation placed upon the friendship of the United States.

I then entered at once upon the object for which I had sought the interview, remarking that I desired to begin a full and frank conversation in relation to Cuba.

The minister replied immediately that the question of Cuba was one of the gravest that now occupied the government; that he had spoken with the president of the council of ministers on the subject and was prepared to hear the views I had to present.

I proceeded to observe that the government and people of the United States felt a lively sympathy in the recent efforts made by the people of Spain in the great work of their national reorganization, and that it was the earnest desire of the President to avoid anything that could embarrass the government of Spain at this time. In this relation I mentioned the scrupulous observance by the government of the United States of all its international obligations, and the strict enforcement of its neutrality laws in respect to the Cuban insurrection; at the same time pointing out the close relations by which the population of the United States is connected with Cuba, the near neighborhood, and the large commercial and social intercourse between them. It was but natural, I added, that a deep sympathy with the Cuban people should have grown up in the United States, especially as so many of our citizens regarded the Cubans as fighting for the same principles of self-government we had ourselves adopted.

That if it were true, as is believed, that a majority of the people of Cuba desired to terminate their relation of colonial dependence upon the mother country, it seemed to the President that in this they were only following the general course of events upon the American Continent since the establishment of our own independence. This manifest and inevitable tendency had been generally recognized by the European powers, including not only Spain herself, but Great Britain, France, Russia, and other nations.

Considering, therefore, our old and intimate relations of friendship with Spain, and the ties of interest and sympathy which bound us to Cuba, the President regarded the present moment opportune for tendering to the government of Spain the good offices of the United States in all proper efforts to arrest the deplorable conflict of which the Island had been the theatre for so many months.

The President appreciated too highly the sense of national honor and the legitimate pride that form such distinguishing traits of the Spanish character to make any suggestion that could awaken the just susceptibilities of the government of his Highness, the Regent, but in the name of humanity, and in the interest of both nations, he hoped that some means of settling the questions at issue might be devised at the earliest possible day.

The minister, interrupting me as if he thought I had gone quite far enough, for the present at least, acknowledged the sincere and loyal manner in which the government of the United States had fulfilled its international duties in regard to the Cuban insurrection; he admitted the extreme difficulty in a free country of preventing individuals from joining either side in a war near its borders, and said that so far as the power of the American government extended, Spain not only had no cause for complaint, but had been most gratefully impressed with the upright and loyal dealing of the President; that he had repeatedly directed their representative in Washington to express to our government their cordial appreciation of its action; that this feeling of grateful sympathy was general in Spain, and found utterance everywhere in public and in private; and that now, more than ever, Spain regarded America with sympathy and confidence. In former days, when the pro-slavery party held the reins of power, there was some anxiety from time to time lest the recklessness of filibusters should involve the two nations in difficulty; but that since the victory of the national cause in the great war, the liberal people of Spain had come to regard the United States as their natural friend.

The Cuban question was one of the utmost gravity and delicacy. It was the intention of the Spanish liberals, who planned and executed the revolutionary movements which have given to Spain its new political life, to make, at the earliest moment, provision for granting self-government to Cuba. But this fatal insurrection broke out at the very moment when it was becoming possible to give to Cuba all the rights she desired. The cry of "Death to Spaniards" was heard in Spain, and it became impossible, in the face of civil war, to carry out the beneficent plan that had been formed. The liberal party in Spain finds itself, to its own infinite regret, forced into a seeming sympathy with the reactionary party in Cuba; and the liberals of Cuba, who ought to be its firm friends, are converted, by the fatality of the situation, into its bitterest enemies. There is no sentiment dearer to the hearts of the liberal leaders than that of freedom to all men; yet they stand before the world, in this Cuban conflict, as opposed to self-government and resisting the abolition of slavery. He considered the insurrection as a most deplorable misfortune and mistake, both for Cuba and for Spain.

If a way could be found to settle all these questions in such a manner as to do justice to Cuba, without infringing upon the honor of Spain, the government would be greatly gratified. There is no intention or desire among the liberals of Spain ever again to work [*exploiter*] the Island of Cuba on the old selfish system. It has been their constant hope and wish to grant to the Cubans the administration of their own affairs and the full fruits of their own labor, preserving their commercial connections, and some shadow of their political relations.

The minister said, in conclusion, that he would report to his colleagues in the government the substance of this conversation at the first meeting of the council. The subject was too grave to be disposed of in a single interview. He would name an early day for a second conference, in which he hoped to be prepared to ask General Sickles to lay before him more definitely the views of the government of the United States in this matter.

It was so evident the minister wished to confine the interview to the overtures I had already made, that I forbore proceeding further with the discussion; and expressing the hope that I would soon have the pleasure of renewing the conference, for which I should await his excellency's invitation, I left the topic, and after a brief interchange of civilities, took leave.

No. 9.

General Sickles to Mr. Fish.

No. 5.] MADRID, *August* 12, 1869.

On Sunday, the day after my interview with the minister of state, I made the prescribed visit of ceremony to the president of the council of ministers, Marshal Prim, at his quarters in the war department. After the customary courtesies had been observed, and with the marshal's consent, which was frankly given, the subject of Cuba was introduced. I said I had an important communication from my government looking to a solution of the question, that I was anxious to present as soon as possible. He asked me if it was the same or substantially the same as the one Mr. Forbes had foreshadowed, to which I replied in the affirmative, when, with much animation and even warmth of manner, he protested that Spain would not entertain the suggestion of an armistice with the insurgents, nor consider the question of the independence of Cuba, while the insurgents were in arms against the government; that Spain would grant a full and complete amnesty as soon as the insurgents laid down their arms; and that being done, the whole subject would be open for consideration; that he was disposed to meet the question frankly and practically; that perhaps he was somewhat in advance of the views of his colleagues, but he had no doubt they were unanimous in the hope that the influence of the United States might be successfully exerted to relieve the question from the embarrassments which now surrounded it. He added that, in regard to emancipation, Spain would prefer to leave that matter to the Cubans themselves, saying, "That is your glory in America, the reward of your philanthrophy, and we do not wish to deprive you of it."

I then sounded the marshal upon the proposal for a conference in Washington, in which Spain, the United States, and Cuba should be represented; but to this he at once demurred, saying Cuba could only be heard here through her deputies elected to the Cortes; that Spain might treat with the United States, not with Cuba.

I then referred to my interview with the minister of state the day before, and enlarged upon the considerations then advanced, adding that every day the conflict was prolonged increased the danger of further complications, and to enable the United States to exert their good offices with advantage to all parties, it was essential that no time be lost; that if the preliminaries could be settled here now between the United States and Spain, and the effusion of blood stopped, the passions of the conflict would be calmed, and the details would then be less difficult of adjustment than at present.

The marshal replied that Señor Silvela had informed him of our interview, and that the subject would be brought before the council that night, and he hoped it would not be long before the minister of state or himself would be prepared to intimate to me the bases upon which Spain would be willing to treat; that, meanwhile, he preferred our conversation should be regarded as unofficial and entirely confidential.

Having already trespassed upon the indulgence accorded to a visit of mere ceremony, with the marshal's permission to resume the subject at an early day, I withdrew, agreeably impressed with his candor and courtesy.

No. 10.

General Sickles to Mr. Fish.

[Telegram.]

AUGUST 13, 1869.

President of council authorizes me to state that the good offices of the United States are accepted. He suggests informally, for your information, four cardinal propositions that will be acceptable, if offered by the United States, as the basis for a convention, the details to be settled as soon as practicable:

First. The insurgents to lay down their arms.

Second. Spain to grant simultaneously a full and complete amnesty.

Third. The people of Cuba to vote by universal suffrage upon the question of their independence.

Fourth. The majority having declared for independence, Spain to grant it, the Cortes consenting; Cuba paying satisfactory equivalent guaranteed by the United States.

As soon as preliminaries are settled, safe conduct through Spanish lines to be given for communication with insurgents.

Prim enjoins uttermost secrecy as to this and all other communications.

No. 11.

General Sickles to Mr. Fish.

No. 6.] MADRID, *August* 14, 1869.

In consequence of Mr. Silvela's illness I did not hear from him until the evening of the 9th instant, when he invited me by note to call at the Foreign Office the next day.

He resumed the subject of our former interview by remarking that he had conferred with his colleagues in regard to the proposals I had made, and was prepared to acquaint me with the views of the cabinet. He then read from a manuscript the remarks which are embodied in the inclosed memorandum of the conversation. I expressed my regret that the Spanish government, by choosing to treat the subject as a purely legal question to be settled according to their own forms of procedure, had apparently closed the door to any arrangement by which the good offices of the United States could be made immediately effective.

The minister replied with great animation that such was not the meaning or intention of the government; he considered that exactly the contrary was true; that by the friendly intervention of the United States a great step in advance had been rendered possible—a simultaneous disarmament and amnesty of the insurgents; that this already was a great progress; a minister who would have discussed such a matter a few years ago would have been dragged through the streets by the populace; that now, on the contrary, we are able to discuss it in a calm and reasonable manner.

Mr. Silvela then entered upon a very full analysis of article 108 of the Spanish constitution, showing that it had two distinct and opposite phases in its relation to the present question; that while by its terms it precluded the government from making any definitive arrangement in regard to Cuba until the Cuban representatives shall have taken their seats in the Cortes, on the other hand it authorizes the government to make any arrangement that might seem expedient after the Cuban deputies arrive, the Spanish government and chambers being then free to negotiate on the basis of a liberal constitution, complete autonomy or independence; and that although it might be said the independence of the island was not contemplated by the constitution, yet giving the article a somewhat latitudinarian construction, it was susceptible even of that interpretation.

I answered that while it would not be proper for me to discuss the constitutional question with his excellency, yet I would commend to his notice that in dealing with the events now transpiring in Cuba, it was necessary to look at them in a practical point of view; that unless some arrangement could be made at once, the conflict might soon reach proportions and involve complications that would greatly increase the difficulties of a settlement; and that notwithstanding the desire of the President to do all in his power to promote a satisfactory adjustment, the interests affected and the strong current of sympathy in the struggle felt in the United States, might cause no little embarrassment, if nothing more could be done until the Cuban deputies took their seats in the Cortes.

Mr. Silvela expressed his entire concurrence with what I had said, but added that it was impossible, in the present temper and spirit of the Spanish people, to proceed hastily in the matter, and that above all it was out of the question for the government, whose highest duty it was to inculcate the most religious respect for the constitution, to give at this time the example of an infraction of it.

He hoped the steps he had indicated would lead, in a legal and regular way, to the object we had all so much at heart, and suggested, in view of the susceptible state of public feeling in Spain and Cuba, that both governments and their agents should observe the strictest reserve in regard to these negotiations, as premature publicity would greatly embarrass them.

It was then arranged that a brief memorandum of this interview should be drawn up and signed by Mr. Silvela and myself the next day, whereupon the minister intimated to me that the president of the council desired to see me, and hoped I would call on him the following morning, which I promised to do.

There is a wide interval between the president of the council and the minister of state in their views, as expressed on the subject of Cuba. The latter confines himself strictly, I presume, to the communications he is instructed by the council to make; while Marshal Prim takes ground in advance of his colleagues, counting, no doubt advisedly, upon their co-operation when necessary.

Inclosed will be found * * * a copy of the memorandum of our interview, dated August 11, but signed to-day, and a copy of article 108 of the constitution of Spain. * * * *

A.

In the conference which took place to-day, the 10th of August, 1869, between the representative of the United States, General Sickles, and the minister of state, the latter of these gentlemen said, that having made known to the government the suggestion made by the minister plenipotentiary of the United States, General Sickles, in the conference of the 31st of July last, in regard to the desire of the President and of the people of those States that the Spanish government might succeed in promptly putting an end to the violent state of affairs that now devastates the Island of Cuba, he thinks proper to state that after the revolution of September had taken place, and conformably to the principles thereby proclaimed, Spain would already have given all constitutional liberties to Cuba if the unfortunate insurrection of Yara and the cry of "Death to Spain," uttered by some Cubans, had not alienated the sympathies of the nation, and obliged the government to accept the impolitic contest to which it was provoked; that a good proof of its desire to settle in a liberal sense the question of the Antilles is shown not only by the election of the deputies of Porto Rico, who are to take their seats in the Cortes Constituyentes at their next session, but also by the 108th article of the constitution, in which, notwithstanding the period in which it was adopted, it was provided that the concurrence of the deputies of that province is necessary to fix the future form of government of the island.

In view of these indisputable facts, and taking account of and appreciating the traditional pride of the Spanish people, the government considers that it can come to no definite decision in regard to the political situation and future government of the Island of Cuba, until the insurgents lay down their arms and cease the struggle.

This being done, the government is disposed to grant a full and generous amnesty to the insurgents, and when quiet is established, to proceed to the freest election of representatives of Cuba.

The national dignity being thus preserved intact, and it being practicable to comply with the article of the constitution, the moment will have arrived for concerting with its representatives the necessary measures in relation to the legal future of the Island of Cuba, submitting them to the indispensable approbation of the Constituent Cortes.

In conclusion, if the United States, by their natural influence in America, are able to contribute to the cessation of the effusion of blood, in the pacification of the Island of Cuba, and its entrance, by the election of its deputies, into the exercise of its rights, the government of Spain cannot but be grateful for these good offices.

General Sickles replies that he will communicate to his government the views of the cabinet of Madrid. Of course he cannot anticipate the views of his government in regard to the bases mentioned by his excellency the secretary of state; and although it will be deeply regretted that a constitutional obstacle prevents the executive from dealing with the main question now and definitively, there can be no doubt that the scrupulous observance of constitutional limitations of authority will be appreciated by the government of the United States. The generous offer of a full amnesty to the insurgents, the recognition of the right of the Cubans, through their representatives, to have a concurrent voice in determining the future of the island, and the promise of a free election for deputies, afford ground for congratulation upon the good disposition manifested by the Spanish government.

Reserving the questions suggested by article 108 of the constitution of Spain, General Sickles, in conformity with his instructions, expresses the hope of his government that in view of the deplorable character of the conflict, and the possible complications incident to a prolongation of hostilities, the cabinet of Madrid will endeavor to reach as promptly as possible a solution of the question, a result which the government of the United States will be happy to assist in promoting.

This exchange of views, the object of the conference, being thus terminated, it was agreed to give to it the character of the strictest reserve.

Signed at Madrid on the eleventh of August, eighteen hundred and sixty-nine.

MANUEL SILVELA.
D. E. SICKLES.

C.

CONSTITUTION OF THE SPANISH MONARCHY.

SECTION 10.—*Of the transmarine provinces.*

ARTICLE 108. The Cortes Constituyentes shall reform the present system of government in the transmarine provinces when the deputies of Cuba or Porto Rico shall have taken their seats, in order to extend to the same, with the modifications which shall be deemed necessary, the privileges set forth in the constitution.

No. 12.

Mr. Fish to General Sickles.

[Telegram.]

WASHINGTON, *August* 16, 1869.

Urge acceptance on basis proposed by the United States. First proposition of Spain that insurgents lay down arms is incapable of attainment as a preliminary. The third, to ascertain the will of the Cubans by a vote is impracticable because of the disorganization of society, and the terrorism that prevails, and the violence and insubordination of the volunteers. There can be no question as to the will of the majority; it has been recognized and admitted. An armistice should immediately be agreed upon to arrest the carnage and destruction of property, and opportunity be granted to communicate with the insurgents, and emancipation of slaves be determined.

No. 13.

General Sickles to Mr. Fish.

No. 8.] MADRID, *August* 16, 1869.

I have the honor to acknowledge the receipt of your instructions Nos. 1, 2, 3, 4, 5, 6, and 7, with the inclosures mentioned in them respectively, except the office copy of No. 2.

My interview with the president of the council was postponed at his instance until the 12th, when I had a long and free conversation with his excellency in relation to Cuba. My telegram of the 13th having already advised you of the result of the conference, I shall condense my report as much as possible.

General Prim said he had conferred freely with his colleagues in regard to the basis I had informally communicated to him, and they were less inclined than himself to agree to our proposal.

I remarked that the official answer of the minister of state to my overtures had acquainted me with the views of the cabinet, and I regretted to be compelled to transmit to my government a reply so little calculated to encourage the efforts the President was disposed to make toward a settlement of the controversy.

General Prim replied that some of his colleagues did not realize, as he did, the difficulty of carrying on a war in America; and that they were greatly influenced by the popular sentiment in Spain, which made no account of any sacrifice of life or money when the national honor was believed to be involved; that Mr. Silvela, being a lawyer, and a parliamentary leader, naturally inclined toward a purely legal and legislative solution, while for his part, if he were alone concerned, he would say to the Cubans, "Go if you will; make good the treasure you have cost us, and let me bring home our army and fleet, and consolidate the liberties and resources of Spain."

I suggested that public opinion in Europe had already anticipated some arrangement by which the independence of Cuba might be conceded; that the continental and English journals in discussing the subject found ample precedent for such a concession by Spain in the action of other European states; that several influential papers in Madrid favored more or less the same views, and I added that the people of Spain had given such proofs of their confidence in the present government, that he had only to carry out the sagacious and practical plan of action he had heretofore indicated, and he would doubtless be sustained in this as he had been in all his measures.

The general rejoined by saying with much animation that the great difficulty in the way was the defiant attitude of the insurgents; that here was the mistake of the United States in proposing an armistice and asking Spain to treat on the basis of independence with insurgents with arms in their hands; and he added emphatically, "I am sure no human power could obtain from the Spanish people the most insignificant concession as long as the rebellion maintains its footing."

Upon this I observed that no one appreciated more highly than the President the elevated tone of the cabinet of Madrid, and that he would be the last to make any proposal derogatory to the honor of Spain; that in his view a measure that would stop the indiscriminate sacrifice of life and property in Cuba, pending negotiations for ulterior arrangements, was prompted as well by considerations of humanity as of policy; that Great Britain had recognized the independence of the United States simultaneously with the cessation of hostilities, and that if, as I was glad to be assured, the future relations of Cuba to the mother country admitted of adjustment hereafter on the basis of the independence of the colony, then surely some means might be devised by which, without offense to Spain, the conflict could be arrested pending the negotiations with the United States, a friendly power offering its good offices to promote a settlement of the question; and I added, with emphasis, that such was the pressure of events, you had instructed me by telegraph to ask for an immediate answer to our proposal, and to say that the President was embarrassed by the delay that had occurred; that I had preferred to make this communication to himself in view of Mr. Silvela's disinclination to discuss the question before the arrival of the Cuban deputies to the Cortes; and that unless he was prepared to forego whatever advantage might be gained through the mediation of the United States, prompt action was necessary.

He then, after some conversation about matters of detail, put in form the substance of the proposition sent to you by my telegram of the 13th, a copy of which I inclose with this dispatch. In the evening, not long after I had left him, the general sent me a note asking me not to send my dispatch until after I had seen him again the following day, at eleven. In that interview, which was brief, General Prim said he had informed the council, soon after we separated, of the communication he had made to me, and they thought he had perhaps gone beyond the limits of the executive power in his proposal; he therefore would qualify the fourth point by inserting "the Cortes consenting," which was accordingly done. I then read to him the text of the telegram as it was transmitted to you, and he found it correct.

You will, of course, observe the duplex form the negotiation receives in the Spanish cabinet. The reserve of the minister of state and the frankness of the president of the council are in striking contrast. The explanation is to be found as well in the solicitude of the minister of state to hold a position easily defended in the Cortes, if the negotiation fail, as in the characteristics of the men; one deals with the question as a successful revolutionary leader wielding almost absolute power, the other purely as a jurist and a parliamentarian.

My dispatches are so far anticipated by my telegrams that I fear these details will not have much interest for you; nevertheless they make up the current record of the transactions of the legation, and as such may be useful.

As I write to you with great freedom of all that seems essential to acquaint you with the situation here, I have marked this dispatch as confidential for obvious prudential reasons.

General Sickles to Mr. Fish.

[Cipher dispatch.]

MADRID, *August* 13, 1869.

President of council authorizes me to state that the good offices of the United States are accepted. He suggests informally for your information four cardinal propositions that will be acceptable if offered by the United States, as the basis for a convention; the details to be settled as soon as practicable.

First. The insurgents to lay down their arms.

Second. Spain to grant simultaneously a full and complete amnesty.

Third. The people of Cuba to vote by universal suffrage upon the question of their independence.

Fourth. The majority having declared for independence, Spain to grant it, the Cortes consenting; Cuba paying satisfactory equivalent guaranteed by the United States.

As soon as preliminaries are settled, safe conduct through Spanish lines to be given for communication with insurgents.

Prim enjoins secrecy as to this and all other communications.

No. 14.

General Sickles to Mr. Fish.

No. 9.] MADRID, *August* 20, 1869.

Yesterday, as soon as I had received the supplemental telegram by which I was informed of the exact text of your instructions, sent by telegraph on the 16th instant, I sought an interview with the president of the council of ministers, which he promptly appointed for this morning at eleven. I have just now left him, after a very full discussion of all the points comprised in your instructions, and although the mail for the next steamer closes early this afternoon, I shall endeavor to send you by this post a report embodying the substance of our conversation.

After communicating to General Prim your views in regard to the first and third of his propositions, requiring the Cubans to lay down their arms, and to declare by a vote the desire of the population for independence, I proceeded to urge your proposal as embodied in your instruction No. 2, already communicated to him by Mr. Forbes, and illustrated its advantages by arguments and suggestions I will not now stop to recapitulate.

General Prim, in reply to the objection made to the cessation of hostilities on the part of the insurgents as a preliminary, said it was not intended as a condition to precede an understanding with the United States; he was ready to agree with me upon the bases of an arrangement contemplating the independence of Cuba, but that he could not give to the arrangement the sanctions of a treaty, nor submit the propositions to the Cortes for their ratification while the insurgents were in arms; he said he had no doubt that whatever might be the result of the conflict, Cuba would eventually be free; that he recognized without hesitation the manifest course of events on the American Continent and the inevitable termination of all colonial relations in their autonomy as soon as they were prepared for independence; but that no emergency and no consideration would reconcile Spain to such a concession until hostilities ceased.

I reminded him that Austria had transferred Venice to France, and assented to its immediate transfer to Italy, before peace was declared; that the independence of all the American States had been recognized at one time and another during the progress of hostilities; and that in coming to an agreement with the United States on the subject Spain would not treat with insurgents, but with a friendly power, offering its good offices to an old ally. To these and like amplifications of the argument he replied with great earnestness and emphasis: "Let the United States be assured of the good faith and the good disposition of Spain, and especially of the frankness and sincerity with which the president of the council has promised to treat with the cabinet at Washington, on the basis of the independence of Cuba, as soon as it is possible to do so consistently with the dignity and honor of Spain; formidable as the insurrection in Cuba may become, it has not yet approached the proportions of any of those conflicts in which governments have found themselves constrained to treat during hostilities. The Cuban insurgents hold no city or fortresses; they have no port, no ships; they have no army that presumes to offer or accept battle; and now, before the period arrives for active operations, when Spain will send the ample re-enforcements she holds in readiness, it is only necessary for the Cubans to accept the assurance of the United States, given on the faith of Spain, that they may have their independence by laying down their arms, electing their deputies, and declaring their wish to be free by a vote of the people."

I have thus rapidly and briefly sketched the leading points of this interview, that you may be put in possession of all of it I can give you to-day by post. I am satisfied the president of the council desires to come to an agreement with the United States on the subject of Cuba, and that the independence of the island is not a serious obstacle to the negotiation.

No. 15.

General Sickles to Mr. Fish.

[Telegram.]

AUGUST 20, 1869.

Long interview with president of council to-day. He said the first proposition of Spain was not a preliminary to an agreement with United States, but was a condition of concessions to the insurgents; and that the third proposition was a condition of the independence of Cuba. I again urged acceptance on the basis proposed by the United States. He said that Spain desired the good offices of the United States, and was prepared to see Cuba free, but that the consent of Spain must be given in a manner consistent with her self-respect. He repeated that an armistice with the insurgents was impossible; that emancipation of the slaves could not be separated from other questions now paramount; and that communication with the insurgents would be permitted after agreement with the United States. Shall report this conversation fully by mail to-day and Sunday. I regard it as essential to a correct appreciation of the views of Spain.

No. 16.

General Sickles to Mr. Fish.

No. 10.] MADRID, *August* 21, 1869.

The report in my No. 9 of the interview with General Prim yesterday was necessarily brief. In giving you the conversation more in detail, I shall endeavor to avoid superfluous repetition.

The president of the council said his idea was that the governments of the United States and Spain should come to an understanding in regard to the question—a full and complete accord; that then the United States should employ their influence with the Cubans to induce them to accept a basis of settlement which should comprise—

1. A cessation of hostilities;
2. An amnesty;
3. The election of deputies;
4. A project of law to be submitted by the government to the Cortes, settling the future of the island.

It was impossible to act officially in the matter while the insurrection still maintained itself. But the arrangement which the two governments were now trying to arrive at was as earnest, as serious, and as binding as if it were in form and manner a treaty.

I asked what would be the result if the United States accepted such a basis of agreement, and the Cubans should refuse to lay down their arms and proceed to the election of deputies, and vote on the question of their independence.

The president of the council said: "In that case, there would be but one solution, continuing the war *á l'outrance*. I do not flatter myself that Spain will retain possession of the island. I consider that the period of colonial autonomy has virtually arrived. However the present contest may end, whether in the suppression of the insurrection, or in the better way of an amicable arrangement through the assistance of the United States, it is equally clear to me that the time has come for Cuba to govern herself; and if we succeed in putting down the insurrection to-morrow, I shall regard the subject in the same light—that the child has attained its majority and should be allowed to direct its own affairs. We want nothing more than to get out of Cuba, but it must be done in a dignified and honorable manner."

I assured the general that nothing was further from the disposition of the President of the United States than to make any proposal that could wound the just susceptibility of the government of Spain; that all the wars by which the American republics had attained their independence were closed by negotiations carried on before hostilities had ceased; and although in any matter affecting its honor every nation must decide for itself, it did not appear to the President that the course of action he had proposed was in the slightest degree inconsistent with the self-respect of Spain, while it avoided many difficulties and afforded the most speedy and practicable solution of the question.

General Prim at once replied: "There is a vast difference between the present insurrection in Cuba and those revolutionary movements by which the republics of the Western Continent gained their independence. In those examples negotiation was resorted to after campaigns had been fought, and battles lost and gained; they had armies in the field and organized governments supporting them. We see nothing of this in Cuba; only mere roving bands, who fly when they are pursued, and who have never been found in numbers sufficient to give or accept battle. It is very possible that in the lapse of time the insurrection may become more formidable; it may raise armies; it may take cities and fortified places; it may demonstrate, what has not yet been in any way demonstrated, that it is supported by the majority of the population. In that case Spain will have something tangible to treat with. But we hope to avoid all this bloodshed, disaster, and ruin by making some amicable arrangement now. It is impossible for us to treat with the Cubans now, but the United States, when once convinced of the good intentions and good faith of the Spanish government, can then assure the Cubans that by following the programme I have indicated, they can have their liberty without firing another shot."

In regard to the propositions of the American government heretofore presented by Mr. Forbes, and to-day renewed by myself, the president of the council remarked that he could only say, it was impossible to precede negotiations by either an armistice or by the abolition of slavery; that the latter would at once follow the emancipation of the island, and that all these things were bound together and could not be separated. "Here, then," he repeated, "are the successive steps:

"1. A settlement of a basis of agreement which shall assure the government of the United States of the good intentions and good faith of the Spanish government;

"2. The United States to counsel the Cubans to accept this arrangement;

"3. Cessation of hostilities and amnesty;

"4. The election of deputies;

"5. Action of the Cortes;

"6. Plebiscit and independence.

"This being all arranged in advance between the two governments, if the United States could but be satisfied of the sincerity of these proposals, and would persuade the Cubans to accept them, the object we both desire could be accomplished. There will, of course, be difficulties in the execution of the plan, but they must be met and overcome."

General Prim concluded with the request that I would communicate his views fully to you, and add that he would be happy to hear and consider any suggestion the government of the United States would make in the way of emendation or modification of matters of detail.

The tone of the Spanish cabinet has been so manifestly conciliatory, and their disposition apparently so earnest for a complete accord with the United States, that I have seen no occasion as yet for any intimation of our future policy, as foreshadowed in your instruction No. 3. It is by no means improbable that this government may, before long, assume a more popular form than it has yet received. If the Cortes fail, at their approaching session in October, as is anticipated by many judicious observers of events, in choosing a king, the most obvious solution is in the popular tendencies of the revolution. This consideration has increased the force of your admonition "not to arouse or excite any just susceptibilities of the government, of the ministers, or of the people of Spain."

The indications of a more tractable popular temper on the subject of Cuba are multiplying. Yesterday I was shown an article in the *Diario de Barcelona* decidedly favoring a cession of the island to the United States for a fair equivalent; with the reservation, however, that is always made in the Spanish journals and in society, as well as by ministers, that the insurrection must first be terminated. The *Diario* quotes from another Catalonian paper, *La Cronica de Cataluña*, favoring the same views. These expressions are the more worthy of notice, appearing in journals of reputation, published in the province which has been supposed to derive the most advantage from the trade with Cuba; and it may be worth while to consider in the course of the negotiation whether some reciprocal commercial advantages might not conciliate Spanish opinion and interests in favor of the independence of Cuba.

In regard to the emancipation of slaves in Cuba it is quite probable that the disinclination of the Spanish cabinet to enter into engagements on the subject at present is attributable in part to the embarrassment such action would cause in Porto Rico, as well as in Cuba, where the slaveholders are generally the most influential partisans of the home government.

No. 17.

Mr. Fish to General Sickles.

[Telegram.]

WASHINGTON, *August* 24, 1869.

The propositions of Spain are incompatible with any practicable negotiation. The representatives of the insurrectionary government are necessary parties to a negotiation. Free communication through the Spanish lines is immediately necessary.

The United States cannot ask the insurgents to lay down their arms unless the volunteers are simultaneously effectually disarmed, and in good faith disbanded. This, if practicable, would require time. We want to arrest the destruction of life and property, and to stop the outrages and annoyances to our citizens. An armistice would effect this immediately, and the terms of the compensation to be made to Spain by Cuba could then be arranged between them under the mediation of the United States.

You may say that we deem an armistice indispensable to the success of any negotiation. Spain may in honor grant this at the request of the United States, and in deference to the wishes of a friendly power, whose good offices she is willing to accept. This being done, negotiations can immediately be opened that will probably result in peace, and her receiving a fair compensation.

No. 18.

General Sickles to Mr. Fish.

No. 12. MADRID, *August* 24, 1869.

* * * * * *

In this relation the recent articles in *La Patrie* and *La France*, semi-ministerial, are not without interest; regarding the insurrection as likely to be successful, the latter journal suggests that Spain yield the independence of Cuba for an equivalent, to be paid by the assumption of a portion of the public debt of Spain, the independence of the island to be guaranteed by the great powers, including the United States.

The Madrid journals continue the discussion of the Cuban question.

The articles in the Epoca are from the editor-in-chief; but for prudential reasons he hesitates to commit the paper to his personal views. I have reasons for suspecting that the newspaper discussion of the subject is stimulated by agents of American parties, who have undertaken the purchase of Cuba from Spain as a private enterprise. I do not learn that the Spanish cabinet, or any responsible persons here, have countenanced the scheme.

Mr. Forbes left Madrid a few days ago for Paris and Hombourg.

I hear from a well-informed source that the minister of finance is well disposed toward our views in reference to Cuba, but that the minister of the colonies is hostile to any arrangement looking to the separation of the colony from Spain. I have not met any of the cabinet except the president of the council and the minister of state. In general, I find less susceptibility to the idea of a transfer of the island to the United States than to the concession of the independence of Cuba. There is an apprehension that the persons and property of Spaniards in Cuba would not be safe under Cuban control. This impression, I hear, prevails in Catalonia.

No. 19.

Mr. Fish to General Sickles.

[Telegram.]

WASHINGTON, *September* 1, 1869.

United States willing to mediate between Spain and Cuba on these terms: First, immediate armistice; second, Cuba to recompense Spain for public property taken; United States not to guarantee unless Congress approve; daily destruction is steadily decreasing value of property for which purchase money is offered; third, persons and property of Spaniards remaining on island protected, but they may at option withdraw. To prevent difficulties, as well as to stop bloodshed and devastation, we must have early decision. These offers withdrawn unless accepted before October 1st. Say that anarchy prevails over much of island. Murders of American citizens are committed by volunteers. Confiscation of their property attempted by Spanish authorities.

No. 20.

General Sickles to Mr. Fish.

[Telegram.]

SEPTEMBER 4, 1869.

Have communicated formally and fully, in a note to minister of state *ad interim*, all your propositions and views in relation to Cuba, and have asked for early and decisive answer. Prim and Silvela still absent.

Spanish government expresses much solicitude about detention of gunboats.

No. 21.

General Sickles to Mr. Fish.

No. 14.] MADRID, *September* 5, 1869.

With this dispatch I have the honor to forward a copy of my note to Mr. Becerra, minister of state *ad interim*, presenting formally your propositions in relation to the civil war in Cuba, which had been the subject of the several conferences with the president of the council and the minister of state heretofore reported, and asking, in compliance with your orders, received by telegraph through our legation in London, on the 29th of August, for an early and decisive answer. I would have preferred, as intimated in my telegram to you of the same date, to await the return of the president of the council and the other absent members of the cabinet, including Mr. Silvela, the minister of state, who are understood to be least opposed to your views, before pressing an immediate decision upon your proposals; but in the absence of any reply to my request for further instructions I did not feel authorized to withhold my note any longer after receiving, through Mr. Motley on the 3d instant, your telegram of the 1st, the latter part of which, however, has not yet been intelligibly transmitted.

Yesterday I had an interview with Mr. Becerra, the minister of state *ad interim*, at his own request. He said he had been informed of the detention of the Spanish gunboats by order of the President, and proceeded to remonstrate against the measure as unreasonable and evincing unfriendly feelings toward Spain. I interrupted him by remarking that I had neither instructions nor official information on the subject, and intimated that inquiries made at Washington through the Spanish minister would doubtless be answered satisfactorily. The minister then said he had telegraphed Mr. Roberts on the subject the day before, but desired also a conference with me, and went on to observe that Spain had manifested her friendship for the United States from the period of our revolutionary struggle for independence down to the recent rebellion, and that now when Spain was endeavoring to establish free institutions, as well for her colonies as for herself, they looked for the friendship of the United States, and deprecated this proceeding as calculated to impress public opinion in Spain unfavorably with reference to the sentiments of the United States. I replied that being without instructions I could only report to my government the observations his excellency was pleased to make on the subject, but that I must remind him of the proofs the President had already given of his friendly disposition in the measures taken to enforce a strict neutrality between Spain and her antagonists in America, and that it should not be forgotten that there were on the one hand sister republics in South America, and, on the other, a people struggling for self-government and emancipation from the traditional severities of Spanish colonial rule.

The minister rejoined that the president of the council had informed him of our conversations in regard to Cuba, and that he quite agreed with the views General Prim had expressed to me in relation to the future of the island, but that Spain could not with honor treat with the insurgents with arms in their hands; and that in this she was governed by the same sense of self-respect as animated the United States in their refusal to treat with armed insurgents during the southern rebellion.

I observed to the minister that I had been for some time prepared to communicate formally to the cabinet of Madrid the propositions of my government in relation to the unfortunate conflict in Cuba, and had only deferred my note until informed officially of his excellency's assumption *ad interim* of the portfolio of foreign affairs; that now, after this interview, I should lose no time in placing before him the views of the President; and that I earnestly hoped they would be acceptable to the Spanish government, and result in a speedy and satisfactory disposition of the whole question, and I added that there seemed to be no good reason why two liberal governments, animated by the most friendly disposition toward each other, should not agree upon a practicable course of action in dealing with the struggle in Cuba, which, in truth, was only the aspiration of the Cubans for the liberties Spain enjoyed, commended to them yet more impressively by the example and experience of the United States.

In rising to take my leave, I alluded to the deplorable character of the conflict, and the unprovoked injuries suffered by American citizens within the Spanish lines, which I remarked would also be the subject of a formal communication at an early day, and to which Mr. Becerra promised to give immediate attention.

General Sickles to Mr. Becerra.

MADRID, *September* 3, 1869.

The undersigned, envoy extraordinary and minister plenipotentiary of the United States of America, had the honor, on the 31st of July last, to inform his excellency Don Manuel Silvela, minister of state of the government of his highness the Regent of Spain, that the President of the United States, animated by sentiments of sincere friendship for Spain, and earnestly desiring to see a speedy termination of the deplorable conflict in Cuba, tendered his good offices to the government of Spain for the purpose of promoting a settlement of the questions at issue, on a basis alike honorable and advantageous to the mother country and to the colony. His excellency the minister of state was pleased, on the 10th ultimo, to reply to this friendly overture, "that if the United States, by their natural influence in America, are able to contribute to the cessation of the effusion of blood, to the pacification of the Island of Cuba, and its entrance, by the election of its deputies, into the exercise of its rights, the government of Spain cannot but be grateful for these good offices."

The undersigned is happy to be able to assure his excellency, the minister of state, that the government of the United States is prepared to exert whatever influence it may have with the insurgents, to promote the pacification of Cuba. Nevertheless, the good offices of the President will be quite unavailing unless both the antagonists are disposed to listen to friendly counsels. This consideration increased the regret felt by the undersigned in having to communicate to his government the further declaration of his excellency, the minister of state, that Spain "can come to no definite decision in regard to the political situation and future government of the Island of Cuba until the insurgents lay down their arms and cease the struggle."

The undersigned is instructed to state that these conditions are deemed by the President incompatible with any practicable negotiation. It is not reasonable to hope that either party to a long and sanguinary contest will voluntarily abandon it without guarantees for the future, in some measure equivalent to the sacrifices it has made. The United States cannot ask the insurgents to lay down their arms unless the volunteers are simultaneously and effectively disarmed, and in good faith disbanded. It is notorious that these irregular troops have sometimes set at defiance the authority of their government and the orders of their superior officers, when the measures of the government have failed to satisfy their vindictive passions and their turbulent demands; and, therefore, the undersigned need not remark upon the insecurity of any reliance upon their forbearance if they have the means and the opportunity of assailing the unarmed insurgents. Besides the difficulties inseparable from disarming these forces on either side, the proceeding, if at all practicable, would consume precious time and delay the measures which ought to be taken to arrest the deplorable destruction of life and property in Cuba. The President is convinced that the suspension of hostilities is indispensable to the success of any negotiation; and since an armistice may with honor be granted in deference to the wishes of a friendly power, he trusts Spain will not refuse this concession. The President is, moreover, constrained to look with deep solicitude for some speedy action on the part of Spain that will put an end to the unprovoked injuries to American citizens which, as the contest is prolonged, become more and more frequent and fatal within the Spanish lines. The excesses which have followed the domination of the Spanish volunteers in some parts of the island, sparing neither non-combatants, nor prisoners of war, nor unoffending citizens of the United States, have aroused feelings of indignation and horror, which the refinement and sensibility of the Spanish nation will be the first to appreciate.

During the insurrection in Cuba the government of the United States has, in the utmost good faith and with great success, exerted its power to perform all its duties and obligations toward Spain, and to maintain its friendly relations with that power. It has been no easy task for the government to restrain its citizens within the bounds prescribed by the obligations of one friendly power to another, and to repress the spirit of adventure and enterprise from entering the field of a prolonged contest where the cry was in favor of liberty, emancipation, and self-government, especially when all the claims of neighborhood, of personal intimacies, and of political sympathies were tending in the direction of material aid to the insurrection, and when these tendencies were warmed into life by the personal presence and the appeals of those Cubans who were either residents of the United States or had sought refuge there from the desolation of their country. The government of the United States maintains that it has faithfully discharged all these duties.

Almost a year has passed since Cuba became the theatre of a war which has for its object the emancipation of the population from their colonial relation to Spain, and the establishment of an independent state. The struggle has commanded the attention, and no small share of the sympathy, of Europe as well as of America. It has already marked its track by devastation and ruin; towns sacked, houses burned, plantations destroyed, and lives lost. On either side the war has been one of desolation, and if continued, it must result in the destruction of the productive capacity of the island and an appalling sacrifice of human life. Measured by its duration, and the means employed to suppress it, the insurrection must indeed be formidable. Numerous and powerful as have been the armaments Spain has sent against the insurgents, they still keep the field in large force, and hold possession of a considerable portion of the island. It is not impossible that the Cubans may be conquered, but they can never again be contented, happy, or faithful subjects of Spain; and assuming that she may eventually subdue the present insurrection, she will find herself in possession of a devastated territory, inhabited by a discontented people. It is true that in comparison with past colonial wars for independence, the insurrection in Cuba has not been of long duration. Yet considering the vastly greater facilities for transoceanic communication and the many improvements in arms and implements of warfare which have done so much to make recent conflicts short and decisive, the struggle in Cuba is approaching the period when, according to the practice of nations, the recognition of the parties to the contest as belligerents cannot be delayed.

The people of the United States cannot be indifferent to the fate of Cuba. The spectacle of a population in their immediate neighborhood, long deprived of cherished franchises, and maintaining, at the cost of terrible sacrifices, an unequal struggle for self-government, could not but touch the sympathies of a generous and free nation. Nevertheless, the President has not been unmindful of the obligations which required him to confine within purely moral limits the manifestation of sentiments not easily to be restrained in popular governments. Nor has he relinquished the hope that Spain, herself regenerated by free institutions, might regard with indulgence the aspirations of the Cubans to enjoy the liberties the people of the parent state justly deem indispensable to their welfare and becoming their renown. The enlightened statesmen of Spain cannot fail to appreciate that the feelings and the affections of the native population of the island are not only estranged, but that they are deeply hostile to the continuance of Spanish rule. Nor can they fail to recognize the advancing growth of that sentiment which claims for every part of the American hemisphere the right of self-government and freedom from transatlantic dependence.

England, bound as she has been to the traditions of the past, tenacious as she has been of her possessions, and conservative of all her rights and interests, has not been unmindful of the force of this sentiment, and has anticipated events by granting self-government to her North American provinces. Denmark, approving the policy of the separation of colonies from the parent state, is endeavoring to part with her insular possessions. Russia has set a recent example of parting with her possessions in America. Nor are these the only governments in the Old World that are preparing their colonies for independence and self-government. It can no longer be a question of national dignity, nor can the proper pride or the just susceptibilities of a great power refuse to consider the question of a voluntary severance of past relations between itself and distant possessions. Spain herself was one of the first of the great European powers to cede voluntarily its distant colonial possessions, for she transferred Louisiana to France, and subsequently ceded Florida to the United States. France, engaged in war, and finding Louisiana liable to military attack, replenished her treasury by its sale, while relieving herself of the burden of the defense of a distant possession. The President trusts that, with these examples, Spain will now be prepared to consider, and to adopt with respect to Cuba, a like course of wise foresight and enlightened statesmanship. In the name of humanity, Spain can afford to arrest this war; and were it not for her traditional pride, and her recognized disregard of all considerations of mere interest where her honor is involved, an appeal might be made to these motives, which, after all, must be regarded by those who would wisely and prudently conduct the affairs of a nation.

History records but one issue to all the wars in North and South America waged during this and the last century by European states to compel the submission of colonies which had asserted their independence. Europe has found more advantage in the commerce of the rich and prosperous nations which have sprung from the colonies than in holding them in costly and precarious subjection. Not a few reasons might be assigned for the belief that, however the struggle in Cuba may be prolonged, it will end like those which have preceded it in America. And the undersigned, with the greatest respect for the enlightened judgment of the cabinet of Madrid, earnestly commends to its consideration the conclusion of the President, that now is the opportune moment for Spain to take the measures necessary for a prompt and satisfactory solution of the questions presented by the situation in Cuba.

After much consideration, and a careful survey of the question in all its relations, the government of the United States is convinced that it is its duty to exert its friendly influence to bring this unhappy contest to a close. Duty to its own citizens, and to their large interests jeoparded by the continuance of the war; the necessity of maintaining quiet within its borders, now seriously disturbed by a struggle carried on so near its shores; friendship for Spain, one of the oldest and earliest of our allies, with whom no interruption of friendly relations has occurred since our entrance into the family of nations; sympathy for the Cubans, who are our neighbors, all alike impel the government to this course.

The President, therefore, has directed the undersigned to offer formally to the cabinet at Madrid the good offices of the United States, for the purpose of bringing to a close the civil war in Cuba, and to propose the following bases of negotiations:

I. The independence of Cuba to be acknowledged by Spain.

II. Cuba to pay to Spain a sum, within a time and in a manner to be agreed upon by them, as an equivalent for the entire and definite relinquishment by Spain of all her rights in that island, including the public property of every description. If Cuba should not be able to pay the whole sum at once in cash, the future payments by installments to be adequately secured by a pledge of the export and import customs duties, under an arrangement to be agreed upon for their collection, in trust, for the purpose of securing both principal and interest of those installments until their final discharge.

III. The abolition of slavery in the Island of Cuba.

IV. An armistice shall take place so soon as the basis of the negotiations shall be agreed upon, and shall continue until the termination of the conference.

The undersigned reserves for a further communication, in case the good offices of the United States are accepted, the views of his government in relation to the proposed conference, and the manner in which the negotiation should proceed. The undersigned will not have complied with all the instructions of his government if he omits to invite the earliest attention of his excellency the minister of state to this communication, in order that the President may be informed, as soon as possible, of the decision of the government of Spain.

The undersigned avails himself of this occasion to convey to his excellency the minister of state assurances of the very distinguished consideration with which he has the honor to be, &c.

No. 22.

General Sickles to Mr. Fish.

No. 15.] MADRID, *September* 8, 1869.

I have the honor to forward to you a copy of my note to Mr. Becerra, the minister of state *ad interim*, in relation to Charles Speakman and Albert Wyeth, executed at Santiago de Cuba. In the further execution of your instructions No. 10, I have in the same communication formally protested against these deplorable excesses, demanding, in the name of humanity, that the war in Cuba, if prolonged, shall not be conducted in disregard of the customs and usages of Christian nations.

The most extravagant rumors are current in relation to my note to

Mr. Becerra of the 3d. It seems the government gave out intimations of its purport, and these have been accepted as indicating the purpose of the United States at an early day to recognize the Cubans as belligerents, if our mediation be not at once accepted. No small degree of excitement has followed, and a sudden fall in the Spanish funds is attributed to the hostile tone of opinion echoed by several influential journals. I inclose some extracts from the "Epoca" and others, that you may see the spirit of the press on the subject.

The president of the council wrote me on the 3d instant from Vichy, expressing his regret that his sudden departure prevented him from seeing me before leaving town, and informing me that he would return about the 20th and resume our conferences. I replied, acquainting him with the urgent tenor of my instructions, and adding that, besides the principal question, recent events in Cuba had increased the solicitude of the President for the prompt action of the Spanish cabinet.

* * * * * * * * *

The republican organization shows increasing vitality and efficiency throughout Spain; the difficulties attending the choice of a king distract more and more the monarchical party; and the opinion gains ground that the further development of the revolution will be in a republican direction, to which public sentiment obviously inclines. Hence the monarchical organs are foremost in their efforts to provoke a misunderstanding with the United States, while the republican journals have been generally friendly, and have united with their leading partisans in deprecating any interruption of the good relations now existing between the two countries.

(For Mr. Sickles' note to Señor Becerra see page 104.)

No. 23.

Mr. Fish to General Sickles.

[Telegram.]

WASHINGTON, *September* 11, 1869.

We hope there is no truth in the rumor that Spain is about to send additional troops to Cuba. It would exhibit a want of confidence in the pending negotiation that might compel the withdrawal of the offer of this government to attempt a reconciliation. It might prolong the struggle, and the destruction of life and property, with questionable influence on the result. It certainly would embarrass the negotiations.

You are at liberty, in your discretion, to communicate this view to the Spanish government. You will advise me by telegraph of their intention with respect to the sending of additional troops.

No. 24.

General Sickles to Mr. Fish.

[Telegram.]

SEPTEMBER 14, 1869.

Telegram received. Have asked Motley to repeat parts not intelligible. Additional troops had been heretofore announced for fall campaign. Anticipated recognition of insurgents as belligerents causes much excitement and ill-temper. Press of all parties urge government to send large re-enforcements of men and ships at once. One batallion has sailed. No doubt active measures are hastened by fear of early recognition. It is reported that Spain has communicated my note of 3d of September to European cabinets and asked their advice and co-operation. I have asked interview with minister, and will report result immediately.

No. 25.

General Sickles to Mr. Fish.

No. 17.] SEPTEMBER 14, 1869.

In a full and frank interview held to-day with his excellency Mr. Becerra, minister of the colonies and charged *ad interim* with the department of foreign affairs, I brought to his notice the rumor, which has been current for some days past, that the Spanish government had opened negotiations with other European powers on the subject of my note of September 3, and asked if there was any foundation for this statement.

His excellency at once replied that there was none; that the government had not communicated my note to any other power; that no answer had as yet been sent to me on account of the absence of the president of the council and the minister of state; and that, in a matter of such gravity, the government could take no definite action before the meeting of the Cortes.

I expressed my gratification that the statement to which I had referred was erroneous, adding that, as the overtures of the United States had been made in a friendly spirit, and with the greatest reserve, if the circle of discussion was to be widened by the introduction of other powers, the government of the United States would desire to be informed of this action.

I then said that, in view of the tender of good offices made by the United States government for the purpose of promoting a prompt and satisfactory termination of hostilities, the President would learn with regret of the intention of Spain to send large re-enforcements to Cuba, inasmuch as this would indicate either that Spain is indisposed to accept our friendly offices, or despairs of reaching a favorable result through the pending negotiations.

His excellency replied that the Cuban question was altogether domestic; that, highly as the government of Spain valued the friendly offices of the United States, it could only proceed in a legal and constitutional way; that it could not yield to the armed insurrection; that its first duty was to restore order in Cuba by force of arms; but, not restricting itself to this, it would at the same time extend to the island the fullest reforms and the widest liberties enjoyed in the peninsula; a general amnesty would be granted; it would make immediate preparations for the election of deputies in Cuba; on their arrival in Madrid the government and the Cortes could, in concert, determine the future destiny of the island, including a scheme for the gradual and entire abolition of slavery. The Spanish government had frankly and gratefully accepted the good offices of the United States; but the bases proposed in my note of September 3 were such as it was out of the power of the Spanish government to accept; that, while recognizing the friendly spirit and the loyalty with which they were offered, they could not be adopted in the present state of public opinion in Spain. That the mediation of any nation in a purely domestic question was incompatible with the honor of Spain; that the permanent committee of the Cortes, representing all shades of politics, had unanimously voted that the independence of Cuba was inadmissible as a basis of negotiation; and that, by the terms of the constitution, no measure could be taken without the consent of the Cortes that might result in any alienation of Spanish territory. His excellency hoped that it might be possible for me to withdraw the note of September 3. He said that this would relieve the Spanish government, and enable it to proceed more expeditiously with the liberal plan which it had adopted.

I replied that the United States, in making the propositions in question, had no purpose of aggrandizement, and only desired to put an end to the calamities that now desolated the Island of Cuba; that if the bases proposed were not likely to accomplish this result, I had no doubt I would be authorized to withdraw the propositions.

In reply to my earnest representations of the necessity for an armistice as the essential preliminary to any satisfactory arrangement, his excellency said that no one could be more anxious for an armistice than he and his colleagues in the government; the difficulty was, how to bring it about in a proper manner.

His excellency then informed me that a report from the Captain General of Cuba had been called for in relation to the cases of Speakman and Wyeth, and, if the facts were as alleged, full reparation would be made to the families of the deceased; and he added that orders had been given to prevent such scenes of cruelty in the future conduct of the war.

The foregoing *résumé* of our conversation, which occupied more than an hour, having been sent to the minister of state *ad interim* for his revision, he has returned it to me with the following remarks: "The dispatch of your excellency contains in its *ensemble* a faithful and sufficiently exact *résumé* of the conference which we had on the 14th. For my part, I have only one point to rectify, and if I explain some others, it is with the desire that there shall be nothing which can give rise to doubts, and not because the explanation is absolutely indispensable. That which I wish to rectify is in regard to the resolution of the permanent commission of the Cortes. That commission unanimously decided to tender to the government all the means at its disposal to extinguish the rebellion, and also to oppose our treating on the subject of Cuba with any foreign power."

His excellency proceeds to explain the meaning of this resolution, and to amplify other points mentioned in the *résumé*. This communication may indeed be regarded as an expression of the views of the cabinet of Madrid in relation to the pending negotiation, and I shall inclose a copy of it with this dispatch.

* * * * * * *

Mr. Becerra to General Sickles.

Translation.]

SEPTEMBER 16, 1869.

Mr. Valera handed me yesterday the copy of the dispatch which you had the goodness to send him through the secretary of your legation, but the dispatch was delivered to me so late that I had not sufficient time to examine it with the necessary leisure, so as to make a slight correction and certain explanations which struck me as proper for the purpose which we propose; that is, to accomplish the pacification of Cuba, and to terminate a civil war, which cannot but prove the more disastrous the more it is prolonged. I beg your pardon for this involuntary delay, and repeat my cordial thanks for the interest you have manifested that this matter may be ended promptly and well, a result which can hardly fail to be reached, those who are managing the matter being animated equally by good faith and the best desires.

The dispatch of your excellency contains in its *ensemble* a faithful and sufficiently exact *résumé* of the conference which we had on the 14th. For my part, I have only one point to rectify, and if I explain some others, it is with the desire that there shall be nothing which can give rise to doubts, and not because the explanation is absolutely indispensable.

That which is to rectify is in regard to the decision of the permanent commission of the Cortes. That commission unanimously decided to tender to the government all the means at its disposal to extinguish the rebellion, and decided to oppose the government's treating on the subject of Cuba with any foreign power. You will perceive that the idea of the commission was no other than to oppose a mediation or intervention in our domestic affairs, which would result in diminishing and tarnishing the sovereignty of the Spanish people, whom the Cortes to-day represent completely, and of whose honor and sovereignty they are so jealous; but the Cortes cannot oppose our coming to a friendly understanding for the termination of the struggle, the cabinet of Washington interposing its good offices, which we accept with gratitude, to induce the Cubans, who, residing in the United States, are in correspondence with the insurgents, to pursuade them to lay down their arms, assuring and promising them that Spain will give them amnesty and full liberties, and will summon to Madrid the legitimate representatives of that ultramarine province. These can set forth frankly their grievances, and make known their aspirations, which being, as they of course will be, those of the immense majority of the islanders, cannot fail to be satisfied without having recourse to violence, and solely by the infallible, legal, and peaceful means which a constitution so free as ours provides.

It is upon this point alone, I repeat, that a rectification is necessary. On the others I am agreed. You will, however, permit me to explain briefly a few of them.

In regard to the negotiations with other powers on the subject of your note, I said the current rumor was false. As Spain will not negotiate with the United States upon a subject like that of Cuba, which relates to its internal policy and government, neither will she negotiate with any other power. If Spain hopes to preserve Cuba united to the metropolis, it is because she trusts that a majority of the islanders regard it still an honor and a privilege to be Spaniards, and because she trusts that the few insurgents will soon be brought to terms, if not by persuasion, by force, however painful it would be to us to continue to employ this means. It is likewise inexact that we have transmitted a copy of your note to any foreign government.

As to the armistice, I do not think I said I desired it, but that I desired peace; but as it is evident that he who desires the end desires the means, it is also true that I desire the armistice if this is necessarily an effective means of obtaining peace. In this sense, I will write to the Captain General of Cuba, but can only suggest to him the propriety of an armistice, if it is to terminate in pacification. I cannot make it an order, because only he who holds the chief command of an armed force, and upon whom depend the lives of so many men and the issue of the campaign, ought to decide if an armistice is proper and opportune.

Finally, with or without armistice, you know what Spain promises and is disposed to grant to the insurgents. They have only to ask for peace, and they will have it; and with peace, all the promises heretofore mentioned truly and loyally fulfilled. If they do not want peace, the war will continue with energy and activity on our part, but pardoning the vanquished and prisoners, and striving to avoid all shedding of blood through revenge, and all reprisals, however horrible and cruel may be the acts of the insurgents.

I have nothing more to add, except to beg anew that you will insist upon being authorized to withdraw your note, and that it may be withdrawn. This will be the best way to enable Spain, without its being said that she yields to any pressure, to give most freely what she offers. In this way it can be gratefully accepted in Cuba, and in this way our moderation (*blandura*) cannot be censured in Spain as unworthy weakness.

Mr. Valera said it might be necessary to add a word or two which had been omitted in our yesterday's interview. Mr. Becerra might put in still stronger language the intention of the government to make full reparation for the outrageous execution of Speakman and Wyeth at Santiago. Admiral Topete was much incensed when he read General Sickles's note on the subject, saying that the matter must be instantly investigated, and if Palacios, the governor, had been guilty of the brutality charged, he should be removed and punished.

Another word might possibly be added in regard to the gunboat question. This is a much graver cause of preoccupation than General Sickles's note. It is true the bases contained in that note are not acceptable, and cannot be entertained; he could say this with certainty now, as both Messrs. Prim and Silvela had answered in that sense;

but neither of them considered the note an unfriendly one, but on the contrary dictated by a sincere desire of the United States to see the struggle brought to an end. But the matter of the gunboats was one of especial gravity. The pretext that they were intended to be used in any way against Peru was not serious; the war with the South American republics was over. The seizure of the gunboats seemed to indicate a hostile interior toward Spain. If this exists, Spain must and will face the situation thus created. "But if we are forced into war with the United States," he said, "we are not so innocent (*candides*) as to think we are going to have any allies in Europe. We expect to fight it out alone, whatever the issue may be. We have made no overtures to any power for help."

No. 26.

Mr. Fish to General Sickles.

[Telegram.]

WASHINGTON, *September* 15, 1869.

If a negotiation were made on the basis of the six successive steps mentioned in your dispatch No. 10, omitting the plebiscit, can the president of council give assurance that if the United States induced the insurgents to lay down arms, and deputies to the Cortes be elected by Cuba, that the Cortes will grant independence? The plebiscit is impracticable, because in the present circumstances and conditions of the island, a popular vote can be no indication of the popular will, and this must be borne in mind with reference to any election to be held for deputies. It is doubtful if the insurgents will consent to lay down arms, but if their early independence can be assured thereby, the United States will make every effort to induce them to do so.

No. 27.

General Sickles to Mr. Fish.

[Telegram.]

SEPTEMBER 16, 1869.

Long interview Tuesday with foreign secretary *ad interim*. Notes of conversation subsequently exchanged. Am now able to send *résumé*.

First. Spain frankly and gratefully accepts good offices of United States, but cannot accept bases proposed, and asks withdrawal of my note of September 3d. Spain desires, without appearance of pressure, to make the concessions she offers to Cuba.

Second. Permanent commission of Cortes now in session, representing all parties, unanimously assure government all the means at their disposal to put down rebellion; they oppose treating about Cuba with any foreign power; not objecting, however, to a friendly understanding with the United States by which their good offices may help to end the struggle.

Third. Spain has not begun and does not contemplate negotiations with any foreign power about Cuba, or the proposed mediation of the United States, nor has my note been communicated to any foreign government.

Fourth. Spain desires to terminate civil war in Cuba, and will agree to armistice if necessary to peace. This measure will be recommended to Captain General of Cuba, but must be left to his discretion.

Fifth. Spain is ready at once to give Cuba ample reforms and widest liberties enjoyed in peninsula, also general amnesty and gradual emancipation of slaves.

These refused, the war will be prosecuted with energy and activity, pardoning, however, the vanquished and prisoners, and striving to prevent all shedding of blood through revenge, and all reprisals, whatever the provocation from insurgents.

Sixth. Reparation promised in cases of Speakman and Wyeth. Orders given to prevent such cruelties hereafter.

Full report will go by next mail. Will telegraph further particulars if desired.

Spain regards Cuban question as purely domestic, and will not, in my judgment, accept mediation. If our offer be withdrawn, and friendly relations continue, our good offices can mitigate the cruel character of the war, promote liberal concessions, and perhaps bring about an armistice.

Two more transports have started for Cuba with troops, from twelve to twenty thousand rumored under arms, besides six war vessels. Will report departures as they occur.

No. 28.

General Sickles to Mr. Fish.

[Telegram.]

SEPTEMBER 17, 1869.

Telegram of 15th received. President of council expected in Madrid on or before 21st. Discretionary authority to withdraw pending offer of mediation will facilitate new negotiation. Information about recognition and gunboats desirable before further overtures. Cortes would probably insist on plebiscit. Perhaps the obstacles to a fair vote may be removed by an armistice or by a simultaneous disarmament of volunteers and insurgents. Suggest answer direct by French cable and duplicate through Motley.

No. 29.

General Sickles to Mr. Fish.

No. 19.] MADRID, *September* 19, 1869.

In the execution of the instructions contained in your telegram of the 13th instant, you will have observed in the report already transmitted in my dispatch No. 17, that I withheld any intimation of the probable withdrawal of our proposed offer of mediation. In the present temper of the cabinet, which more or less reflects an excited public opinion, the suggestion would have had no influence in preventing the movement of re-enforcements to Cuba, whilst it might have increased the obvious disquietude of this government to be subjected to any appearance of pressure at this moment.

Nevertheless the interview of the 14th had not proceeded far before the minister himself stated that Spain would be embarrassed in the execution of the liberal policy it contemplated in relation to Cuba, unless my note of the 3d instant, proposing the mediation of the United States, were withdrawn, and that he therefore hoped this might be done. It will not escape your notice that, in my reply, I waived any allusion to the withdrawal of the note, and confined myself to the expression of a mere opinion that my government would not hesitate to withdraw the proposals it had made, if convinced that these would not contribute to the pacification of Cuba; that our offer had been made for that purpose only, and without any motive of present or ulterior advantage to the United States.

It is needless to trouble you with further details of the interview, as the synopsis forwarded by telegraph, day before yesterday, together with the brief report already transmitted in my No. 17, and Mr. Becerra's note inclosed with it, will put you in possession of all that transpired, except the arguments and observations of the minister and myself respectively in support of our views. The conference was marked by the same cordiality that has heretofore agreeably characterized my intercourse with the Foreign Office.

I have not yet deemed it opportune, in view of the commotion caused by our proposed mediation on the basis of independence, to suggest to Mr. Becerra the modifications of our offer communicated in your instructions by telegram through Mr. Motley, dated 1st instant, and received correctly on the 5th. These modifications, as well as the new bases mentioned in your instructions, received by telegraph on the 16th instant, will be the subject of an early conference with the president of the council when he returns to Madrid.

* * * * * * *

I inclose with this dispatch a decree organizing a commission to consider and propose within thirty days a plan of political and administrative reform for Porto Rico, including the abolition of slavery. It is preceded by a decree dissolving a former commission, and establishing another to prepare and submit forthwith the necessary changes in the penal code of the Peninsula to make it applicable to the colonies. The report of the colonial minister, preceding the decree in relation to Porto Rico, is not without interest in its recognition of the cogent reasons demanding radical changes in Spanish colonial government, and thorough reforms in colonial administration. Other decrees are foreshadowed, establishing freedom of worship in Cuba, and providing for the election of deputies to the Cortes; although several times announced semi-officially as forthcoming, they have not yet appeared.

I am assured by the president of the Cortes that among the first subjects brought before that body will be the cruel and vindictive manner in which the war in Cuba is prosecuted, and he feels confident the Cortes will require the most energetic measures to be taken by the government to prevent hereafter the outrages which have been so justly denounced by the United States. Captain General Concha, Marquis of Duro, has likewise expressed to me his abhorrence of the treatment of prisoners of war and other captives in Cuba, and will move actively in the matter on the assembling of the Cortes, where his high military reputation and personal character will exercise their just influence. Other prominent personages have given me similar assurances.

I have sent confidential instructions to the consuls at Cadiz, Barcelona, and Malaga to inform me of all movements of troops embarked for Cuba, and of vessels of war leaving those ports for the Spanish West Indian fleet. I have already received a report from General Duffie, announcing the departure of one thousand five hundred infantry from Cadiz, and that five or six hundred more are there preparing to embark. The departure of the frigate Almansas from Carthagena, bound for Havana, is announced to-day. I have not sent to our consuls at Carthagena or Santander for information, as they seem to be Spaniards.

MINISTRY OF TRANSMARINE AFFAIRS.—STATEMENT.

SIR: By a decree of September 29, 1866, a commission was appointed whose duty it was "to examine and propose a reform of the penal laws in force in our transmarine possessions," and also to propose "the principles and rules whereby judgments in criminal cases shall be governed" in those territories.

This commission, taking as its basis the penal code which is in force in the peninsula, and accepting as its object the application of said code in our transmarine possessions, has labored to facilitate the same by means of some reforms in the text. But these labors do not embrace the whole code, nor do they refer to the enforcement of the penal code, which was, and justly so, one of the principal ends for which the commission was appointed.

It is important to carry out this intention, and it would be a matter of great regret, if, by reason of its being unduly extended, any obstacle should be placed in the way of its speedy accomplishment. Hence, the undersigned minister is of opinion that the duties of the aforesaid commission being considered at an end, another should be appointed to examine and propose the various reforms and modifications whereby our penal code may be applied to our various transmarine territories, and at the same time to prepare a provisional law for the application of the code, deferring the elaborate preparation of a law for judicial procedure until some future time.

In this manner, limiting its task to the examination of the common penal law, and to the form of its immediate application, the committee will be able to accomplish this as speedily as the government of your highness and our brethren beyond the sea desire and need.

With these considerations the undersigned minister has the honor to submit to the approval of your highness the accompanying plan of a decree.

The Minister of Transmarine Affairs,
MANUEL BECERRA.

MADRID, *September* 10, 1869.

DECREE.

In accordance with the suggestion of the minister of transmarine affairs, made with the approval of the council of ministers, I decree as follows:

ARTICLE 1. The commission which was appointed by the decree of September 29, 1866, to examine and propose reforms in the penal laws in force in the transmarine possessions of Spain, is hereby dissolved.

ART. 2. Another commission is appointed in its stead, to consist of a president, five voting members, and a secretary, who shall have the right to vote, and it shall be the duty of said commission, first, to propose as speedily as possible such alterations as may be necessary in the penal code now in force in the peninsula, in order to apply the same to the various Spanish territories lying beyond the sea; secondly, to prepare, likewise with all speed, a provisional law for the application of the same code; thirdly, to examine and propose the basis of a law for judicial procedure in criminal cases for the said territories.

ART. 3. The ministry of transmarine affairs will furnish the commission with the data and information which it possesses, and will further give the necessary orders for the execution of this decree.

Done at Madrid, September 10, 1869.

FRANCISCO SERRANO.

MANUEL BECERRA,
Minister of Transmarine Affairs.

STATEMENT.

SIR: The day being at hand for our legislative body to renew its labors, and the legitimate representatives of Porto Rico being now present in the metropolis, the time has arrived for the fulfillment of the just duty and of the solemn obligation imposed upon us by the September revolution toward the Spaniards beyond the sea.

Spain is not limited to the peninsula which is bounded by the Mediterranean and the Atlantic. The community of race and traditions which is manifested by a common language and a glorious history, never tarnished by disloyalty, clearly shows that nations are made principally by means of moral bonds of union far stronger than misfortunes and errors. If governments that distrusted the national spirit by which they disdained to be actuated, hoped more from the always doubtful efficacy of external and violent means than from the attractive virtue of national solidarity, never appealed to in vain among our people, it is now time to seek, in the free manifestation of the aspirations of all, that potent union and that dauntless courage whereby we may recover the position which history claims for us, and which of right belongs to us in the council and assembly of enlightened nations. Sovereign Spain cannot deprive any of her members of that portion of sovereignty which is their due.

The revolutionary movement, therefore, was very soon made in our transmarine possessions, and gave rise to legitimate as well as encouraging hopes. But, in an unfortunate hour, by reason of inveterate feelings of distrust, by reason of the excessive exaggeration of past offenses, perhaps also by reason of inordinate aspirations, this movement, which ought to have been as measured, as regular, and as productive of good as in the peninsula, stepped beyond the limits within which it should have confined itself, raising the flag of rebellion in Cuba, to violate the sacred integrity of the Spanish nation.

In presence of such a danger the honor of the country, the duty of the government, the vital interests of the revolution, peremptorily demanded the defense of the territory, and, as a consequence of the state of hostilites, the much to be regretted but necessary postponement of reforms, so that these might not be confounded with the timorous and arbitrary reforms of past times, nor fail to appear solemnly consecrated by the action and free consent of all interested in them, thus strengthening with firmer bonds than those of force the lasting union of Cuba and Spain.

But if such invincible obstacles temporarily prevent the Spanish revolution from exercising its political influence in the most precious of our Antilles, this is not the case in Porto Rico, and the government being free from the well-founded apprehensions which the state of affairs in Cuba cause it to entertain with respect to that island, when the question is to radically change the political and social system there prevailing, it is proper to show how energetic, honest, and sincere is its desire to admit the colonies to the full enjoyment of their rights, and to an untrammeled participation in the great conquests of modern civilization.

A deplorable and pertinacious tradition of despotism, which, if it could ever be justified, is without a shadow of reason at the present time, intrusted the direction and management of our colonial establishment to the agents of the metropolis, destroying, by their dominant and exclusive authority, the vital energies of the country, and the creative and productive activity of free individuals.

And although the system may now have improved in some of its details, the domineering action of the authorities being less felt, it still appears full of the original error, which is upheld by the force of tradition, and the necessary influence of interests created under their protection, which doubtless are deserving of respect, so far as they are reconcilable with the requirements of justice, with the common welfare, and with the principles on which every liberal system should be founded.

A change of system, political as well as administrative, is, therefore, imperatively demanded. To declare and respect the inalienable rights of persons, municipalities, and provinces, to seek to bring about administrative centralization, allowing the widest freedom of action to municipal boards and provincial deputations, as legitimate, immediate, and direct organs and representatives of the people electing them; to simplify the complicated mechanism of the superior administration, restoring to those natural centers the powers which of right belong to them, and as a political guarantee of still greater importance, firmly to establish the public representation, at one time near the colonial government, at another near that of the metropolis, or in both at once, if it should be possible and necessary—such is, in brief, the general intention of the undersigned minister.

But, in order that these intentions may be duly fulfilled, and that their results may be felt by all alike, it is indispensable to solve one of the most difficult social problems, at once the danger and the glory of our epoch. Errors arising from a false view of life sacrificed for more than three centuries the personal liberty of thousands of beings to the idea of preparing for them a greater degree of happiness after death. Mistaken notions of economy were joined to these, seeking in forced labor that wealth and production which are found far more abundantly in free labor. But neither do the eternal laws of morality, which permit not even a good end to be attained through unjust means, nor does the mission of the state, which, as the supreme organ of right, ought to respect it under all circumstances and above all interests, permit the existence of slavery, with its horrors and dangers, to continue any longer, without an act of immorality and injustice. This was recognized by the commissioners appointed to propose political, moral, and social reforms in Cuba and Porto Rico; without for this reason forgetting, as the undersigned likewise will not forget, the just respect due to material interests created under the protection of ancient institutions and laws. No progress, no advancement of humanity is ever accomplished by an absolute disregard of a previously existing state of things, unjust though this may have been; for, notwithstanding its injustice, it has given rise to human relations, the consideration of which it is neither right nor prudent, much less politic, to lay aside, thereby reaching a solution which will only be productive of lasting disturbances.

Besides this, the serious difficulties presented by every social change; the discretion with which liberty should be accorded to persons whom it was considered a crime to call human beings, and for whom labor has been a permanent sign of servitude, disappear almost entirely where the white and civilized population is much more numerous than the colored, and where the majority of the latter have been able to earn a subsistence, and even competence and wealth by free labor, which experience, as well as the teachings of economical science, has shown to be the most beneficial and productive. In order happily and speedily to effect these important changes, which, notwithstanding the urgent call for them, must receive serious and conscientious study, the undersigned proposes to your highness the appointment of a commission composed of persons of high character, and having a knowledge of the real necessities of the country, who, in a brief and determined space of time, but not insufficient for those who must already have formed their opinions, shall propose such reforms and plans as may be necessary to harmonize the social, political, and administrative situation of the Island of Porto Rico with the imperative demands of justice and morality, and, as far as possible, with the principles laid down in the democratic constitution of the Spanish nation, which ought to be applied, as soon as possible, to those remote countries.

With the foregoing considerations, the undersigned has the honor to submit to the approval of your highness the accompanying plan of a decree.

MADRID, *September* 10, 1869.

The Minister of Transmarine Affairs,
MANUEL BECERRA.

DECREE.

In view of the statements made by the minister of transmarine affairs, with the approval of the council of ministers, I decree as follows:

ARTICLE 1. A commission is hereby appointed, whose duty it shall be to discuss and propose to the minister of transmarine affairs the principles in accordance with which shall be made all plans of laws for political and administrative reform, and for the abolition of slavery in the Island of Porto Rico.

ART. 2. This commission shall consist of a president, and the minister of transmarine affairs shall act in this capacity; of fifteen voting members, and the under secretary of the ministry, who shall act as secretary, with voice and vote. The voting members shall elect the vice-president.

ART. 3. The commission shall remain in office for thirty days precisely, from the moment of entering upon the discharge of its duties, which shall take place three days after the publication of the present decree.

ART. 4. The ministry of transmarine affairs will furnish to the commission such data and information as it may possess, and the necessary orders will be given for the execution of this decree.

Done at Madrid, September 10, 1869.

FRANCISCO SERRANO.

The Minister of Transmarine Affairs,
MANUEL BECERRA.

No. 30.

Mr. Fish to General Sickles.

[Telegram.]

WASHINGTON, *September* 23, 1869.

The good offices of the United States were tendered in a spirit of mutual friendship, and in the interest of humanity, of Spain, of Cuba, and of the United States. If the tender be not acceptable to Spain you may withdraw it, and you may say that those good offices will be ready whenever they can tend to a settlement of the unhappy contest that is devastating Cuba, and injuring the commercial interests of this and of other nations.

The gunboats were arrested on the request of Peru, who claims to be at war with Spain. We cannot deny the condition of war as an abstract fact, inasmuch as we have offered, and both parties have accepted our mediation. Peru claims that although these boats may not go to Peru they will release from employment other portions of the Spanish navy, and strengthen her in case the pending mediations do not result in a peace. Our position of impartial neutrality compelled their detention.

No step has been taken toward a recognition of the belligerency of the insurgents of Cuba. But this government cannot forestall its future necessities. If belligerency be recognized at all, it will be because the necessities of the case and the complications of the controversy force it upon us. Your dispatch No. 14 this day received. Your instructions in dispatch No. 2 from this department directed you to read those instructions to the minister, and to leave a copy with him.

No. 31.

General Sickles to Mr. Fish.

No. 21.] SEPTEMBER 25, 1869.

Your telegram of the 23d instant having called my attention to the direction contained in your instructions No. 2, to read those instructions to the minister of state and leave the office copy with him, it becomes proper for me to state more fully than I had deemed necessary my authority and reasons for adopting another form of communication. Your instructions No. 3 required me to avail myself of Mr. Forbes' assistance in this negotiation, and in the event of his reaching Madrid, and notifying the Spanish cabinet informally of the nature of our propositions, before my arrival, to govern myself in their formal and official presentation somewhat by his report and advice. On my arrival in Madrid Mr. Forbes informed me that he had communicated to the president of the council the propositions contained in your instructions No. 2, and that he had not received them favorably; that General Prim's colleagues in the cabinet were yet more disinclined toward our views; that in his (Mr. Forbes's) judgment Spain would not negotiate upon the bases we proposed, and that to communicate them formally would not only result in their prompt rejection, but embarrass further negotiations.

On this report, and on the advice of Mr. Forbes, which was confirmed by my own information, I deferred the formal communication of your instructions No. 2, and informed you of my determination and the reasons for it in my dispatch No. 4 of the 12th ultimo. Subsequent interviews with the president of the council and the minister of state only made more apparent the wide difference between your views and the present policy of Spain, and I proceeded at once to ascertain, by means of frank and informal conversations with the president of the council, the bases on which Spain would be willing to negotiate. These I had the honor to report in my telegram of the 13th, and in my dispatches Nos. 8, 9, and 10, of the 16th, 20th, and 21st ultimo.

The serious obstacle to the negotiation appearing to be not in the independence of Cuba, but in the preliminaries—Spain being unwilling to accept the formal mediation of the United States, or to agree to an armistice, or in any manner to recognize the insurgents as parties to a negotiation—I would have preferred to confine myself for the present to the informal presentation and discussion of our propositions and views, in the hope that I might thereby promote an accord between the two governments and avoid a formal refusal to entertain our offer of mediation.

Your telegram of August 29, instructing me that the propositions of the president of the council afforded no practicable basis of negotiation, and that the president desired an early and decisive answer to our offer of mediation, made it my duty at once to communicate it formally to this cabinet. This I proceeded to do in a note to the minister of state rather than in the form your instructions No. 2 had indicated, because the conferences which had taken place meanwhile had advanced the negotiation considerably, and if I had not availed myself of the latitude given me in your instructions No. 3, I would have surrendered an obvious advantage gained in the initiative already taken, besides affording the minister an opportunity to ignore our offer altogether, by simply declining to receive the copy of your instructions, as is usually done when cabinets do not choose to engage in a discussion.

It was, moreover, necessary, in the execution of your further instructions, to communicate views not embodied in your No. 2, and yet depending upon it for their relation to the discussion. In doing this it seemed to me preferable, if not essential, to embody all I had to say on the subject in a note which had for its apparent object a reply to the communication made to me on the 10th of August by the minister of state, and thus present the whole case to this government in a form that avoided the inconvenience and the risk of two communications, one of which might not be received at all.

It is quite true, as was foreseen, that this cabinet find our offer embarrassing to them, and ask that the communication may be withdrawn; yet it is now quite at the option of the United States to have the formal and definite answer of this government to their offer of mediation, which, from the tenor of your recent instructions, appeared to be most desirable.

In respectfully submitting this explanation, and commending it to your candor, I have only to add that in all my proceedings, and especially in the exercise of the discretion confided to me, "every consideration of humanity, as well as of interest," admonished me "so to shape this negotiation within the line of your instructions as to bring it to a successful result, if possible."

No. 32.

General Sickles to Mr. Fish.

No. 22.] MADRID, *September* 25, 1869.

On Thursday, the 23d, I had an interview at the Foreign Office, by request of the minister of state, with Mr. Silvela and Mr. Becerra. The minister of state asked me if I had received any instructions from my government in regard to the withdrawal of our offer of intervention in the affair of Cuba. I replied that I had not—and this led to some desultory conversation which need not be reported, as the same matters were discussed more fully with the president of the council the next day.

Mr. Silvela then spoke of two letters which he had just received from America; one from the Spanish consul at New York, announcing the departure of an armed vessel from Cedar Keys for Cuba with six guns, four thousand rifles, and two hundred men; and the other from Mr. Roberts, detailing the difficulties which the American government threw in the way of the departure of the Spanish gunboats in New York. He enlarged upon the apparent unfriendliness of this action.

I replied that Cedar Keys was so insignificant and remote a point that there might well be some exaggeration in the report that had reached the Spanish consul; that even if it were true, it only proved that the insurgents, prevented by the government from fitting out expeditions in the principal ports of the United States, sought these remote and obscure places along our immense coast line which it was impossible to guard entirely. The government of the United States had loyally and with great success exerted itself to preserve a strict neutrality in the war which Spain was carrying on with Cuba. It had arrested and broken up numerous expeditionary parties; it had very recently arrested two more expeditions and subjected the participators to trial; it was not possible to do more than it had done.

Mr. Silvela very frankly admitted the zeal and good faith with which the American government had fulfilled its obligations; he only mentioned this case because the two letters had come together. It was not that he meant to complain of this isolated case of the escape of an expedition; but he thought the matter of the gunboats a very important one in its bearings on the good relations of the United States and Spain. The Cortes were soon to assemble; as soon as they were opened, one of the earliest interpellations would be in relation to Cuba. The government is anxious to put the matter properly before the chambers; they hope to be able to say that the United States have offered their friendly offices to give a more humane character to the war. To check the bloodshed and devastation which have marked it; to their humanitary intervention Spain can properly consent, out of consideration to a friendly power; the war being divested of its savage character, an armistice would be soon attainable, for, say six months; after that it is most probable that hostilities would never be resumed; then could come a final understanding, peace, election of deputies, and the future of the island amicably settled. All these steps must be taken successively; they cannot be precipitated without unduly exciting the public mind. In this view, the matter of the gunboats is a great embarrassment. If the embargo should still remain at the opening of the chambers, it will be difficult to persuade the Cortes or the people that the government of the United States is not hostile to Spain. They will say the United States have two weights and measures; they allow the Peruvian monitors to go—they retain the Spanish gunboats. The material assistance which the one or two gunboats now ready would afford our fleet in Cuban waters would be very slight compared with the moral advantage which the release of them would give the government in the plan which it has marked out for the pacification of the island in accord with the United States. Mr. Silvela hoped I would make these views known to my government.

I promised to communicate the views of his excellency, as I had formerly those of Mr. Becerra. I was still without instructions and without official information in regard to this matter. I was sure, however, that it would appear that the action of my government had been based upon the same principles of strict neutrality that had actuated them in all other similar cases. Our neutrality laws are very stringent and always rigidly enforced; they have been put in action repeatedly for the benefit of Spain, and there could be no just cause for complaint if they were now executed apparently to her disadvantage.

The same evening I addressed a note to the president of the council, whom I had not seen since his return to Madrid, on the 21st instant, asking him to name an hour when I might pay my respects. He designated the following afternoon. In the mean time I received your telegram of the 23d, and, as you will observe, after making the inquiries necessary to answer your telegram of the 15th instant. I took occasion to express your views upon the topics referred to in the former, omitting, however, any allusion to the recognition of the insurgents as belligerents. That subject was not introduced by the president of the council. The interview was cordial and occupied more than an hour.

General Prim began by referring to the animated and excited discussion which had taken place in the public journals during his absence, in reference to Cuban affairs, and expressed his gratification that a calmer temper was now beginning to assert itself. He thought there was a certain gain perceptible from this recent excitement. Six months ago the question could not be discussed in Spain; now it is a general topic of discussion. At first there was but one side, now there are evidently two; a decided sentiment in favor of the emancipation of Cuba is growing up; let the national honor be saved, and he thought there would be no serious difficulty in accomplishing the emancipation of the island. His news from the Captain General was very good; he expected with the assistance of a few additional battalions to break the military power of the insurrection; in the course of this autumn the government expected to be able to begin the work of political reform. The one thing necessary is to bring about as soon as possible the cessation of hostilities.

Referring to my former conversations with General Prim I asked whether, in his opinion, the elections to be held for deputies and the plebiscitum were indispensable conditions to the independence of the island; I enumerated the difficulties to be encountered in this proceeding, if the insurgents laid down their arms, and the volunteers maintained their organizations, and asked what were the intentions of the government in this respect.

The general answered that the election of delegates to the Cortes was an absolutely indispensable preliminary; that there was no other possible method of accomplishing this object without a violation of the constitution; that the Americans, with their traditional regard for constitutional law, would be the last to expect this. In answer to my question about the volunteers, he said that their disarmament would take place simultaneously with the cessation of hostilities; he had already taken his measures, and given orders to the Captain General for that purpose, and there would be no difficulty or delay about the matter. The government did not propose to have a repetition of the scenes which took place in the time of General Dulce. I expressed my gratification at this information, and hoped that the government had also taken measures to prevent those barbarous and cruel executions that had hitherto marked the progress of the war. This was one of the causes that most embarrassed the government of the United States, as the sufferers in these outrages were not only the Cuban insurgents, but also Americans, and in many instances persons entirely innocent of any participation in the insurrection.

General Prim stated that he had given very severe and positive orders on that subject to the Captain General that these scandalous scenes should be prevented at all hazards, and that General De Rodas had answered avowing his intention of putting a stop to such occurrences, and of resorting to the punishment of death, if necessary, to accomplish this.

I said I would beg to commend to the consideration of the Spanish government the propriety of adopting the system of cartel, and treatment of prisoners according to the rules of ordinary warfare; that this would at once divest the war of its savage character, and make more practicable the projects of pacification which the government entertained.

General Prim said that it was necessary to proceed gradually and surely. The government was now occupied with various decrees, carrying its liberal policy into effect in Cuba. A decree would soon be issued initiating the gradual abolition of slavery, by giving freedom to all negroes born after date. The government would also soon announce a plan of administrative and municipal reform for Cuba. All this without waiting for the termination of the war.

General Prim then referred to the question of the Spanish gunboats in New York, repeating the considerations already advanced by MM. Silvela and Becerra.

I rejoined that I had already communicated to my government the point of view of the Spanish cabinet; that the action of the United States was founded on the demand of the Peruvian government; that a state of war existed between that nation and Spain; that the United States were bound to take cognizance of this, not only as a neutral nation, but still more as a mediator between the two parties, accepted as such by both; that the Peruvians claimed that these gunboats might be used either to prey upon their commerce or to relieve the Spanish fleet in the Gulf, and enable it to attack them; that the neutrality laws of the United States are so strict, and their execution so rigid, that even if the government of the United States had taken no action in the matter, the vessels might have been stopped by judicial proceedings on competent information from any source. I added that these incidents furnished but another reason for putting an end as soon as possible, either by peace with Peru, or an armistice in Cuba, to such causes of annoyance.

General Prim said he did not consider the claim of Peru serious; the war with that power was virtually ended; it was an absurd and foolish war, left by the late government of Spain, and which the present government was determined to close at once. "Not another shot will be fired in it, and that the Peruvians know as well as we. We cannot be induced to recommence that war."

I declined to discuss the validity of the claim of Peru; the action of my government was founded on the requirements of our neutrality laws, and with reference to strict and impartial justice between the two antagonists.

I then said that I had communicated to my government the views of the Spanish cabinet, as expressed in the conversations of Mr. Silvela and Mr. Becerra, and the note of the latter in reference to the offer of the friendly intervention of the United States, made in my note of the 3d September; that this offer was made in a spirit of friendship, and in the interests of humanity, of Spain, of Cuba, and of the United States. If the tender be not acceptable to Spain, I was authorized to withdraw it; but that I was reluctant to do this while there seemed any possibility that our services could be made available for the purpose in view. I therefore asked General Prim whether he had any modifications to propose which would make the bases I had submitted acceptable to the government of Spain.

General Prim replied that while recognizing the good faith and friendship with which this offer was made, he must say that at this moment it embarrassed the Spanish government. "We can better proceed, in the present situation of things, without even this friendly intervention. A time will come when the good offices of the United States will be not only useful but indispensable in the final arrangements between Spain and Cuba. We will ascertain the form in which they can be employed, and confidently count upon your assistance."

I then said I would withdraw the bases proposed by my government, and while both nations would reserve their full liberty of action, the good offices of the United States would be ready whenever they could tend to a settlement, upon a just and honorable basis, of the unhappy contest that is devastating Cuba, and so injuriously affecting the United States and Spain.

I shall reserve for another dispatch the observations suggested by the present situation here in its relation to the Cuban question. Reinforcements are not sent off as fast or as largely as was announced to be the purpose of the government. Not more than three thousand have sailed, and these, for the most part, recruits. There are manifest indications of a formidable republican movement, and to meet this the government will require all the forces at its disposal. The resources of the government are so far exhausted, and its credit so low, that it is now using the reserves appropriated to the payment of the interest on the public debt due in December, and must soon suspend specie payments altogether. In a word, the political and financial difficulties of the situation are so critical that a change in the policy of this cabinet with regard to the question of Cuba may be looked for at any moment.

No. 33.

General Sickles to Mr. Fish.

No. 23.] MADRID, *September* 29, 1869.

I have the honor to transmit herewith copies of three telegraphic dispatches sent by this legation to the Department of State on the 23d, 24th, and 25th days of September instant.

General Sickles to Mr. Fish.

[Telegram.]

MADRID, *September* 23, 1869.

Résumé of interview to-day with minister of foreign affairs at his request. Minister of colonies present.

Spain embarrassed by our proposed mediation. Hoped our offer would be withdrawn or modified. Spain would proceed in accord with the United States to settle Cuban question by the successive steps this cabinet had heretofore indicated, including armistice. Detention of gunboats retarded progress, and would prejudice Cortes and public opinion against accepting good offices of United States. They expressed wish for reply before Cortes meet, October first.

Have asked interview with president of council. Serious disturbances anticipated here. Opposition parties anxious to send troops to Cuba. Government holds back; fears republican demonstrations; wants money; taxes unpaid.

General Sickles to Mr. Fish.

[Telegram.]

MADRID, *September* 24, 1869.

Your telegram of 23d received. In the exercise of the discretion given in your instructions, number three, and for prudential reasons that will be reported in my next dispatch, the offer of mediation was communicated first verbally and afterward by note. Nothing has occurred to disturb my friendly relations with the Spanish cabinet. They object only to our mediation in a domestic question.

General Sickles to Mr. Fish.

[Telegram.]

MADRID, *September* 25, 1869.

Resumé of interview last evening with president of council.

Plebiscitum not insisted upon. Election of deputies required by constitution; indispensible preliminary to independence. Measures already taken to disarm volunteers simultaneously with cessation of hostilities. Severe and positive orders given to stop the scandalous execution of captives and like cruelties. General de Rodas promises to do so at all hazards.

A decree will be promulgated forthwith for the gradual abolition of slavery. Government will proceed with liberal reforms without waiting for termination of war.

Spain recognizes the good faith and friendship of our offer of mediation. Nevertheless, it is a serious embarrassment. Spain, at present, can proceed better without intervention. It is necessary to wait till a more practicable temper prevails. It would not be long before our co-operation would be not only useful, but indispensible in the settlement of the question. He would then indicate the form in which Spain could avail herself of our friendly intervention. The recent excitement had advanced the growing sentiment favoring Cuban independence. The national honor saved, no serious obstacle prevented the emancipation of the island.

The Spanish cabinet distinguish between *mediation* and *good offices*. To prevent recognition of belligerents, they seem anxious to hold us to our offer of good offices, while declining mediation as long as there is hope of suppressing insurrection.

No. 34.

Mr. Fish to General Sickles.

No. 10.] WASHINGTON, *October* 12, 1869.

Your dispatches to No. 22 were received this morning. Immediately on receipt of them I sent to you, in cypher, the inclosed telegram, thinking that you would desire, when opportunity should offer, to correct the misapprehension under which the Spanish cabinet were evidently laboring, as to the action of the United States in the detention of the Spanish gunboats. In support of the statements in my telegram, I inclose also a translation of the note of Mr. Goñi, dated the 23d May, 1868, requesting the detention of the monitors, and also a translation of his note of the 24th of November, consenting to their release.

I need not state to you, who are familiar with the laws of the United States, and with the faithful manner in which we perform our international obligations, that the President had no option on the receipt of such a note as the first note of Mr. Goñi in regard to the detention of the vessels, and that after the receipt of his second note on the same subject it was manifestly his duty to let the vessels go.

I also inclose a translation of the note of Mr. Freyre, the Peruvian minister, requesting the detention of the gunboats which Spain is constructing in New York. And inasmuch as, since the Peruvian monitors were first detained at New Orleans, at the request of Mr. Goñi, there has been no change in the relations between Spain and Peru, (though the President hopes those relations may be soon changed into those of permanent peace, through the good offices of the United States,) the President could only act towards Spain, at the request of Peru, as he had acted towards Peru, at the request of Spain. Independently of his duty as a neutral, the laws of the United States left him no option, nor did they even permit him to inquire into the question which appears to have been raised at Madrid, whether the gunboats were to be used against Peru. Your answer, however, to that question, that they would release in the Antilles vessels which might be employed against Peru, is consistent with the facts as represented to this department by the minister from Peru. If you have not already done so, it will be well to bring these facts informally to the notice of the Spanish cabinet when opportunity offers.

The necessity of preparing this note for the mail which leaves to-day forbids me to enter more at length upon the several subjects treated in your dispatches.

Mr. Goñi to Mr. Seward.

[Translation.]

LEGATION OF SPAIN AT WASHINGTON,
Washington, May 23, 1868.

The undersigned, envoy extraordinary and minister plenipotentiary of her Catholic Majesty, has the honor to present to the consideration of the honorable Secretary of State what follows:

It is already a notorious fact, as published by the daily press in the United States, as well as in that of Peru, and neither contradicted nor denied, nor called in question by any one, that the armor-clad ships Catawba and Oneota, bought by Messrs. Swift & Co., of Cincinnati, have been purchased for the government of Peru, to which they at this time belong, and that they are preparing for departure, more or less early, bound for that republic from the port of New Orleans, where they now actually are. This being understood, the undersigned, repeating the verbal reclamations which he has at various conferences made upon the subject, now addresses himself to the honorable Secretary of State, invoking his recognized uprightness, his loyalty toward friendly nations, and the noble perseverance with which he has upheld respect for the laws of neutrality, to the end that he may hinder the departure to sea of the monitors Catawba and Oneota, while the state of war exists between Spain and Peru.

The undersigned, on the present occasion, thinks he may hope for the most efficient action from the honorable Secretary of State, for most especial and extraordinary reasons. First, if the state of war still subsists, it is not by fault of the Spanish government, which has shown dispositions propitious to the adjustment of a peace worthy and honorable for all parties, having always met the friendly invitations given by the Hon. Mr. Seward, and in consequence suspending active hostilities. Secondly, that the government of her Catholic Majesty having now presented the question of peace in a positive manner to the honorable Secretary of State, it ought to trust, and does trust, that while Peru and the allied republics do not proffer themselves to enter upon the negotiations proposed, the government of the United States will not consent that in this country any detriment shall occur to the rights of Spain in derogation of the laws of neutrality.

The undersigned avails of this occasion to reiterate to the honorable Secretary of State the assurance of his highest consideration.

FACUNDO GOÑI.

Hon. WILLIAM H. SEWARD, *&c., &c., &c.*

Mr. Goñi to Mr. Seward.

[Translation.]

LEGATION OF SPAIN IN WASHINGTON,
Washington, November 24, 1868.

At one of the latest conferences in relation to the monitors Catawba and Oneota, purchased for the government of Peru, the honorable Secretary of State of the United

States, after again presenting some observations expressed in his note of the 9th of July, referring to this matter, was pleased to make manifest to the undersigned that the Spanish government could, without obstacle of any kind, consent to the departure of those vessels in consideration of two special circumstances, to wit:

1st. That complete peace existing in fact between Spain and Peru, and this peace in fact being very shortly to be converted into peace according to law, as recent communications received at the Department of State demonstrate, and especially the protocol of the conference which on the first day of September last was observed in Lima by the representatives of the four allied republics, in view of so near and probable an event, the acquiescence of the Spanish government would be justifiable in respect of the immediate departure of the monitors, which need to avail themselves of the fair weather of the southern hemisphere, and would moreover signify a deference very remarkable and worthy of esteem.

2d. That this government having assurance that the monitors are not to exercise any hostilities against Spain, not only because of the disposition which animates the government of Peru, but also because the minister of that republic has made so solemn promise thereof, as the honorable Secretary of State has been pleased to assure the undersigned in the said note of the 9th July, that Spain cannot entertain, in this respect, the least reason for withdrawal or apprehension.

In consequence of the precedent manifestation of the Secretary of State, the undersigned finds himself fully authorized to declare that the present government of Spain, desirous, as the representative of the new political situation created in that country, to give proof of its friendly attitude towards the Hispano-American republics of the Pacific, ceases to oppose the departure to sea of the monitors Catawba and Oneota, hoping only that the honorable Secretary of State will please to assure him, in conformity with the offers made by the minister of Peru, that the said vessels will not attempt to commit any act offensive to Spanish interests during their voyage to the Pacific.

The undersigned has the honor to communicate the foregoing to the honorable Secretary of State of the United States, and awaiting reply to the present note, avails of this fresh occasion to reiterate the assurance of his highest consideration.

FACUNDO GOÑI.

Hon. WILLIAM H. SEWARD, *&c., &c., &c.*

Mr. Freyre to Mr. Fish.

[Translation.]

LEGATION OF PERU,
New York, July 31, 1869.

The undersigned, envoy extraordinary and minister plenipotentiary of Peru, has the honor to inform the honorable Secretary of State of the United States, that it is well known, not only through the newspapers, but from other sources, the authenticity of which cannot be doubted, that the Spanish government has ordered the building of thirty steam gunboats, equipped for war, to be effected in this country; their agents have contracted for fifteen in the ship-yards of Mystic River, Connecticut; for ten in Poillon's yards, in Brooklyn, four of which have already been launched, and are receiving their engines from the foundery of Delamater, in Thirteenth street, North River; and five are being built in one of the yards at Greenpoint. It is announced that they will soon leave, to reinforce the naval squadron now stationed round the Island of Cuba.

The undersigned will not ask the destination of these gunboats; it is enough to know that they are armed vessels of war, belonging to the government of Spain, to justify him, as the representative of a republic at war with that nation, in protesting against the departure of these vessels, and in requesting the ever just government of North America, as a neutral exercising the right imposed by the law of nations, to order the detention of the thirty gunboats mentioned, and not allow them to leave the places where they now are, under any pretext whatever.

The undersigned insists on prompt attention to this business, as one of the vessels will be ready in ten or twelve days, and the others will be finished soon.

In fine, the undersigned, in giving this information to the honorable Secretary of State, hopes a flagrant violation of the laws of neutrality may be prevented on American soil, against the republic of Peru; for with these additional vessels, Spain may use all her other naval forces against the republics on the Pacific coast, in case hostilities be renewed.

With these remarks, the undersigned has the honor to offer to the honorable Secretary of State of the United States the expression of his most distinguished consideration.

MAN'L FREYRE.

Hon. HAMILTON FISH,
Secretary of State, &c., &c., &c.

No. 35.

General Sickles to Mr. Fish.

No. 26.] OCTOBER 16, 1869.

I have the honor to transmit herewith a copy of my note addressed to the minister of state, Mr. Silvela, on the 28th ultimo, and a copy and translation of his reply, dated the 16th instant.

General Sickles to Mr. Silvela.

SEPTEMBER 28, 1869.

The undersigned, envoy extraordinary and minister plenipotentiary of the United States of America, had the honor, on the 31st of July last, in compliance with the instructions of his government, to offer to the government of Spain the good offices of the United States, in the measures that should be found most expedient for the pacification of the Island of Cuba.

His excellency the minister of state, in a subsequent conference, communicated to the undersigned the reply of the cabinet of Madrid to the overture; and the undersigned, having duly transmitted the same to his government, informed the minister of state, on the 3d of September instant, of the views of the President in regard to the bases suggested on the part of Spain in that conference; and at the same time the undersigned communicated to the cabinet of Madrid the bases proposed by the United States for the adjustment of the questions pending between Spain and Cuba. These propositions were deemed by the President to be most advantageous to all the interests compromised by the deplorable conflict in the Island of Cuba, and it was believed the arrangement would be acceptable to the government of Spain.

His excellency the minister of state, acknowledging for the cabinet of Madrid the sincerity and friendship of the offer made by the United States, has intimated to the undersigned that the bases proposed by the United States cannot be accepted by Spain, and that even the friendly intervention of another power would embarrass the Spanish government in proceeding with the liberal measures it proposes to initiate, to meet the requirements of the situation in the Antilles.

The undersigned, therefore, in conformity with his instructions, withdraws the offer of the good offices of the President of the United States, heretofore communicated to the government of his Highness the Regent; and, while both nations will reserve their full liberty of action, if the occasion shall hereafter arise when the United States may contribute by their friendly co-operation to the settlement of the questions at issue in Cuba, the undersigned is instructed to state that the President will be happy to assist in promoting a result so conducive to the interests of Spain and of America.

Mr. Silvela to General Sickles.

[Translation.]

OCTOBER 8, 1869.

I have received your excellency's polite note of the 28th of last month, to which matters of the gravest importance have prevented an earlier reply.

In this note, in accordance with the instructions of the government of the United States, your excellency withdraws the offer of good offices with the insurgents of Cuba, with which that government was pleased to favor us, in the desire to put an end to the civil war which afflicts that transatlantic province. The Spanish government had accepted with gratitude these humanitary good offices. What it did not accept, because it could not accept them, were all the bases upon which they were founded, bases which evidently, as it now appears, constituted the essential condition of the offer. The Spanish government could not accept these bases, the first of which was the independence of Cuba, because, even if they had wished it, it was not within their competence to consent to a dismemberment of the territory of this monarchy, without the permission and authorization of the Cortes; but the Cortes, far from permitting and authorizing this, manifested by a unanimous resolution of their permanent commission that they were ready to lend their entire support to the government, in an elevated and dignified policy in the Cuban question, calculated to preserve the integrity of the territory and the national honor, and were disposed to convoke the national representation to strengthen the action of the government.

The Spanish government, nevertheless, as I have already said, had accepted the good offices, hoping that in the first place, they would be exercised by the government of the United States using their influence with the promoters of the insurrection, who had sought refuge in the territory of the republic, to induce the insurgents to lay down their arms. The Spanish government proposed spontaneously to present to the Constituent Cortes for their deliberation, in accord with the deputies of the island, measures which should tend to give to the Cubans the liberties their condition may require, in harmony with those proclaimed in Spain—a complete amnesty for those who have fought against the mother country, the gradual emancipation of the slaves, and the right of the free to hold public offices, and to share in making the laws. The humanitary good offices were accepted with gratitude upon these bases. If the United States now withdraw them, it is apparently because they consider as an inflexible basis of any negotiation the declaration of independence, to which neither the respect which the government professes to the constitution of Spain, nor other considerations not less important, permit us to accede. But as, the offer of good offices being withdrawn, the Spanish government can do no less than consider the bases and conclusions on which they were founded as having passed out of view, this is sufficient to cause the Spanish government to recognize the fairness of the government of the United States, and the respect which is due to the sovereignty of a people which has been its friend and ally from the beginning of its glorious history.

Your excellency, moreover, observes in ending your note, that while the President of the republic reserves his liberty of action, he will be happy if he can contribute in anything to the pacification of Cuba, a result equally advantageous to the interests of America and of Spain.

This frank and noble declaration is extremely satisfactory, and I beg that your excellency will present to the President the thanks of the Spanish government. At the same time I venture to indicate two acts which it is in his power to accomplish, and which will serve as an illustration of these loyal and friendly purposes toward Spain.

The first is, to exercise all his natural influence upon those who, having taken refuge in American territory, foment the rebellion, to the end that they, following the generous initiative of the Spanish government, contained in the Gazette of the 28th of September, may induce their followers to abstain from giving a savage character to the conflict with the outrages and ferocious crimes with which they have been hitherto stained. The Spanish government having manifested its purpose to confine the contest within the limits prescribed by modern civilization, orders having been given to the authorities to proceed with all the moderation required by humanity, it would be truly monstrous if the insurgents should continue the barbarous conflict which they have begun, and should keep on perpetrating the excesses which outrage the consciences of honorable men, rendering themselves wholly unworthy of the generous hospitality which the republic dispenses to those who, under the name of the Cuban Junta, stand forth as promoters of the insurrection. The Spanish government having spontaneously set this example, and being resolved to act in a civilizing and humanitarian sense, a wide field is opened to the United States to show their sympathies and their good-will toward a government and a nation which proceeds in this manner, notwithstanding the conduct of the rebels.

The second act, which may illustrate the sincerity of the President's offers, is in regard to the gunboats constructed in the United States by the order and at the expense of Spain, not to go against Peru, nor even to fight the insurgents of Cuba, but to defend our coasts against the aggressions of filibusters and pirates.

The strongest argument which your excellency has used on various occasions to endeavor to demonstrate the importance of the insurrection, has been the extent of its duration; but this argument will have no weight while the insurrection receives continual increase and nutriment from abroad; while it does not remain isolated and without other partisans and champions than the Cubans themselves. Only when the insurrection persists in this manner can it be urged that it is rooted in the country, that the majority of the Cubans desire to be independent, and even that they are worthy to be so, and are possessed of sufficient means, vigor, and energy to form a nationality and a separate state. At this time, in the present state of things on that island, Spain cannot believe nor admit that the majority of the Cubans incline to separation from the mother country, but that a turbulent and blind minority, excited and aided by adventurers and speculators of other countries, by filibusters and pirates, guided by evil passions and not by patriotic purposes, aspire to overcome the general will of their own countrymen, and that is the sole cause of the discord which we deplore. At this time Spain does not and cannot see in Cuba the profound sentiment and true capacity of independence, and therefore, if she should consent to a separation from that rich and ancient colony, she would not have the great consolation of thinking that she was giving existence to a new nation, but the deep remorse of weakly abandoning her own children; of leaving unprotected a people of her own language and race to miserably perish and disappear.

These reasons are sufficiently strong to be esteemed at their just value by a government so enlightened as that which your excellency here worthily represents, and in whose friendly co-operation Spain still trusts to give peace to Cuba, and with peace, those ample liberties which our constitution grants to every Spanish citizen of either hemisphere.

No. 36.

General Sickles to Mr. Fish.

No. 27.] MADRID, *October* 16, 1869.

With this dispatch you will receive a copy of my note of the 28th ultimo to the minister of state, withdrawing the offer of the good offices of the President, heretofore tendered to Spain, for the settlement of the Cuban question; also, a copy of Mr. Silvela's reply, dated on the 8th instant, and received to-day. [See General Sickles's No. 26, page 56.]

An early answer was promised by the minister; and having already informed you of my action, in my telegram of the 29th ultimo, I waited for the reply of the Spanish government before transmitting a copy of my note.

A reply was sent to me on the 9th instant, identical with the one inclosed, except that it contained the extraordinary statement that I had withdrawn my note of the 3d of September. I called upon Mr. Silvela immediately, and informed him that this assertion was inadmissible, and if persisted in would compel me to put on record a positive contradiction of a statement which had no color of foundation in fact. He explained his meaning to be that the withdrawal of the offer of good offices was, in his opinion, synonymous with the withdrawal of the bases of settlement proposed by the United States, and he had given to this inference the form of assertion expressed in his note.

I assured the minister that, in attributing to me any purpose of withdrawing my note of the 3d ultimo, he had altogether misapprehended the tenor of my communication of the 28th; that the objections were insuperable to a proceeding which would mutilate the record of an important transaction, in which the President had performed a public duty imposed upon him by grave events; that the withdrawal of our good offices rendered unnecessary the further discussion of the bases proposed; that my communication of the 3d ultimo was not, however, confined to the suggestion of these bases; it embraced also a statement of the reasons which constrained the President to regard the bases proposed by Spain as inconsistent with any practicable negotiation; it included besides an exposition of the motives which had prompted the offer of the good offices of the United States, and it presented, moreover, the general considerations deemed by the President to be essential in determining the means for the pacification of Cuba.

The minister, although inclined to extend the range of the discussion by arguments in support of the soundness of his deduction, did not insist upon the correctness of his statment. He asked me to send him an informal note, pointing out the matter to which I objected, and promised to give immediate attention to the subject. I wrote him unofficially the same evening; and on the 12th, Mr. Diaz del Moral, of the state department, called upon me and submitted the draught of a proposed amendment, which I rejected, as it was a repetition in other phraseology of the original misstatement. Yesterday Mr. Diaz called again, and proposed a modification of the paragraph, omitting altogether the statement that my note had been withdrawn, which removed any objection to the reception of the reply of the minister. To-day the original of the accompanying copy was received at the legation, and the one first sent was returned to the Foreign Office.

I have thought proper to inform you of all these particulars, because it has been repeatedly stated in semi-official journals and in official circles in Madrid, with the apparent sanction of this cabinet, that my note of the 3d of September had been withdrawn, in compliance with the demand of the Spânish government, and this misrepresentation has been telegraphed all over Europe and the United States.

I inclose also with dispatch No. 26, a copy of the instructions sent to the Captain General to prevent in future the atrocities which have disgraced the war in Cuba; also, the decree establishing freedom of worship in the Antilles, to which reference is made in the reply of the minister of state. [For inclosures see Mr. Plumb's dispatch of October 26, page 156.]

The republican demonstration has recently occupied the attention of this government to the exclusion of all other matters.

* * * * * * *

There is no doubt, however, that recent events have made the president of the council stronger than he has yet been, at least in authority, if not in popularity, and that his views will more than ever shape the policy of Spain.

No. 37.

General Sickles to Mr. Fish.

No. 31.] MADRID, *November* 3, 1869.

Two changes in the cabinet are announced. Mr. Martos replaces Mr. Silvela in the state department, and Mr. Figuerola, who had before occupied the post, succeeds Mr. Ardanaz in the treasury. Additional gravity is given to the ministerial crisis by the resignation of Admiral Topete. It has not been accepted, as appears by a decree of the Regent published in the Gazette of this morning, because the reasons assigned for the resignation are altogether personal. It is not believed, however, that the admiral will resume his portfolio, as the real differences between the president of the council and the minister of marine are well understood to be political. The retiring ministers belong to the "liberal union" party, of which the Regent became the chief on the death of O'Donnell. Their successors are taken from the ranks of the "radicals," a new name adopted since the recent fusion of the "progresistas" and "democratic monarchists," under the leadership of the president of the council. It is understood that the "union liberals" declined to accept office in the reorganization of the cabinet, and it is claimed that the new administration is homogeneous in its politics. Besides the dissensions growing out of the candidature of the Duke of Genoa, who is not supported by the "union liberals," it is probable that other differences, as, for example, the relations of the government to the church, contributed to the rupture. It remains to be seen whether the new cabinet will command the same support in the Cortes enjoyed by the late administration, for although all sides profess to regard the preservation of the coalition as essential, there are serious doubts of its practicability. The loss of the union liberal vote in the Cortes, which is somewhere between sixty and seventy, would still leave the radical cabinet a majority in the chamber; but the weight of character, and especially the powerful influence in the army attributed to the Regent's party, will greatly increase the strength of the opposition to General Prim's administration, if he fails to conciliate this important element of the coalition that has hitherto sustained him.

* * * * * *

The commission organized to prepare and report for the consideration of the Cortes a plan of administrative reform for the island of Porto Rico, of which I advised you in my dispatch No. 19, has been dissolved. The Marquis de la Esperanza, one of the deputies of Porto Rico, and a member of the board, informed the secretary of this legation, Colonel Hay, that the commission was unable to agree upon any plan. The disagreement between the government and the provincial members included among others the questions of slavery, tariff, and taxation. The decree dissolving the commission, which appeared recently in the Gazette, assigns as the reason for the measure, that the time limited for the sittings of the board has expired. I shall inform you of whatever else may transpire on this subject. It is probable the matter will soon be brought up in the Cortes by the deputies from Porto Rico.

No allusion has been made to the matter of the gunboats since the receipt of your telegram and instructions upon that subject. I have preferred to wait for such an opportunity to correct the misapprehension you mention, rather than introduce the subject myself.

* * * * * *

Although the Cortes have been in session for a month, the Cuban question has not been considered, nor even mentioned, otherwise than incidentally, in the public sittings. With every mail from the Havana the announcement is repeated that the insurrection is suppressed, yet the embarkation of reinforcements continues. The consul at Cadiz reports the departure of 1,428 troops since the middle of October. Of these, three hundred were marines, taken by the ship of war Zaragoza. The remainder were sent by the transports Porto Rico and Lopez de la Cá-Lopez.

* * * * * *

No. 38.

General Sickles to Mr. Fish.

No. 33.] MADRID, *November* 14, 1869.

The subject of Porto Rico was brought before the Cortes yesterday by one of the deputies of the island, Mr. Padial.

I inclose herewith a report of the debate, taken from the official Gazette. You will find in the speech of the colonial secretary, Mr. Becerra, an exposition of the principles adopted by this government, in shaping their plans of colonial administration. The deputies from Porto Rico differ widely in their demands, and it is evident the government will take advantage of these dissensions and do as little as possible in the way of reform.

The colonial minister declared on the 8th instant, in the Cortes, that the government would not bring forward any measure of reform for Cuba until the last hostile band was dispersed, and the insurgents had lost all hope. You will perhaps find some interest in a comparison of that view of Mr. Becerra with his expressions on the 6th of October, and I inclose reports of his remarks on both of these occasions.

* * * * * *

[For inclosures see extract of above dispatch, document No. 115, page 161.]

No. 39.

General Sickles to Mr. Fish.

No. 34.] MADRID, *November* 17, 1869.

Last week, while in the diplomatic tribune of the Cortes, I received a ceremonious visit from the president of the chamber. Señor Rivero took occasion to assure me of the great interest he felt in the continuance of good relations between the United States and Spain, and of his earnest desire to assist in promoting whatever might tend to strengthen the ties between the two countries. He concluded by asking me to meet the secretaries of state and of the colonies at dinner at his house. This interview was reported in the journals of the same evening and on the following day. The dinner took place on Sunday last, and has likewise been chronicled in all the ministerial organs.

The secretaries of state and of the colonies, the late secretary of state, Mr. Silvela, the present and late under-secretaries of these departments, and several deputies, were among the guests invited to meet me. The secretary of this legation, Colonel Hay, was the only other member of the diplomatic corps present. I would not feel authorized to report the conversation that followed if Mr. Martos, Mr. Becerra, and Mr. Rivero had not distinctly stated that they wished me to regard all they said as the frank and unreserved expression of their official as well as of their personal sentiments, which they hoped I would communicate to my government. Mr. Martos spoke of the common interests shared by the United States and Spain in Cuba. He said that whatever retarded the prosperity of the island was injurious alike to both countries; that the welfare of Cuba was of more commercial importance to the United States than to the mother country; that Spain, having adopted the most democratic constitution in Europe, was more than ever disposed to enter into intimate relations with the United States; that the government intended in good faith to extend to Cuba the same free institutions enjoyed by Spain, including the right to elect not only their deputies, but also their municipal and provincial councils.

Mr. Becerra remarked that the Cubans were better prepared for free institutions than the average population of Spain; that he had been urged to order the immediate election of Cuban deputies to the Cortes, but he had refused to do so, for the reason that now an election would only represent the views of the peninsular party, whereas the government desired a full expression of the opinions of the whole population.

I asked what objection could be made to the immediate consideration of the Cuban question by the Cortes; that the Cubans, unfortunately, had no hope of any change for the better while they remained a colony of Spain; they did not believe, if they gave up the contest, that Spain would do anything to lighten their burdens or improve their political condition; that one mode of removing these impressions would be for the Cortes to settle at once the form of the future government of the island.

To this Mr. Martos replied that the council of ministers were occupied with the subject, and that he had advocated, and would continue to advocate, both as a minister and a deputy, the extension of the largest liberties to Cuba; that the government could not, however, ignore the fact that the colony was in rebellion, and nothing could be conceded to force; that the well-known opinions of the cabinet were a guarantee that in legislating for Cuba they would adhere to the principles of the constitution they had assisted to frame. This would be seen in the forthcoming ministerial measures of colonial reform in Porto Rico, which would be presented to the Cortes next week.

I mentioned that the United States had abolished slavery during the war of the rebellion; that Congress and the President, while the war was pending, had, by various acts of legislation and by proclamations, adopted measures indicating the purposes and future policy of the government in reference to the rebel States; that in this it was not believed there was anything inconsistent with the dignity and self-respect of the nation. And that if Spain would now, by a timely measure, adopted by the Cortes, make known the plan of government for Cuba, I had no doubt that if the measures were such as ought to satisfy the legitimate aspirations of the people, it would do more to put an end to hostilities than all the reinforcements they had sent.

Mr. Becerra replied the rebellion would very soon be at an end; that the force now in Cuba was really larger than was necessary to overcome the insurgents; that at least forty thousand regular troops were in Cuba, and that the real object of further reinforcements was to maintain order when it should become necessary, on the termination of hostilities, to disband the volunteers and afford protection to the lives and property of the Cubans.

Mr. Martos added that he was most anxious the President should be convinced of the determination of this government to act with the utmost liberality in all that related to the interests of Cuba; that in this they hoped to have always the good will and friendship of the United States.

Expressing my profound regret to see the armies of free Spain in conflict with their natural allies, who were contending for self-government in Cuba, I added that although my government had done all that a friendly power could do to put an end to the struggle, the President still desired, as sincerely as ever, that measures might be matured which would insure the speedy pacification and future prosperity of the island.

Mr. Becerra, assuming that my intimation pointed to an armistice, replied that if, during the war of the rebellion in the United States, any mediator had proposed to the cabinet of President Lincoln an armistice with the rebels, with a view to negotiations, he was sure the offer would have been instantly rejected and the government would have said, "The insurgents must lay down their arms before we can listen to any propositions." He proceeded to repeat some of the arguments he had, on a former occasion, addressed to me officially on this subject, and added that now, when the republic of the United States had become the giant the minister of Charles III had predicted, it could not forget the friendship of Spain in its infancy.

Mr. Martos observed here, that as soon as the present government came into power they sent General Dulce to Cuba, with instructions to make the largest concessions to the Cubans. He granted them liberty of the press, and they used it to denounce the government of the revolution. He recognized their right to hold public meetings, and they employed it to despoil Spain of her territory. It then became plain that what the Cubans wanted was not liberty, for that was offered to them, but independence, and that Spain could not yield to force without dishonor.

The president of the Cortes, Mr. Rivero, here interposed, and referred to his record as a democrat, and as a constant supporter of the Union throughout the struggle with the South; he wished to see the United States and Spain allies; they had the best constitutions in the world; they had principles and interests in common; the Cuban question would be settled on the basis of self-government and commercial reciprocity as soon as the war ended, for then the Spanish government would be in a condition to act and to treat, and in this happy result the United States might be all-powerful, first by their influence with the Cubans in advising them to confide in the good faith of the pledges of the government of the revolution to do justice to Cuba; secondly, by means of the good understanding between Spain and the United States which afforded a sure basis for the exercise of their good offices.

I said the great difficulty in the way was the distrust of the Cubans in any change in the colonial policy of Spain; that upon this subject the constitution was silent, and all depended upon the pleasure of the Cortes. The Cubans seemed to have no hope for the future, except in independence.

Mr. Becerra replied that already the government had given pledges of its sincerity, in the decree establishing freedom of worship; that he and his colleagues had publicly declared they would proceed with the gradual abolition of slavery, and that reserving for the home government the regulation of purely national concerns, the Cubans should have as much control over their local affairs as is enjoyed by any Spanish province under the constitution.

In these views Mr. Martos and Mr. Rivero concurred, the former remarking that he well knew the native Cubans, or "insulars," as he called them, were far more numerous than the "peninsulars," and that, as a consistent democrat, which he claimed to be, the wishes of the majority should be respected in the determinations of any government in which he held office, whenever those wishes were legitimately made known by regularly chosen deputies from the island.

In reply to some observations I made on the injurious commercial restrictions to which the trade between Cuba and the United States was subjected, the excessive postal charges maintained by Spain, and the absence of any extradition treaty between the two countries, Mr. Martos assured me of his readiness to take up these questions at any time, and to deal with them in the manner best calculated to promote the interests ot both nations. Mr. Becerra at the same time remarked that he hoped I would myself bear in mind, and impress the fact also upon my government, that Spain was no longer controlled by the reactionary and antiquated ideas of the Bourbons, but by statesmen who appreciated and sustained the most advanced views of the epoch on all questions of colonial policy, trade, and international intercourse. "We do not," said he, "say these things in the shade, but in the light; we have spoken frankly to the representative of a nation that we know deals openly with all, and assured of this, we have not hesitated to throw aside the reserve habitually maintained in ordinary diplomatic conversations."

* * * * * *

No. 40.

General Sickles to Mr. Fish.

No. 37.] MADRID, *December* 3, 1869.

I have the honor to inclose herewith the text of two cable telegrams sent from this legation on the 28th November and 2d December, 1869.

The concluding paragraph of the latter dispatch was the only portion deemed necessary to be transmitted in cipher.

General Sickles to Mr. Fish.

[Telegram.]

MADRID, *November* 28, 1869.

Dispatch mentioned in private letter not received. Nothing new about that matter. Am authorized by minister of colonies to inform you that government measures for Porto Rico will include local self-government, free press, public schools, impartial suffrage, gradual but speedy abolition of slavery, civil and political rights without distinction of color, domiciled foreigners to vote for town officers after six months' residence, and for members of provincial council after one year. And that these reforms will in good faith be extended to Cuba, when hostilities cease and deputies are chosen in compliance with article one hundred and eight of Spanish constitution.

General Sickles to Mr. Fish.

[Telegram.]

MADRID, *December* 2, 1869.

Interview with foreign secretary at his request. He said that Spain had yielded to the expressed wishes of the United States in withdrawing objection to the departure of the monitors on the assurances given by Peru. And he asks that the President will in like manner use his good offices with Peru, to the end that the objections to the departure of the gunboats may be withdrawn upon the same conditions.

He wished me to assure you that Spain now desires the most friendly relations with all the American republics, and intends in her colonial policy to begin immediately the most liberal reforms.

I presented the views contained in your instructions, and suggested the prompt restoration of peace with Peru as the best solution.

No. 41.

General Sickles to Mr. Fish.

No. 38.] MADRID, *December* 5, 1869.

In reply to the interpellation made the week before by Señor Rodrigo, the president of the council yesterday read to the Cortes a statement showing the forces and *materiel* of war sent to Cuba since the commencement of the insurrection. I inclose herewith a translation of this interesting document, which appears in the Gaceta of this morning, together with the remarks of General Prim and Señor Rodrigo.

* * * * * * *

[From the Gaceta, December 5, 1869.]

The president of the council said: Last Saturday Señor Navarro y Rodrigo addressed certain inquiries to the minister of war which I could not answer immediately. I said, however, that there had gone to Cuba some thirty thousand men, and to-day I will read a statement of the land and sea forces, and of the material which has gone to Cuba since the revolution, because this proves the vitality and energy of the government and of all Spain exercised in the preservation of the Island of Cuba.

The first forces which went there were 771 volunteers; then 5,400 men of the regular service; afterward the series of battalions which were asked for by General Dulce, (may he rest in peace!) 1,000 went from Baza, 1,000 from Chiclana, 1,000 from San Quintin, and 1,000 from Simancas, who were so thoroughly equipped that they were able to take the field immediately on their arrival. Since that the successive departures have reached a total of 20,966 of the army of the peninsula; of marines, 2,600; of recruits, 1,371; and of volunteers, 9,563; which gives a total of 34,500 men, according to the accompanying statement. I would call attention to the fact that this immense sum would represent a great effort for any nation whatever.

Statement of the forces embarked for the Island of Cuba since the beginning of November, 1868, when the intelligence of the insurrection arrived:

Enlisted volunteers of the conscription funds	771
Enlisted from the army	5,411
Battalion of the chasseurs of Baza, preserving their peninsular organization	1,000
Battalion of the chasseurs of Chiclana	1,000
Battalion of San Quintin	1,000
Battalion of Simancas	1,000
Sixth battalion of marines	650
Volunteers from the army	456
Battalion chasseurs of Leon, with peninsular organization	1,003
Battalion chasseurs of Aragon, organized with regular troops	1,002
Battalion chasseurs of Andalusia, organized with regular troops	1,000
Battalion chasseurs of Antequera, organized as they were in the peninsula	1,000
From the regular army	651
Battalion of Catalan volunteers, organized and equipped in Barcelona, and two companies of guides from Madrid	1,206
From different arms of the army	476
Battalion chasseurs of Reas, organized with regular troops	1,000
From different arms of the army	420
From the Basque provinces	600
Recruits	280
First battalion of third regiment marines	650
From the army	1,500
Pizzaro chasseurs	1,000
Hernan Cortes chasseurs	1,000
From special arms of the service	500
Recruits	140
Battalion of marines	650
From the army	547
Battalion of marines	650
First battalion volunteers of Madrid	1,049
Half second battalion volunteers of Madrid	506
Battalion volunteers of Covadonga	1,000
Battalion volunteers of Cadiz	820
Battalion volunteers of Santander	1,000
Second battalion volunteers of Barcelona	1,037
Belonging to the second half of the second battalion of volunteers of Madrid, of Cadiz, recruits, and Basque contingent	1,310
Third battalion volunteers of Barcelona	1,035
Total	34,500

There have gone also 14 ships of war, among them two iron-clad frigates; a complete equipment for a regiment of mountain artillery, with 24 pieces, 24 caissons for artillery of 8 centimeters bore; 20 Krupp steel guns of 8 centimeters bore; 4,000 projectiles for the same; 5,000 kilograms of powder; 7,400,000 cartridges of 14½ caliber, model of 1857 and 1859; 1,000,000 metallic cartridges for needle guns; 10,500,000 caps; 15,000 kilograms of lead; 9,600 carbines, model of 1857; 3,600 muskets, model of 1859; 8,000 Enfield rifles; 3,000 Berdan; 500 short carbines; 1,000 lances; 2,000 sabers.

This is an amount of material which seems impossible to have gone from Spain.

There have been sent 12,530 different articles, composed of medicine chests, mattresses, &c., &c.

Fifteen hundred seamen have also gone. I hope Señor Navarro will be satisfied with my explanation.

* * * * * * * * *

Señor Navarro y Rodrigo said: * * * I take pleasure in noting the declarations with which his excellency introdued the statement which he has made, that these facts exhibit the energy, the vitality, and the will of the Spanish people in the defense of the Island of Cuba, in the preservation of this province within the great Spanish nationality; and the great and heroic efforts which the government and the representatives of the nation are disposed to make to preserve this island forever within our nationality.

In addition, I must declare that no idle curiosity impelled me to ask for these data. An important debate will soon take place here, perhaps the most important that can occupy the constituent Cortes, in respect to the constitution of Porto Rico, and then I shall have occasion to refer to some of the data furnished by the minister of war.

No. 42.

General Sickles to Mr. Fish.

No. 46.] MADRID, *December* 29, 1869.

I inclose a statement of the forces composing the "army of Cuba," recently published, to which I have added estimates of the numbers of the several arms, derived from semi-official sources. The effective strength of the army is said to be well kept up by the recruiting service in Spain. It is true that many recruits have been sent forward during the last four months, besides the re-enforcements; but it would be safe, I think, to assume that the figures of the field reports are much below the estimate transmitted. The publication is doubtless made to satisfy the people of Spain that the government is doing all in its power to put down the insurrection, and the omission of any precise statement of the actual numbers present for duty seems intended to invite the inference that the respective organizations are maintained at the full standard. At all events, there is no doubt that the estimate is much below the number of troops raised for service in Cuba since the insurrection.

During the past week several journals have stated that a note has been sent to the Spanish government announcing the resolution of the President to recognize the insurgents in Cuba as belligerents. "La Politica,' the organ of the "union liberals," with whom the regent and the late secretary of state, Mr. Silvela, are identified, goes so far as to indicate your line of argument, and the views of a Spanish writer on international law, Riquelme, represented to have been cited by yourself in support of the conclusions of the President. The "Imparcial," a ministerial journal, heretofore edited by the present under-secretary of state, Mr. Gassett, has denied the statement. The "Epoca," also, which was fore most last September in sounding the alarm when our good offices were formally tendered, has contradicted the story on my authority, at least so far as this legation is informed. Nevertheless, the assertion is repeated by its authors, who claim to have obtained their information from diplomatic sources.

There is evidently much anxiety felt, and not without reason, in regard to the effect which will be produced in the United States by the failure thus far of the present campaign in Cuba, from which such decisive results were confidently predicted. If, with the exhaustive efforts made by this government to re-enforce the land and naval forces operating against the insurgents, they still, as it seems, hold their own, the impression in the United States cannot be more favorable to their cause than the despondency which is already apparent here in all except official circles. The main reliance now is on the services anticipated from the gunboats, in depriving the insurgents of resources from abroad.

No reference has been made by ministers publicly to the President's message, nor has it been mentioned in any of the interviews I have had with the president of the council, the secretary of state, or the colonial minister. The journals continue to discuss, and generally to deprecate, the expression of the sympathy of the government and people of the United States for the cause of the insurgents, as well as the President's declaration of the right of the government of the United States to determine when it may rightfully proclaim its neutrality in a conflict between nations, or between a colony struggling for independence and the parent state. It is remarkable that in all these discussions, and generally in this country, it is assumed that Spain never conceded the rights of belligerents to the so-called Confederate States. The Queen's proclamation of June, 1861, is forgotten; and the large and profitable commerce carried on between Havana and the blockaded ports of the South, in enemies' ships which changed their flag in Cuban waters, is quite ignored.

The British minister, Mr. Layard, informed me night before last that he had been instructed by Lord Clarendon to second my suggestions to this government in relation to the abolition of slavery in Cuba and Porto Rico. I replied that all I had said on the subject was unofficial, and so understood by the cabinet; that I had furnished the colonial secretary with a memorandum of the history and results of emancipation in the United States, and had otherwise endeavored to fortify his apparent disposition to deal with the question of colonial reform in a large and liberal sense; that I was, however, rather discourged by the procrastination of the committee of the Cortes, and of the secretary himself, who seemed, after all, inclined to yield to the representations of the reactionists. Mr. Layard said he had spoken to Mr. Martos on the subject, who had remarked that the government could do nothing in the way of reform or enfranchisement for Cuba while the rebellion was flagrant, without alienating the Spanish party in the island; but that changes of administration in Porto Rico would be radical, and would probably include a measure for the gradual abolition of slavery.

If this be done, the peninsular party in Cuba will have fewer motives to resist the independence of the island; for with slavery abolished in Porto Rico, there would remain little hope of perpetuating it in Cuba. Administrative and social reforms once established in the Antilles, the Spanish element in the islands—that is to say, a portion of the slaveholders and the persons employed in the colonial administration—would have neither the disposition nor the means to resist much longer the realization of the wishes of a great majority of the people of Cuba and Porto Rico. * * * * *

Estimate of the Spanish forces composing the "Army of Cuba," compiled from the statement published in La Iberia of December 26, 1869, and from semi-official sources of information.

The strength of battalions, batteries, and squadrons, conforms to the regulations of the Spanish service.

INFANTRY.

Eight regiments of infantry of the line, two battalions of eight hundred each	12,800	
Twenty-five battalions of light infantry, one thousand each	25,000	
Two battalions of the guard—all veterans—one thousand each	2,000	
Two battalions of militia (estimated)	1,600	
Eleven battalions of infantry, organized in Cuba, (estimated to be of the same strength as peninsular light infantry)	11,000	
		52,400

ARTILLERY.

One regiment, two battalions of four batteries each—eight companies.	1,000	
One regiment of mountain artillery, two battalions of four batteries each—eight companies	1,000	
		2,000

Field artillery being organized, force not stated.

CAVALRY.

Twenty-five squadrons—fifty companies of one hundred and fifty each (full strength in Spanish army)	7,500

ENGINEERS.

One battalion—ten companies of one hundred and fifty each	1,500

MARINES.

Four battalions	4,000
	67,400
Beside these forces in the field, there are more than forty thousand volunteer troops doing garrison duty	40,000
Grand total	107,400

RECAPITULATION.

Infantry, fifty-six battalions	52,400
Artillery, four battalions, sixty-four guns	2,000
Cavalry, twenty-five squadrons	7,500
Engineers, one battalion	1,500
Marines, four battalions	4,000
Volunteers doing garrison duty	40,000
Total	107,400

No. 43.

Mr. Fish to General Sickles.

No. 20.] WASHINGTON, *December* 30, 1869.

I have received your dispatches Nos. 36, 37, and 38, dated the 1st, 3d, and 5th instant, respectively.

I have read attentively the account which your No. 36 gives of an interview between Mr. Martos and yourself, concerning the Spanish gunboats at New York. The views expressed by the minister of state on that occasion are just and liberal, and the assurance that Spain intends to initiate and develop immediately the amplest and most liberal reforms in the colonial policy is received with great satisfaction.

No. 44.

Mr. Fish to General Sickles.

No. 22.] WASHINGTON, *January* 7, 1870.

I have received your dispatch of the 13th ultimo, No. 40.

The information it conveys of the comments of the Madrid journals on the portion of the President's message relative to Spanish affairs, as well as of the political situation of that country, is very interesting.

In a conversation recently held with Mr. Lopez Roberts, the Spanish minister to Washington, in which allusion was made to the statement contained in the final paragraph of your dispatch, to the effect that the prisons of Spain are open now to the recruiting officers, who are authorized to furnish pardon to offenders willing to enlist for service in Cuba, that gentleman assured me that the class of offenders referred to embrace only those who have been imprisoned in consequence of political offenses against the government. If, however, upon inquiry, you should obtain information conflicting with the above assurance of Mr. Lopez Roberts, you will be expected to duly advise the department thereof.

No. 45.

General Sickles to Mr. Fish.

[Telegram.]

MADRID, *January* 9, 1870.

I deem it proper to state, in view of misapprehensions caused by the published abstract of my correspondence just now received, that I see no objection to the publication of the whole of it; and, personally, I prefer that all be communicated, at least to the Senate, if not the country.

No. 46.

Mr. Fish to General Sickles.

No. 26.] WASHINGTON, *January* 26, 1870.

Your dispatch No. 46, containing an account of the "army of Cuba," has been received, and has been read with attention.

The public interest felt in the United States in the Cuban struggle has decreased since the flagrant violations of laws by the agents of the insurgents became known, and alienated the popular sympathy.

Had the Cuban Junta expended their money and energy in sending to the insurgents arms and munitions of war, as they might have done consistently with our own statutes and with the law of nations, instead of devoting them to deliberate violation of the laws of the United States; and had they, in lieu of illegally employing persons within the dominion of the United States to go in armed bands to Cuba, proceeded thither unarmed themselves to take personal part in the struggle for independence, it is possible that the result would have been different in Cuba, and it is certain that there would have been a more ardent feeling in the United States in favor of their cause, and more respect for their own sincerity and personal courage.

You are yourself a personal witness of the strength of the sympathy which the President and all the members of the cabinet felt for them before they made these unlawful demonstrations.

I observe that you think that the Spanish campaign in Cuba has thus far failed. Your standpoint of observation is a good one, and I trust that you will keep the department constantly advised of Madrid opinions on this subject; especially as the news received here, though fluctuating, indicates in the main the reverse.

This government has to this time succeeded in maintaining its freedom of action on this question. Strong pressure has been made on the one side to induce it to recognize a state of belligerency; and, on the other, to induce it to declare that it will not recognize such a state. It has declared, and still maintains, that it will be governed in its action entirely by the facts as they occur.

It is proper, at the same time, to bear in mind the obligations to which the commerce of the United States will be subjected in case a state of war shall be recognized; but should Spain, after her great and exhaustive effort, fail to restore a state of peace on the island, the President must reserve to himself a complete liberty of action in that event.

In your interview with Mr. Layard, I notice that, to his statement that he had been instructed by Lord Clarendon to second your suggestion to the Spanish government in relation to the abolition of slavery, you replied that all you have said upon the subject had been unofficial. This naturally causes some surprise in this department, where, from the commencement and through all the stages of negotiations and correspondence, the instructions to make the abolition of slavery a *sine qua non* have been given in the most positive manner.

It is not to be supposed that your remark to Mr. Layard was intended in the broad sense in which it may be interpreted, as implying an absence of instructions from the department on this important subject. If, when the offer of our good offices was withdrawn, you were not instructed to continue to urge the question of abolition, it was because your dispatches indicated that the Spanish cabinet were not then in a mood to listen to suggestions from Washington. I have regarded it, and still regard it, as your duty under your existing instructions, at all times, whenever in your judgment a fitting opportunity offers, to do all in your power to secure complete emancipation not only in Cuba but also in Porto Rico.

It becomes more apparent every day that this contest cannot terminate without the abolition of slavery. This government regards the government at Madrid as committed to that result. You have several times received positive assurances to that effect from more than one member of that cabinet. They have also promised large and liberal reforms in the Spanish colonial policy. As late as the 3d of December last, the foreign minister thought these promises of enough importance to make them the subject of a cable telegram.

You will, therefore, if it shall appear that the insurrection is regarded as suppressed, frankly state that this government, relying upon the assurances so often given, will expect steps to be taken for the emancipation of the slaves in the Spanish colonies, as well as for the early initiation of the promised reforms, and you will then communicate to Mr. Layard the fact that you have done so.

II.—CORRESPONDENCE TRANSMITTED TO THE SENATE DECEMBER 20, 1869.

No. 47.

Mr. Hall to Mr. Seward.

No. 82.] MATANZAS, *November* 18, 1868.

I am mainly indebted to a Cuban gentleman, of conservative political opinions, for the statements contained in this communication in reference to the extraordinary events at present transpiring in this island and the opinions prevailing in this locality.

As far as my own information extends these sentiments are impartial and reliable. The belief that they may prove of interest in the present emergency, induces me to communicate them to the department:

The news of the late revolution in Spain was received here with surprise, and no little enthusiasm by the native Cubans and many Spanish liberals; the Cubans thought they could discern the dawn of a new era, and a radical change of Spanish policy in the government of this island, a feature full of hope for the cause of liberty and enlightened progress, to be realized without resort to arms and bloodshed.

The excitement caused by the information first received soon passed away, and public attention became fixed upon the institution of slavery and the course likely to be adopted by the Madrid government in regard to it. Naturally, every shade of opinion has been expressed, from the extreme radical—in favor of its immediate abolition—to the propagandist—devoted to maintaining and perpetuating the institution.

The diversity of opinion in regard to slavery is worthy of notice; the more intelligent of the Cubans, including a small number of slaveholders, are in favor of immediate abolition; they contend that it is not only an obligation due to justice and humanity, but a measure of sound policy that would be attended with less danger to the peace and good order of the island than others of prospective emancipation; that it would obviate all inducement to insurrection on the part of the blacks, and that any perturbation of the present system of labor could be easily arranged without materially reducing the productions of the island.

They claim, too, that the African slave-trade will only finally and definitely cease with the unconditional abolition of slavery in the island, where, alone, it meets with any encouragement.

They believe that while slavery exists there will be no government established here in which they can have a voice; that the island will continue to be governed by a repressive, censorious system, under pretext of preserving order; in other words, the forcible submission of the blacks, to the exclusion of all the rights and privileges of free government.

The generality of slave owners, Cubans as well as Spaniards, favor a plan of emancipation that will extinguish the institution in ten years, all born from and after the date of the decree to be declared free; they believe that by this plan the social transition may be gradually and insensibly effected, without serious injury to proprietors, whose interests are, or should be, considered identical with the general welfare of the island. This conservative class care very little about the advantages of free government, as long as they are protected in their material interests, and the immediate abolition of slavery is not attempted; they believe, also, that during the proposed period of ten years, European emigrants may be induced to come to the island and adopt agricultural pursuits; meanwhile they trust that the tranquillity of the island will remain unaltered and its resources developed.

A few Cuban and many Spanish proprietors oppose all plans interfering with their favorite institution; the most that they will consent to, and that with much reluctance, is a decree of freedom to all born from and after a date yet to be fixed upon. This class still persists in reviving the African slave trade, to which many of them owe their fortunes. It is known that they have sent commissioners to Madrid to protest against any plan of abolition or emancipation, differing from their own, that may be proposed. They desire the perpetuation of slavery, under the conviction that not only their own prosperity depends upon it, but because the independence of the island would be next to an impossibility while the present system remains unchanged. With the loss of the island they know that Spain and her subjects would lose the languid influence they still maintain in the western hemisphere.

While the whites at the clubs, in public places, and at their own houses, discuss this question with little reserve, the other race, free and slave, listen in silence, not a few of them appearing to understand the question as well as their masters. It is believed that should a just and equitable system of emancipation be adopted they will remain quiet, but should other counsels prevail their peaceable submission can hardly be expected.

Almost simultaneously with the revolution in Spain, and apparently without concert with it, an insurrection broke out in the eastern and central department of the island.

Notwithstanding the difficulties that occur in obtaining reliable information from that direction, the reserve of the government, keeping back important news, which afterward comes into circulation with all kinds of exaggerations, there appears to be little doubt but that the insurrection is of a much more formidable character than we were at first led to suppose, having its ramifications throughout the island, and its programme nothing less than absolute independence of Spain.

A state of poverty and decay has been noticeable in those departments during the past two years, the evils of which have been greatly aggravated by the system of taxation adopted a year since, and applied with little discretion or judgment to the more indigent portion of the rural population, principally engaged in raising cattle, cultivating tobacco, and cutting timber.

The discontent caused by the unusual and inappealable measures culminated in a "pronunciamiento" of the town of Yara, a short distance from Bayamo, headed by Don Pedro Vicente Aguilera, a landed proprietor of wealth, who, it is reported, at the same time gave freedom to two hundred of his own slaves.

Simultaneously with this movement other "pronunciamientoes" occurred in Tunas, Manzanillo, and Manibio, under the leadership of the well-known Cubans Cespedes, Arteaga, and Chamizo, to which, it has been reported, some small detachments of Spanish troops have united.

The wild character of the country where the insurrection has broken out, the entire want of railroads and even common roads, are greatly in favor of the "insurgents." It is well known, however, that they are deficient in arms, munitions, and effective organization, with which to oppose the forces that have been sent against them; still it is reported that their numbers are now about equal to that of the entire Spanish force in the island.

It is generally admitted that should the government not succeed in checking this insurrection it will prove ruinous to the best interests of the island. Many, however, are confident that every motive for its continuance will cease with the arrival of General Dulce, the publication of a general amnesty, the adoption of a liberal and just policy in regard to the inhabitants of the insurrectionary districts carried out in good faith, and a definite settlement of the slavery question. It is believed that such a course will alone put an end to the present unsatisfactory state of affairs, the insurrection having already assumed such proportions as will make it very difficult, if not impossible, for the government to subdue it by force.

In addition to the foregoing, I beg leave to state that in this consular district good order prevails without any evidence of a rebellious spirit among any portion of the inhabitants; however, should the insurrection extend itself in this direction it is difficult to predict the consequences. The removal of General Dulce is looked for with great anxiety.

No. 48.

Mr. Hall to Mr. Seward.

No. 83.] MATANZAS, *December* 17, 1868.

Since addressing the department on the 18th ultimo, I have to report that a marked change is noticeable in the political condition of this part of the island. The same difficulties for acquiring information still exist. There are any number of rumors and exaggerated reports put in circulation by both parties, but it appears to be generally admitted that up to the present time the government has made no progress in quelling the insurrection, allaying the excitement of the inhabitants, or inspiring confidence.

The only attempt to revolt in this vicinity appears to have occurred at Jaquey Grande, near the terminus of the Matanzas railroad, where it is reported some three to four hundred insurgents met a few days ago, but not having obtained the arms that had been promised them they returned to their homes. With this exception there has been no demonstration of importance, but there is every indication that a general plan of insurrection exists in this and other principal cities, if not throughout the whole of the island.

In this city and vicinity there is much excitement among the Cuban population, and it is believed that only a want of arms prevents their rising against the authorities, while the Spanish, or loyal, portion of the inhabitants are becoming exasperated to such a degree, that it seems next to impossible for two such antagonistic elements to exist much longer, side by side, without coming into conflict.

It appears, also, that in other parts of the island the insurrectionary movement gains strength and adherents; even the conservative class of Cubans, that a month ago hoped and predicted a settlement of all difficulties, with the arrival of General Dulce, now fear, and even admit, that the affair has progressed so far that there can be no recession, and whether as a question of months or years, it can only terminate in separation with Spain.

The question of slavery appears, meanwhile, to have been lost sight of; the insurgents, however, rely upon the assistance of the free blacks in case of need.

Arrests are numerous; parties in custody of soldiers and police are frequently seen in the streets, many of them from the surrounding country destined to the prisons of this place or the fortresses of Havana.

* * * * * *

There is a general distrust in commercial circles; business is greatly paralyzed, notwithstanding the promise of an abundant crop, just coming into market. There is no disposition on the part of any one to make investments—in fact, all would be glad to realize and remove their means out of the island—evidently fearing that the worst has not yet come.

I have endeavored in the foregoing to give the department an impartial and reliable account of the present state of affairs in this district, and hope it may be of interest.

No. 49.

Mr. Hall to Mr. Seward.

No. 89.] MATANZAS, *February* 25, 1869.

I have the honor to accompany herewith copy of a letter received to-day from Mr. James H. Horner, consular agent at Sagua la Grande.

* * * * * * *

Mr. Horner to Mr. Hall.

SAGUA LA GRANDE, *February* 23, 1869.

In order to comply with your request to furnish you with reliable information respecting the insurrectionary movement in this vicinity, I have been obliged to wait till now, as the reports heretofore received have been very much exaggerated.

There are, however, some facts that may possess interest, and one is that Sagua la Grande, and the jurisdiction of that name, are under *martial law*, and are declared in a *state of siege*.

Day before yesterday the insurgents in the number of 1,800 (reported) were attacked by about 400 infantry, and 100 cavalry volunteers, in the estate "San Miguel," near Villaclara. The rebels were hidden in the cane fields, and the government troops charged upon them, and the rebels set fire to the cane in many places at once, thinking to envelop the troops in the flames. The fire drove both parties to the batey, (yard,) and the rebels hid themselves in the buildings, where they were hunted and shot down in great numbers. The official report states, or will state, that there was a "horrible butchery." The government forces lost fourteen in killed. The loss of the other side is not stated.

To-day the passenger train from the "Encruzijada" to the Boca, and which passes through Sagua, has been captured, at least it is so supposed, as the train ought to have arrived at 8.30 a. m., and now, at 9 p. m., it has not arrived, and nothing has been heard of it. An engine was sent to ascertain the cause of the detention, and was fired upon by the insurgents, and obliged to return without accomplishing its object.

The prison here has been fortified by surrounding it at some distance with sugar hogsheads, set on end and filled with earth. The "pass" of the river (ford) is defended by the guards with a field-piece.

The rebels have destroyed several bridges between this and Las Cruces, thus interrupting our railroad communication with Cienfuegos.

A few days since a fight took place at Colonia de Santo Domingo, between the insurgents and the forces of the government, the result of which is not known, but believed to be important.

Should there be any disposable vessels of war of the United States at Havana or Matanzas, I think it would be favorable to American interests here to have an occasional visit from them during the present state of affairs.

I suppose no steps have been taken to allow the United States flag to be used here, as it is in Cardenas and Cienfuegos. If the place should be taken, it might, if it could be used, afford some protection to the families of foreigners.

No. 50.

Mr. Hall to Mr. Washburne.

No. 4.] HAVANA, *March* 11, 1869.

* * * * * *

I have the honor to accompany herewith a copy and translation of a document, purporting to be a decree of the Cuban insurgents assembly, abolishing slavery in this island.

* * * * * *

[Translation.]

The institution of slavery, introduced into Cuba by Spanish dominion, must be extinguished along with it. The assembly of representatives of the center, having in view the eternal principles of justice, in the name of liberty and the people that it represents, decrees:

1. Slavery is abolished.
2. The owners of those that have been slaves will be indemnified in due time.
3. All those who by this decree obtain their freedom will contribute their efforts to the independence of Cuba.
4. To this end, those who may be found apt and necessary for military service will enter our ranks, enjoying the same compensation and the same consideration as other soldiers of the liberal army.
5. Those who are not destined to military service will continue while the war lasts at the same labors in which they are now employed, to preserve estates in a productive condition, and thus provide subsistence to those who offer their blood to the cause of common liberty, a duty imperative alike on all those citizens now free, of whatever race, exempt from military service.
6. A special regulation will prescribe the details in regard to the execution of this decree.

Patria y Libertad, Camagney, February 26, 1869.

The assembly: Salvador de Cisñeros, Edwardo Agramonte, Ignacio Agramonte, Francisco Sanchez, Antonio Zambrana.

General A. CASTILLO.

No. 51.

Mr. Hall to Mr. Hunter.

No. 17.] HABANA, *March* 27, 1869.

I have the honor to transmit herewith a copy and translation of the proclamation of Captain General Dulce, relative to vessels approaching the island with hostile intentions, having men, arms, or munitions of war on board.

I would respectfully call the particular attention of the department to the extraordinary features of this proclamation.

[Translation.—Official.]

SUPERIOR POLITICAL GOVERNMENT OF THE PROVINCE OF CUBA.

It being necessary for the better service of the state, and with the firm determination that the insurrection already held in check by the force of arms in the interior shall receive no exterior aid that may contribute to its prolongation, and to the ruin of property, industry, and commerce—using the extraordinary and discretional powers in me vested by the supreme government of the nation—I decree the following:

Vessels which may be captured in Spanish waters or on the high seas near to the island having on board men, arms, and munitions, or effects that can in any manner contribute, promote, or foment the insurrection in this province, whatsoever their derivation and destination, after examination of their papers and register, shall be *de facto* considered as enemies of the integrity of our territory, and treated as pirates, in accordance with the ordinances of the navy.

All persons captured in such vessels, without regard to their number, will be immediately executed.

DOMINGO DULCE.

HAVANA, *March* 24, 1869.

No. 52.

Mr. Fish to Mr. Lopez Roberts.

WASHINGTON, *April* 3, 1869.

I am directed by the President of the United States to invite your serious attention, and through you that of your government, to a proclamation of his excellency the Captain General of Cuba, of the 24th of last month, an authentic copy of which has this day been received at this department.

That instrument, in its preamble, refers to the existing insurrection in Cuba, and declares that the measures which it proposes for the suppression of that insurrection are necessary for that purpose. Those measures are: "Vessels which may be captured in Spanish waters or on the high seas near to the island (Cuba) having on board men, arms, and munitions, or effects that can in any manner contribute to promote or foment the insurrection in this province, whatever their derivation or destination, after examination of their papers and register, shall be *de facto* considered as enemies of the integrity of our territory, and treated as pirates in accordance with the ordinances of the navy.

"All persons captured in such vessels, without regard to their number, will be immediately executed."

It is to be regretted that so high a functionary as the Captain General of Cuba should, as this paper seems to indicate, have overlooked the obligations of his government pursuant to the law of nations, and especially its promises in the treaty between the United States and Spain of 1795.

Under that law and treaty the United States expect for their citizens and vessels the privilege of carrying to the enemies of Spain, whether those enemies be claimed as Spanish subjects or citizens of other countries, subject only to the requirements of a legal blockade, all merchandise not contraband of war. Articles contraband of war, when destined for the enemies of Spain, are liable to seizure on the high seas, but the right of seizure is limited to such articles only, and no claim for its extension to other merchandise, or to persons not in the civil, military, or naval service of the enemies of Spain, will be acquiesced in by the United States.

This government certainly cannot assent to the punishment by Spanish authorities of any citizen of the United States for the exercise of a privilege to which he may be entitled under public law and treaties.

It is consequently hoped that his excellency the Captain General of Cuba will either recall the proclamation referred to, or will give such instructions to the proper officers as will prevent its illegal application to citizens of the United States or their property. A contrary course might endanger those friendly and cordial relations between the two governments which it is the hearty desire of the President should be maintained.

No. 53.

Mr. Hall to Mr. Fish.

No. 22.] HAVANA, *April* 2, 1869.

I have the honor to transmit herewith a copy of a private letter received to-day from ——— ———, a highly respectable merchant, residing in the Remedios district.

*   *   *   *   *   *   *   *   *

I have thought it my duty, without expressing any opinion of my own in regard to the justice of his remarks, to transmit to the department a copy of his letter, merely stating that as far as my information extends, they agree in the main with the views of a majority of other American merchants residing here and at other parts of the island.

*   *   *   *   *   *   *   *

Mr. ——— to Mr. Hall.

CAIBARIEN, *March* 25, 1869.

In answer to your interrogatories regarding the welfare of American citizens in the outports of the island, I would say that they are thus far being treated by the government with all due consideration; more cannot be asked or expected than they are receiving, and in turn, all American-born citizens are conducting themselves in a manner that cannot be otherwise than satisfactory to the authorities.

In general, American citizens residing here are against this disorderly and unpromising insurrection, which is causing so much harm to the island and to all interested property holders. Not only Americans, but all foreign residents are desirous that the government shall succeed, and trust no sudden change which would be disastrous to all.

The amount of American capital in the outports is very heavy, and would suffer greatly if any change took place. Being well informed of the material of the insurgent party, the larger portion of whom are unprincipled persons, badly organized, and without discipline, I think certainly cannot succeed and the government will soon put them down. In the four districts of Sagua, Cienfuegos, Villaclara, and Remedios, they have succeeded in breaking up the large bands, and now those that still rove in these districts are comparatively few and in bands of very small numbers, being driven from place to place, fleeing like robbers, and by their atrocious actions lately committed in these districts deserve severe treatment.

It would be very detrimental to the interests and safety of American residents for our government to take any steps in acknowledging the insurgents as belligerents, and it is the universal wish of Americans here that they should not. The insurgents certainly are declining, and they are very far from being in a position to be recognized.

*   *   *   *   *   *   *   *   *

No. 54.

Mr. Lopez Roberts to Mr. Fish.

[Translation.]

WASHINGTON, *April* 5, 1869.

The undersigned, envoy extraordinary and minister plenipotentiary of Spain, thinks the time has now arrived to address to the honorable Secretary of State of the United States a few observations in reference to facts which he has heard of through the public papers, and through official communications received from the consuls of Spain in different ports of the United States, and from public rumor—facts which affect the interests and dignity of the nation which the undersigned has the honor to represent, and which, of course, must be of interest to the government of the American nation, whose friendly relations with Spain he is pleased to recognize, and which he deems his agreeable duty to preserve.

Of the facts alluded to, some consist of urgent and clamorous instigations, which the disloyal Spaniards of Cuba, in rebellion against its nationality, and in exile for that crime, are trying to promote in various ways, for the purpose of creating an opinion in favor of their evil cause among the people of the United States, by inserting in the public papers false reports of events said to have occurred in that island, and boasted victories, always contradicted, of the rebel arms. Others referred to are calls of meetings, pompously announced and numerously attended, where speeches are made, abounding in extravagances and absurd falsehoods, intended to captivate the understanding and mislead public opinion, by imposing upon the credulity of the people and alluringly flattering their instincts. And we may add to this kind of excitement the stimulus of musical concerts, public collections of money to aid the rebels, and even sermons and prayers in certain churches, calling for divine aid for the triumph of the cause, after public announcements to increase the attendance, which proves that, instead of Heaven's aid, they are trying by this ostensible sanctity to seduce the multitude and secure the moral and material aid of man.

Facts of another kind, which are referred to, are a natural sequence of those mentioned, and prove that their promoters were not disappointed in their expectations. In fact, the honorable Secretary of State has been informed by the undersigned that frequent communications have been received at this legation from consuls of Spain at various ports of this republic, stating that piratical expeditions are in preparation against the legitimate government of Spain in Cuba; that arms and ammunition are sent there in sailing vessels and steamers, and other acts in positive violation of international law have been perpetrated; and although the undersigned knows, for the honorable Secretary of State has so informed him, that orders have been given to the proper officials of the government of the Union to stop such outrages, and cause a strict observance of the laws, yet it is certain that, in spite of his zeal these officers have not been able to prevent some expeditions from reaching their places of destination, as is publicly known, and that others have been captured by Spanish cruisers, near the coast of Cuba, with positive proof of their criminal intentions.

So advanced are these rebel refugees in their plans of hostility, and so much confidence have they in the popularity of their cause, that the so-called board of directors established in New York has assumed the fancy title of *the independent government of Cuba*, and has dared to send an agent to Washington, with the vain hope that he will be received by this government as the representative of the rebels.

But this is not in question at present; nor does the undersigned look upon it seriously, or presume that the government at Washington will consider it so; but he proposes to establish the truth of the facts, so as to show what the insurrection in Cuba is, and what it means, and the nature of the fancied entity which the rebel refugees in New York insist on calling the *revolutionary government.*

The rebels have no communication with each other; they occupy no place as a center of operations; nor have they, in the whole island, a single city, a single town, a single village or hamlet, nor even a point on the coast, where they might collect their forces and date their orders and proclamations; but they fly from our troops and never offer battle, except when forced to do so; and their only mode of warfare is to apply the incendiary torch to estates, thus reducing to ashes and ruins the whole wealth of the island, if not prevented by Spanish soldiers.

Such are the armies and such is the government that pretend to offer themselves to the American people as the champions of civilization and of liberty.

The undersigned has already stated that he does not deem these explanations necessary to convince the enlightened government of the United States, and he believes it superfluous to add, that the government of Spain would not accept any other signification that might be given to the persons and things, even laying aside these facts and antecedents. His sole intention is to lament the evil effect this pernicious doctrine might have on public opinion in the United States, a doctrine propagated by persons who maliciously distort facts, using prevarications, complaining of want of liberty, rising against the government of their nation, just at a time when all the liberty they could desire, or all that was enjoyed by the entire nation, had been granted them—franchises which the government at Madrid offers to them again, as soon as order shall be restored.

Neither is the intention of the undersigned to protest against the right of American citizens, each and every one of them, to express their opinions in any way they please, provided it be in accordance to law, for the Spanish people have recently acquired the same right; yet the Spanish government, while claiming it for their people reciprocally, is no less obliged to comply with the laws and attend to friendly relations between nations; otherwise it would think it had not done its duty, if it did not publicly declare its religious respect for the sovereignty and integrity of a friendly nation.

Fortunately, the traditions and antecedents of good correspondence between the governments of the United States and Spain could not be more satisfactory.

While Spain recalls with grateful pleasure the many occasions, during the civil war in the United States, when reciprocal testimonials of friendly deference and cordial courtesy were passed between the two governments, and that she is perhaps the only nation against which the government at Washington has not had occasion to present subsequent claims for acts of doubtful neutrality, the American nation ought to remember the noble conduct displayed by the government of President Milllard Fillmore, in 1851, on an occasion identical with that of the present, when a number of rebels conspired against their country by organizing filibustering expeditions in the United States.

The noble and loyal act of that administration, doing its duty with honored frankness, not only toward Spain, but toward its own people, showing them how to act without violation of rights, is worthy of being mentioned here in a copy of the proclamation issued on that occasion:

A PROCLAMATION.

Whereas there is reason to believe that a military expedition is about to be fitted out in the United States with the intention to invade the Island of Cuba, a colony of Spain, with which this country is at peace; and whereas it is believed that this expedition is instigated and set on foot chiefly by foreigners, who dare to make our shores the scene of their guilty and hostile preparations against a friendly power, and seek by falsehood and misrepresentation to seduce our own citizens, especially the young and inconsiderate, into their wicked schemes, an ungrateful return for the benefits conferred upon them by this people in permitting them to make our country an asylum from oppression, and in flagrant abuse of the hospitality thus extended to them;

And whereas such expeditions can only be regarded as adventures for plunder and robbery, and must meet the condemnation of the civilized world, while they are derogatory to the character of our country, in violation of the laws of nations, and expressly prohibited by our own statutes, which declare that if any person shall, within the territory or jurisdiction of the United States, begin or set on foot, or provide or prepare the means for, any military expedition or enterprise, to be carried on from thence, against the territory or dominions of any foreign prince or state, or of any colony, district, or people with whom the United States are at peace, every person so offending shall be deemed guilty of high misdemeanor, and shall be fined not exceeding three thousand dollars, and imprisoned not more than three years:

Now, therefore, I have issued this my proclamation, warning all persons who shall connect themselves with any such enterprise or expedition, in violation of our laws and national obligations, that they will thereby subject themselves to the heavy penalties denounced against such offenses, and will forfeit their claim to the protection of this government, or any interference on their behalf, no matter to what extremities they may be reduced in consequence of their illegal conduct. And therefore I exhort all good citizens, as they regard our national reputation, as they respect their own laws and the laws of nations, as they value the blessings of peace and the welfare of their country, to discountenance and, by all lawful means, prevent any such enterprise; and I call upon every officer of this government, civil or military, to use all efforts in his power to arrest, for trial and punishment, every such offender against the laws of the country.

Given under my hand the twenty-fifth day of April, in the year of our Lord one thousand eight hundred and fifty-one, and the seventy-fifth year of the independence of the United States.

MILLARD FILLMORE.

By the President:

W. S. DERRICK,

Acting Secretary of State.

The undersigned is pleased to believe that a similar declaration is now opportune; and though the Spanish nation does not doubt the cordial friendship of the United States, yet a public and solemn avowal of the inclination and intention of the government to observe the laws and preserve justice toward Spain would have the salutary effect of dissipating false illusions and discouraging dangerous deceptions.

No. 55.

Mr. Fish to Mr. Lopez Roberts.

WASHINGTON, *April* 17, 1869.

The undersigned, Secretary of State of the United States, has the honor to acknowledge the receipt of the note of Mr. Roberts, envoy extraordinary and minister plenipotentiary of Spain, of the 5th instant.

In this note, Mr. Roberts, after stating various circumstances, sets forth a proclamation, issued on the 25th of April, 1851, by Mr. Fillmore, then President of the United States, and expresses the opinion that a similar declaration is now opportune.

After a careful examination of Mr. Robert's note, the undersigned fails to perceive the necessity, or the propriety at this time, of a proclamation by the President of the United States, such as Mr. Roberts desires.

The publication of an instrument of the character asked by Mr. Roberts would be the exercise of a power by the President which is resorted to only on extraordinary occasions, and when peculiar circumstances indicate its necessity. Such a power is not to be invoked lightly, or when the laws are in unquestioned vigor and efficiency, are respected by all persons, and are enforced by the ordinary agencies.

When Mr. Fillmore's proclamation was issued in 1851, the internal peace and quiet of the Island of Cuba were undisturbed; there was no insurrection of its inhabitants, no rebellion or revolution in progress within the island against the authority of Spain. There was, however, a movement on foot within the United States, indicating the intent of certain parties to organize within the territory of the United States an armed expedition with the design of invading the island, attempting to incite an insurrection, and to overthrow the authority of Spain there.

Under such circumstances, Mr. Fillmore issued the proclamation referred to, giving another instance of the watchfulness and earnestness of this government in regard to its obligations to all friendly powers.

The circumstances of the day are wholly different from those which made that measure not only proper, but the natural, if not the necessary manifestation of the policy and the conduct of this government from its organization. A portion of the people of Cuba, for more than six months, have been in arms against the government of Spain over that island, and they are seeking, as they allege, relief from oppression. How just their complaint may be, or what the oppression is from which they desire relief, the undersigned does not purpose to discuss. He only refers to the objects of the insurrectionary party, as that party alleges them to be, to illustrate the entire difference between the events existing when Mr. Fillmore issued his proclamation and those which now exist.

At present this government is not aware of any invasion of the Island of Cuba, or of any other possessions of Spain threatened from the United States, nor is any such believed to be in the course of preparation. Mr. Roberts has, on several occasions, intimated to the undersigned the existence of individual or private attempts in different parts of the country to violate the neutrality laws of the United States. In every such instance, as Mr. Roberts very justly admits in his note, the proper officers of the government have been called upon immediately to vindicate the supremacy of the law, and no single instance is known or is believed to have arisen in which their interference, thus invoked, has not been efficient to prevent the apprehended violation.

The government of the United States has very recently experienced the effects of a precipitate recognition of belligerent rights to a revolutionary movement whose powers of resistance and of endurance were sustained by the recognition on the part of a government at peace with the United States within a little more than two months after the outbreak of the insurrection. But having from its very origin been foremost in the assertion of neutral rights, and in setting the example of enforcing a strict neutrality, this government does not intend at present to depart from its traditional policy, but will execute, in good faith, the wise and efficient laws that have been enacted for the observance of its international duties of neutrality and friendship.

Individuals, tempted either by the hope of gain or instigated by those engaged in the insurrection now pending in Cuba, may be led covertly to undertake unlawful enterprises. Such ventures are not confined to any one country or to any age. They always and everywhere occur with the opportunity. At this moment similar enterprises aimed at Cuba are well understood not to be limited to this hemisphere, but have also been set on foot in transatlantic countries.

The proximity of the United States to Cuba has heretofore and must continue to tempt reckless and adventurous persons to embark in such undertakings. But, in the future, as in the past, every intimation from the Spanish government or its agents of the existence of any design of an unlawful enterprise against Spain, will be met by the most vigorous interposition of the proper officers of the government, and the undersigned has no doubt that such interposition will be sufficient, without invoking the extraordinary power of the President to issue a special proclamation.

The sympathy of the people of the United States has ever manifested itself in favor of another people striving to secure for itself more liberal institutions, and the right of self-government; this sympathy recently obtained strong expression when Spain threw off an existing oppression and placed herself among the more liberal governments of the world. It is now enlisted, beyond doubt, and strongly in favor of a more liberal government in Cuba than that which the policy of past ages and of the deposed government of Spain had fastened upon the people of that island, and it cannot be denied that there pervades the whole American people a special desire to see the right of self-government established in every region of the American hemisphere, so that the political destiny of America shall be independent of transatlantic control. This is no new desire; it arises from no recent events, nor is it now for the first time made manifest. This government has ever been watchful and hopeful, but not aggressive; the desire of the American people for self-government by others has been, and is, held firmly, but consistently with the friendly relations which the United States desire to maintain with all other governments, and especially with those who still claim control over neighboring possessions.

The undersigned has not specially referred to the facts and circumstances cited by Mr. Roberts, such as appeal to public opinion, false or exaggerated statements, public meetings, musical concerts, sermons and prayers, as indicative of the necessity of the proclamation which he requests.

The freedom of speech, of the press, and the right of the people peacefully to assemble, whether for political purposes or for entertainments, or to hear sermons, or for prayer, cannot be called in question, nor admit of any interference.

The experience of this country of nearly a century has demonstrated the harmlessness of extravagant speech, and even of falsehood, when the right of speech and the freedom of the press are untrammeled.

The government cannot, and will not, attempt to influence the thought or the sympathies of its citizens; it will limit itself to the interposition of its power against every improper or unlawful exercise of any sympathies likely to lead to the infraction of its proper obligations to Spain and to other friendly powers.

Having set the example of the most perfect laws of neutrality, both in theory and in practice, the government of the United States will continue to administer them in the utmost good faith and with vigor in every instance where it shall be duly informed of any threatened violation of them.

No. 56.

Mr. Hall to Mr. Fish.

No. 33.] HAVANA, *April* 22, 1869.

During the past few days a number of decrees, many of them very lengthy, have been issued by the Captain General of the island, all in reference to, or tending to the confiscation of the property of such persons as are in any way connected with the insurrection, whether in the island or abroad.

These decrees are published in the Official Gazette; the most important of them is dated 1st instant, but was published for the first time in the Gazette of the 16th instant.

It is not improbable that this decree may be enforced retroactively to the prejudice of some of our own citizens, in view of which I herewith accompany a translation.

* * * * * *

[Translation.]

SUPERIOR POLITICAL GOVERNMENT OF THE PROVINCE OF CUBA.

It is the duty of every government to provide for the security of the territory confided to its command.

That of this province, attacked by an unjustifiable insurrection that is depopulating and ruining many of the rich districts of the island, makes indispensable the adoption of every efficient measure for annihilating the enemies of our nationality by depriving them of all the resources upon which they depend for sustaining their aggression.

With this in view, and the possibility that sales of property may be effected for illicit ends, such sales (contratos) are declared, in conformity with our laws, to be null, and in use of the extraordinary and discretionary powers with which I am invested by the supreme government of the nation, I decree the following:

ARTICLE 1. Contracts for the sale of immovable and semi-movable (slave) property, before going into effect, will from *this date* be presented to the government for revision.

ART. 2. In compliance with this disposition, the contracts made in Havana will be presented to the secretary of the superior civil government, and those effected in other jurisdictions of the island, to governors and lieutenant governors.

ART. 3. The presentations referred to will be made by the parties when the contract is a private one, and by the notary (escritano) when it becomes a public instrument; and before it has been drawn up, in the first case, the original document will be presented; in the second, the memorandum (or minutes) of the instrument.

ART. 4. After the contract has been *vizaed* by the government it shall not be altered or modified in any manner without its (the government's) previous revision, under penalty of the nullity of the alteration in case of infraction.

ART. 5. Sales of produce and other articles of commerce for exportation, as also the transfer of shares of corporations and societies, are also subject to the revision referred to.

ART. 6. In the cases of sales, referred to in the last preceding article, through the medium of a broker, the latter will present the contract for revision in the mercantile form in which it is extended. If no broker intervenes, the presentation will be made by the contracting parties.

ART. 7. The officers of corporations that are authorized by their respective regulations to authenticate transfers of stocks, will effect such transfers with the authorization of the government, and for this purpose they shall render an account of the transfers proposed by the parties interested, expressing in their communications directed to the government the names and residence of the contractors, and the number and value of the stocks to be transferred.

ART. 8. In order not to embarrass in any manner the sales of real estate and semi-movable (slave) property, and still more mercantile transactions, the government will concede or refuse its approbation to the former within four days, and on the sales of produce within twenty-four hours from the presentation of the documents.

ART. 9. All contracts for the sale of every description of property made without the revision of the government will be null, and private individuals, merchants, brokers, presidents and directors of corporations not complying with the stipulations of this decree will incur the penalties established by the penal code, comprehended in chapter 5, title 8, of book 2.

DOMINGO DULCE.

HAVANA, *April* 1, 1869.

No. 57.

Mr. Fish to Mr. Lopez Roberts.

WASHINGTON, *April* 30, 1869.

I am instructed by the President to inform you that this department has received from the United States consulate in Cuba a decree dated the first day of April current, and promulgated by the Captain General of the island, on the 15th of this month, which virtually forbids the alienation of property in the island, except with the revision and assent of certain officials named in the decree, and which declares null and void all sales made without such revision and assent.

In view of the intimate commercial relations between Cuba and the United States, and of the great amount of American property constantly invested there in commercial ventures, as well as in a more permanent form, the President views with regret such sweeping interference with the rights of individuals to alienate or dispose of their property, and he hopes that steps may be speedily taken to modify this decree so that it shall not be applicable to the property of citizens of the United States, and thus prevent disputes and complaints that cannot fail to arise if its execution is attempted as to such property.

No. 58.

Mr. Hall to Mr. Fish.

No. 37.] HAVANA, *April* 30, 1869.

I have the honor to accompany herewith a translation of a document published yesterday in the "Diario de la Marina," of this city, as taken from the "Redactor," of Santiago de Cuba, purporting to be a proclamation of Count Valmaseda to the inhabitants of that jurisdiction.

* * * * * *

I have received a letter from the acting consular agent at Manzanillo, dated the 24th instant, from which I take the following extract:

Since my last report of the 10th instant, I have to advise that Count de Valmaseda, since the 14th instant, has taken the offensive, and has sent from his encampment, near Bayamo, four different battalions to scout the country, pursuing the insurgents in the spirit of his proclamation of that date.

* * * * * * *

[From the Diario de la Marina, April 29, 1869—Translation.]

The Redactor, (of St. Jago de Cuba,) in its number of 21st instant, publishes the following important proclamation of General Count Valmaseda:

Inhabitants of the country! The re-enforcements of troops that I have been waiting for have arrived; with them I shall give protection to the good, and punish promptly those that still remain in rebellion against the government of the metropolis.

You know that I have pardoned those that have fought us with arms; that your wives, mothers, and sisters have found in me the unexpected protection that you have refused them. You know, also, that many of those I have pardoned have turned against us again.

Before such ingratitude, such villany, it is not possible for me to be the man that I have been; there is no longer a place for a falsified neutrality; he that is not for me is against me, and that my soldiers may know how to distinguish, you hear the order they carry:

1st. Every man, from the age of fifteen years, upward, found away from his habitation, (finca,) and does not prove a justified motive therefor, will be shot.

2d. Every habitation unoccupied will be burned by the troops.

3d. Every habitation from which does not float a white flag, as a signal that its occupants desire peace, will be reduced to ashes.

Women that are not living at their own homes, or at the house of their relatives, will collect in the town of Jiguani, or Bayamo, where maintenance will be provided. Those who do not present themselves will be conducted forcibly.

The foregoing determinations will commence to take effect on the 14th of the present month.

EL CONDE DE VALMASEDA.

BAYAMO, *April* 4, 1869.

No. 59.

Mr. Fish to Mr. Lopez Roberts.

WASHINGTON, *May* 10, 1869.

I have the honor to inclose a copy of a proclamation said to have been issued by General Count Valmaseda, in Cuba.

In the interest of Christian civilization and common humanity, I hope that this document is a forgery. If it be indeed genuine, the President instructs me, in the most forcible manner, to protest against such a mode of warfare, and to ask you to request the Spanish authorities in Cuba to take such steps that no person having the right to claim the protection of the government of the United States shall be sacrificed or injured in the conduct of hostilities upon this basis.

[For proclamation above referred to, see inclosure to dispatch No. 37, from Mr. Hall to Mr. Fish, April 30, 1869, *ante.*]

No. 60.

Mr. Fish to Mr. Hale.

No. 158.] MAY 11, 1869.

I inclose for your information a copy of a note to the Spanish minister at Washington, dated April 3,* relative to a proclamation by the Captain General of Cuba, for the detention, search, and seizure of neutral vessels on the high seas. The British government have furnished us, through Mr. Reverdy Johnson, with a copy of their instruction, by telegraph, to the British minister at Madrid, to protest against this proclamation. I am happy to be able to add that we have intelligence that the proclamation has been modified.

* * * * * * * * *

I further inclose a copy of another note to Mr. Roberts, of the 10th instant, protesting against the infamous proclamation of General Count Valmaseda, of which a copy accompanies it. You will please make similar representations to the Spanish government.

* * * * * * * * *

No. 61.

Mr. Hall to Mr. Davis.

No. 56.] HAVANA, *May* 18, 1869.

I have the honor to accompany herewith a copy of a letter this day received from * * * *, Nuevitas, giving account of late military operations in that vicinity.

* * * * * * * * *

Mr. * * * * * * *to Mr. Hall.*

NEUVITAS, *May* 14, 1869.

* * * * * * * * * * * *

The train arrived here on the 12th instant, having left Puerto Principe on the 9th. It was three days coming down a distance of forty-eight miles, guarded by over two thousand troops. On their way to Puerto Principe they were thirteen days, the rebels harassing the column continually, and burning down the bridges ahead of the column.

---

* See *ante,* No. 52. † See *ante,* No. 59.

At Alta Gracia the insurgents made a stand to dispute the passage of the troops, in which engagement the Spaniards had four officers and twenty soldiers killed, and forty wounded—among the officers killed, a lieutenant colonel. The whole line of the railroad is occupied by troops to prevent the insurgents from damaging the road.

The insurgents have established a government at Guaimare. Carlos Manuel Cespedes is the president, Francisco Olguilera, vice-president, and General Manuel de Quesada general-in-chief, of all the rebel forces. They have formed a regular legislative body, and have passed an act to ask our government to admit them into the Union. I have been informed that documents to this effect have been forwarded to their so-named minister in the United States, Mr. Morales Lemus, to present them to our government.

The Spaniards are full of hopes, thinking that the rebellion must soon succumb. But, on the other hand, the rebels are sanguine of success, always expecting aid from the United States. I do not see that the Spaniards gain more advantages than heretofore, holding what ground they occupy militarily, and nothing more. It is true that the railroad to Puerto Principe will give them the great advantage of supplying that city with provisions. But the whole line has to be guarded by troops, it taking three or four days to get the train through, a distance of only forty-eight miles.

* * * * * * * * * * *

No. 62.

Mr. Plumb to Mr. Fish.

No. 15.] HAVANA, *May* 28, 1869.

As there may be no more reliable means of obtaining an idea of the true situation of a country experiencing political disturbances than a study of the measures adopted by the established government, in its endeavors to repress such movements, I beg to inclose to you herewith translations which I have caused to be made of two decrees of considerable importance, which have been published here within the past few days.

The first, inclosure No. 1, is the official sanction by the home government at Madrid, under date of 27th ultimo, of an arrangement made by the Captain General of this island, in February last, with the Spanish Bank of Havana, in connection with various Spanish capitalists of this city, for a credit to be drawn against, at pleasure, by the Captain General, of eight millions of dollars, reimbursable to the bank from the proceeds of certain extraordinary war taxes and export duties imposed by the decree.

This credit, I have heard, is now about exhausted, three months having elapsed. What the amount realized toward its reimbursement has been, I am not informed.

The principle set down in this measure by the home government is, that the island must pay the expenses arising from its present situation.

The second, inclosure No. 2, is a decree or circular order, issued on the 24th instant by Captain General Dulce, directing the seizure of all horses on the estates within a certain district, comprising the eastern portion of the western department, or half division of this island.

The order is apparently designed both to deprive the insurgents of a resource they are now using, and to aid the Spanish forces to more rapid military movements. At the same time the measure would seem to bear hardly upon both loyal and disloyal estate owners alike.

* * * * * * * * *

[Translation.]

DEPARTMENT OF ULTRAMAR—DECREE.

In view of the communication of the 24th of February last, in which the superior civil governor of the Island of Cuba gives account of the resolution which, in the character of provisional, he issued by decree of the 22d of that month, and which appears published in the Gazette of Havana of the following day, establishing an export duty, an increase in the import duty, and another increase in industrial and commercial taxes, in order to meet the extraordinary expenses caused by the insurrection in the said island;

In view of the decree referred to, issued at Havana, on the 22d of February last;

In view of the act of the meeting of contributors, held before the superior civil governor of the Island of Cuba, signed by Messrs. Juom Poey, Julian de Zulueta, Edwardo A. Mijares, the Marquez of Cáuepo Florido, Marnestó Pulido, Rafael R. Forices, Juan A. Calomé, Augustin Saavedra, Manuel de Armas, José E. Moret, J. M. Zaugroniz, Francisco Talomé, and Pedro Sotolongo, from which it appears that the opinion unanimously adopted was that of entering into an agreement with the Spanish Bank of Havana, by which the latter should loan to the government of the nation, and in its name to the superior civil governor of the island, the sum of eight millions of dollars, according as the same might be successively called for, in currency of the class which it at present has in circulation, to be reimbursed weekly with the proceeds of the increased duties before mentioned, the bank relinquishing interest or remuneration for the advance;

Considering the urgency of procuring resources for military operations, to which for the moment it is indispensable to resort for the re-establishment of peace in that province, is an imperative reason which should excuse the superior authority of the island from limitation to the rules established for proceedings of public interest under ordinary circumstances. Considering that it is of high and transcendent importance that the extraordinary expenses imposed by the present situation of the Island of Cuba shall not be raised entirely by an operation of credit, but that, on the contrary, they be covered by resources equally extraordinary, raised by the country itself;

Considering that similar motives of a peremptory and urgent character, as those which justify the proceeding of the superior civil authority of Cuba, excuse the omission of consultations and formalities established by the legislation in force for affairs of this nature under normal circumstances;

The executive power, in council of ministers, has thought proper to decree the following:

ARTICLE 1. The project of agreement entered into between the Spanish Bank of Havana and the committee of the industrial and commercial proprietors, to which the communication subscribed by the individuals composing the same, of the 12th of February last, refers, is approved, the bases of which are the following:

1. The obligation or agreement on the part of the bank to deliver to the government of the nation, and in its name to the superior civil governor of the Island of Cuba, according as the same may be asked for, up to the sum of eight millions of dollars in currency of the class which the said institution has in circulation.

2. The relinquishment on the part of the bank of all interest or remuneration on account of the advance referred to, limiting itself to obtain from the government the reimbursement of the expense occasioned by the different issues of bank bills which it may be found necessary to make on account of this negotiation, and the loss which may be caused to it by the reduction of its bills to the coin which may be asked from it by the treasury.

3. For the reimbursement of the eight millions, and the other sums for which, under the foregoing basis, the government may become indebted, a temporary war tax shall be levied, which shall commence to be in force from the 1st of March of the present year, and will terminate precisely at the moment that said engagements shall have been covered.

4. The proceeds of the said tax be paid weekly into the administration of the bank, and under no circumstances shall they be destined to any other attention or purpose.

5. The bank is authorized to issue bills of ten and five dollars, in sufficient sums for the necessities of circulation, recommending at the same time to the classes represented by the acting committee, that they oblige themselves to receive the bills of the bank in all forms of payments.

6. The restriction to ten dollars per person of daily exchange of bills for specie, in order to facilitate to the bank the issue of the new bills, indispensable in the present negotiations.

ARTICLE 2. In accordance with the foregoing agreement, the decree of the superior civil governor of the said 22d of February is approved, by virtue of which from the 1st of March last, the following extraordinary war taxes are imposed:

1. An export duty to be exacted by all the custom-houses of the island, at the time of export for Spain or foreign ports, of fifty cents on each box of sugar; one dollar and two and a half cents on each hogshead of brown sugar; one dollar on each bale of leaf tobacco; fifty cents per one thousand on manufactured cigars.

2. An additional tax of five per cent. on the amount of the present import duties, which shall also be collected by the custom-houses.

3. For one sole time during the present fiscal year, an additional tax of twenty-five per cent. on the quota for the treasury of the contributions on industry and commerce,

excepting those contributors whose quotas are less than two hundred and fifty dollars per annum.

ARTICLE 3. The minister of ultramar will issue the proper orders for the execution of the present decree.

ADELARDO LOPEZ DE AGALA,
Minister of Ultramar.

MADRID, *April* 27, 1869.

[Translation.—Official.]

SECTION FIRST—SUPERIOR POLITICAL GOVERNMENT OF THE PROVINCE OF CUBA.

[Circular.]

Under date of the 14th instant his excellency the Captain General says to me what follows:

EXCELLENT SIR: Under this date I say to the commanders general of operations at Santa Clara and Sancti Spiritus, as follows:

EXCELLENT SIR: In order to take away from the insurgents the means of providing themselves with horses from the sugar estates, pasture grounds, and other farms in the country, whether delivered by owners who sympathize with their disreputable cause, or who may be forced to give them up from the natural fear that their properties may be burnt, I have thought proper to direct that your excellency order the military commanders, chiefs of columns, to collect all serviceable horses and mares which may be found upon all the farms that are not sufficiently guarded, in order to avoid their being taken away by the insurgents. In the execution of this measure, details and lists should be made out with the just price of every animal that is to be delivered by the owners, or may be gathered, leaving duplicate accounts, signed by the commissioners and attested by the chief of the column or the military commander, one of which must be kept by the chief, and the other remitted to the respective lieutenant governor. The horses will be used by the columns for baggage trains, spare ammunition, allowances, and equipments, and to mount the force so as to be able to go in pursuit of the insurgent parties in the same manner that they move, that is, mounted, and by this means the persecution will be more active, and will give the desired results. Your excellency will dictate the most decisive warning, so that this disposition may be fulfilled with the due formalities, in the understanding that whatever claim may be made of me for informalities in operation, I am disposed to demand of the chiefs the most rigid responsibility, without any complicity whatever, in a measure that affects so much property that must always be respected, and that only in the extreme circumstances in which the island finds itself, and the destruction of the parties obliges me to take for the prompt pacification of the invaded territories. The horses which the columns do not require will be remitted to the headquarters in order that the lieutenant governors may keep them in a close and secure pasture ground at a place where warlike preparations are being made, or upon proprieties that are defended, which owners will make use of them, and to whom an account will be given of those which are delivered to them, brought forth from the general records in order that they may be responsible for them whenever claimed for.

I give an account of this disposition to his excellency the superior political governor, in order that he may, on his side, give the respective instructions to the lieutenant governors, giving them, also, his instructions, so that they may send a copy of the detailed and estimated lists to the proper authority, in which they will explain in a clear and distinct manner the destination given to each horse, so that the animal or its value may be claimed at any time from the person to whom it may be intrusted. The chief of the columns will remit to my authority the detailed and estimated list of the horses which may remain at his charge from any source, with the name of the owners to whom they belong, that of the farm, &c., in order to record the due responsibility, having a special care to give information of the increase or decrease that may occur resulting from combats with the enemies, on the understanding that the surplus will have also the destination already mentioned, making out a list of those so seized. The decrease of those which happen to die or remain useless in the battle-field, should they not be replaced with those which are seized, will be claimed at the stations which are established, the commissioners of which will deliver them with the due formalities, under receipt, expressing the signs, estimate, value, owner, &c., in order to guide themselves when they are claimed for. All which I say to your excellency for your punctual accomplishment, expecting, from your careful observance, that you will take all such measures as to avoid the abuses, which, unfortunately, are very frequent in this sort of measure, which I am disposed to repress with strong arm, and which will second your proper dispositions, which I have the honor to transmit to your excellency for the effects expressed, doubting not that a measure of the kind will be seconded by your authority, tending to the prompt pacification of the island, in which all good Spaniards and the sensible persons of the country are interested; which I transmit to your excellency for your knowledge and the most exact fulfillment in the post which concerns you, bearing in mind that I will demand the most strict responsibility from all whom it may concern, should the least abuse happen to be committed, or if for want of scrupulousness or careful observance on the part of the functionaries to whom it may concern, to intervene in the collection or custody of the horses gathered and delivered, well-founded claims on the part of the proprietors should be occasioned.

God preserve your excellency many years! Havana, May 24, 1869.

DOMINGO DULCE.

To LIEUTENANT GOVERNOR

Of Santa Clara. Cienfuegos. Remidios, Trinidad, Sagua, Sancto Spritus, Malon.

No. 63.

Mr. Plumb to Mr. Fish.

No. 20.] HAVANA, *June* 2, 1869.

Under pressure from the volunteers, General Dulce this morning resigned his command as Captain General of this island in favor of the second in command, General Espinar, and leaves for Spain to-morrow.

* * * * * * *

No. 64.

Mr. Hall to Mr. Fish.

No. 95.] MATANZAS, *June* 3, 1869.

The lawless example of the Havana volunteers in deposing General Dulce has been quickly followed by those of this place, who last night forcibly deposed Brigadier Lopez Pinto, duly appointed by the provisional government of Spain, as governor of this important jurisdiction. The governor incurred the enmity of these volunteers some weeks ago, in refusing to accede to their demand for the surrender of an individual named Manuel Despau, who had made himself conspicuous, as well as obnoxious to the volunteers on account of his insurgent proclivities, and was captured on board of a vessel in the harbor, when about leaving the island.

No one outside of the volunteers pretends to doubt his being an efficient, intelligent, and humane officer, disposed to do justice to all in the exercise of his authority, and as far as I can learn, it would seem that aside from the affair above referred to, his only offense in his personal friendship for General Dulce.

At about nine o'clock last evening the volunteers began to collect in the square fronting the palace, evidently by preconcerted arrangement. At about two o'clock a committee, composed of the senior officers of the different battalions, called on the governor and demanded his resignation, which after some parleying and several communications passed between the committee and the corps of volunteers that were formed in the square, was acceded to by the governor, and the command surrendered to Colonel Domingo Leon, of the regular cavalry, and next in rank. The volunteers also demanded and obtained the displacement of the political secretary, Enriquez, and the chief of police; substituting others of their own selection. It appears to be a part of their programme to displace every Cuban holding any official position whatever, as also every "peninsular" Spaniard whose family connections might lead him in any way to sympathize with the natives of Cuba.

Nearly all of the municipal and many of the subordinate custom-house offices are held by Cubans.

The Matanzas volunteers number about two thousand five hundred men. There are among them many persons of respectability and influence, but in the ranks there are some of the worst elements of the Spanish (peninsular) part of the population—men of brutal and sanguinary instincts, that would, if left to themselves, riot in fire and blood. Fortunately, up to the present, the occurrences referred to have passed off quietly, save the insulting epithets and "mueras" that were applied to the deposed officials by the tumultuous volunteers. There is a wide belief that in some way General Lersundi is responsible for these demonstrations; that through him certain parties at Havana instigated the volunteers at that place to depose General Dulce, having previously attempted to force his resignation by thwarting every conciliatory measure that he would have adopted. It is believed also that the movement initiated at Havana, and imitated here, will be repeated at other places of the island, until all the principal positions are in the hands of his adherents; and, finally, that the movement is in the interest of Doña Isabel II, and favorable to her restoration to the Spanish throne. I refer to these as among the many rumors now circulating here, without vouching for their truth.

As a natural consequence of these demonstrations, an unusual alarm prevails among the Cuban and foreign population of the place. Nevertheless, I have the statements of influential Spaniards that it is unfounded, and that there will be no further disorderly demonstrations, but of this I am confident that they cannot give any assurance.

Colonel Leon, the governor, is well known here, having discharged the duties of the same position, when vacancies have occurred at different periods during the past four or five years. His private character is unexceptionable, but it is to be doubted whether his influence with these volunteers would suffice to prevent excesses in emergencies requiring the exercise of strong authority, which are sure to arise.

* * * * * * * *

No. 65.

Mr. Plumb to Mr. Fish.

No. 23.] HAVANA, *June* 4, 1869.

On the 2d instant, a Captain General of Cuba was displaced from his command by the resident Spaniards of the island. This event, without precedent here, opens an epoch in the history of this Spanish possession. Some fifty years ago a similar event occurred in Mexico. An insurrection had been for some time in progress there, and either induced by the course of events at home, or from dissatisfaction at the conduct of the war, the resident Spaniards deposed the viceroy. A new viceroy was sent out, but arrived too late, and no other representative of the mother country ever succeeded to the place. The resident Spaniards there, as soon as they cut loose from entire obedience to the home authority, turned the scale in favor of independence.

Their design was to control local affairs themselves, but they were soon swallowed up in the greater number of the creole population.

So here, an insurrection has been for some time in progress, commenced and sustained solely by the creole population. The Spanish residents of the island, probably both from the effect of events at home and from dissatisfaction at the conduct of the war, have been for some time, if I rightly judge, inclined to the idea of taking the management of affairs here, in the name of the mother country, more or less into their own hands. They are residents, identified to a great extent with the prosperity of the island, having their business and their property here, and, as the island has to pay its own expenses, contributing largely, many of them, to the burden of the support of the war, both by their money, and now by their time as volunteers. They desire to see the war ended, and to have the former tranquillity, upon which their prosperity depends, restored.

They may believe, especially as liberal institutions are urged in Spain, that they have as full right and are as capable to manage the affairs of the island, of which they are the loyal residents, as officials without any local interests or responsibilities, sent out from home to make their fortunes from the public revenues, not in commerce and industry, here. Yet, until now, the resident Spaniards in business or having property here have had little more chance than the native Cubans to participate in the government of the island. All the offices, mainly, have been filled by frequently renewed officials, sent out for that purpose from Spain. The consequence has been that the public burdens are felt to be unnecessarily increased, and now the feeling has been engendered that the military operations against the insurrection have not been energetically conducted by those who, if they fail here, not having any identification with the island, simply return home to the mother country, leaving the Spanish residents to their fate, or, in some instances, it may be believed that these officials have been too lenient, or have inclined too much in favor of the insurrection, which, if it is successful, would place the control of the island in native Cuban rather than resident Spanish hands.

At the same time there is an under-current of serious difference in the Spanish views. Some of the Spaniards resident here incline to the liberal reforms now proposed in Spain. Others cling to the old monarchical institutions. Some, perhaps an influential party, would like to see Isabella or the Bourbon dynasty restored, and may dream of yet presenting her with the jewel of this rich possession; and the clerical influence may have considerable weight. Yet there is, apparently, among the reflecting portion of the Spanish residents, a consciousness of the grave peril of any separation from the line of due recognition of the legitimate authority of the home government.

Be all these considerations as they may, the rubicon has now been passed, and by a demonstration of the volunteers of this city on the night of the first instant, for which, however unpremeditated and unorganized it may have been, the Spanish residents are responsible, Captain General Dulce, as is publicly and fully known, was forced at once to resign the command of this island, as the representative of the government of Spain.

By his resignation, signed on the morning of the 2d instant, he transferred the command, not of his own free will, but at the demand of a committee of the officers of the volunteers, to the second in authority on the island; and not because he was the second in the line of legitimate authority, or was more especially satisfactory to the volunteers or to Spanish sentiment, but because General Dulce, the representative of the home government, was not satisfactory, and to save appearances, and preserve, as far as possible, the line of legality, the second in command was mutually agreed upon. A little later, the officer so selected may be deemed unsatisfactory to the Spanish residents, or to their material expression in force, the volunteers, and may be in his turn set aside; and so even a new Captain General sent out from Spain may be rejected. At the same time it should not be understood that in these steps the Spanish residents are in entire accord. They are, however, necessarily acquiescent, and have, as a body, to bear the responsibility.

My predecessors have informed the department of the extension given by the recent Captain General Lersundi, the predecessor of General Dulce, after the present insurrection commenced, in the absence of sufficient troops from Spain, to an organization that had been in existence here since the time of the Lopez expedition, when it was originated to aid in the defense of the island, of local militia, called volunteers, composed of the Spanish residents of the island, who, coming to the island mainly as young men to seek their fortune by industry or commerce, furnish a larger proportion than usual of able-bodied, stalwart, and, after a little time, acclimated men.

These organizations of local militia, perhaps confined heretofore to four or five regiments in this city, and one or three in some of the other principal towns of the island, have remained, since the motive of their creation at the time of the Lopez expedition passed, without special purpose or importance, and without power or other duty than that of occasional parade.

When the present insurrection broke out, however, General Lersundi found himself obliged to confront it with but about five thousand regular Spanish troops then on the island. He felt compelled, therefore, to call for assistance upon the loyal Spanish residents of the island. The existing volunteer organizations formed a convenient nucleus, which, by the creation of new regiments and the extension of the system generally to all the towns on the island, has now placed under arms, and in a condition for effective local service, a body of about ten thousand men in this city, and perhaps thirty thousand men altogether, upon the island, which can easily be increased in this city to a considerable extent.

These volunteers, as I understand, have mainly furnished their own arms and uniforms, and serve, when on duty, without charge for their time.

It was not originally understood that they were to go to the field, and they are reluctant to do so, but a few regiments from this city and other places have, however, been sent.

As the regular troops that were here, and those that have since arrived from Spain—say twenty-five thousand in all, have been sent to the field, the militia or volunteers have taken their places in doing duty as guards in the fortresses of the Morro, the Cubañas, and others here, and at the palace.

At the present time, beside a small regiment of cavalry, there are, as I understand, only some two or three hundred regular troops in this city. Thus, for the power to enforce his authority in this city, and to a greater or less extent in the towns on the island, the Captain General, the representative of the government of Spain, has had to depend, not, as heretofore, upon the military arm of Spain, represented by a body of regular troops, but upon the Spanish residents of the island, voluntarily organized into local militia.

Necessarily, in the haste and the need of the recent increase of this organization, it has become composed largely of a very different material from the élite of the young men among the Spanish residents, which made the organization in past times, it is said, similar in composition to some extent to the Seventh Regiment of the city of New York. While the colonels of the volunteers are nearly all men of position and wealth, as are also many of the other officers and of the privates, there is also much of a reckless and turbulent element, over which the officers frankly confess they have but little control.

The feeling among the volunteers is intensely Spanish, and there is great hatred and bitterness against the Cubans. Until after General Lersundi left, at the beginning of January last, no demonstrations were made by the volunteers. The liberal policy at first inaugurated by his successor, General Dulce, however, greatly incensed them, and was very unsatisfactory to the Spanish residents generally. They believed only in severe measures against the Cubans, or the insurgents, which are considered here as almost identical terms. The feeling of hatred extended also, it is said, to Americans, who were supposed to sympathize especially with the insurrection.

General Dulce is said to have believed that by making liberal propositions, giving amnesty, and the adoption of liberal measures, he could induce the Cubans who had revolted to return to their allegiance. It is also said that he was informed by leading Cubans, that if he would concede the independence of the island they would unite cordially with the Spanish residents in its self government. But separation from the mother country General Dulce refused, and the Cubans, either not putting faith in the efficiency or probable continuance of the liberal reforms promised by the new government at Madrid, rejected entirely all the propositions he made to them.

General Dulce then withdrew his proclamation of amnesty and entered upon the opposite course. But it has appeared that he has been unable fully to regain the confidence of the Spanish residents, and there has been much murmuring at his alleged clemency, and latterly, at what was charged as the inefficient prosecution of the war against the insurgents.

My own opinion is, that General Dulce is entitled to great credit for the extent to which he has held out, in the face of great difficulties and of personal peril to himself, against the pressure upon him for the adoption of more sanguinary measures.

In January last, shortly after the arrival of General Dulce, while there were yet large numbers of Cubans, openly sympathizing with the insurrection, still remaining in this city, the volunteers, on the occasion of some performance having the effect to excite partisan political passion on the side of the insurrection in one of the theaters here, on the second night of the performance made an indiscriminate attack upon the audience in the theater, composed largely of Cubans, many of whom must have been armed, as some shots were returned by them, and a large number of revolvers, it is stated, were found thrown under the seats of the theater when the audience had been driven out. General Espinar, now named as Captain General, it is said, deserves credit for his energy in terminating this demonstration. A few nights afterward, while the excitement still continued, the volunteers, who own their arms and carry them to their houses, collected in large numbers near the Louvre, a popular coffee-house, having a large open saloon on the ground floor, frequented in the evening by hundreds of people taking refreshments, and under the alleged provocation of a shot from the roof of the house, made an attack upon the place, firing indiscriminately into the crowd. Several lives were then lost, as on the previous occasion, and among them one American, who happened to be passing by.

Afterward, the same night, the volunteers sacked the house of Mr. Miguel Aldama, a wealthy Cuban, who was supposed to sympathize with the insurrection. Officers finally interfered and succeeded in quelling the disturbance. General Dulce, on this occasion, issued a proclamation, severely reproving the volunteers for their conduct, but I have not heard that any due punishment has been meted out.

Some time afterward, on the occasion of the execution of two insurgents, cries in favor of the insurrectionary leaders by one of them led to instantaneous firing upon him and upon the crowd present by the guard of volunteers, and a number of persons were killed.

On another occasion, upon the occurrence of a sudden excitement, shops were hastily fired by armed volunteers and several lives were sacrificed.

At an early period this insubordination also found expression in cries from bodies of the volunteers, in front of the palace, of death to the Captain General, and the feeling that, in the absence of regular troops, the reins of control over the volunteer force were entirely lost by General Dulce, has caused wide-spread anxiety, it is said, even among the Spanish residents themselves.

When a large number of prominent Cubans and supposed sympathizers with the insurrection, who had been arrested by the Captain General, and had been held for some time in confinement in the Cabañas fortress, were about to be sent to Fernando Po, General Dulce found great difficulty in effecting their departure, from the opposition of the volunteers, who demanded more general executions. As the volunteers have to be relied upon to perform guard duty at this as well as the other fortresses, it required great delay and management, as well as much resolution, to effect the extrication of these prisoners and their safe embarcation, as is currently reported.

Similar difficulties have been met with in effecting the release of other prisoners from time to time, and on several such occasions the volunteers have given expression to their dissatisfaction by cries afterward, when being dismissed in front of the palace, of death to the Captain General.

Recently, since my arrival here, such demonstrations have been repeated. On Sunday morning, the 23d ultimo, according to public report, after the sailing of the Spanish steam frigate Carmen for Spain, having on board the Cuban prisoners captured on the English vessel, the Galvanic, was known, some companies of volunteers, on being dismissed in front of the Captain General's palace, after serving on guard duty during the night at the Cabañas where the prisoners had been confined, gave way to their insubordinate demonstrations by crying death to the Captain General, and on being remonstrated with by their colonel, crying death to him. These prisoners, who were sent to Spain to serve out their sentence there, it is taken, were taken from the fortress in the night and with great difficulty.

It appears to be considered here that sending a prisoner to Spain is equivalent to his early release, and this is objected to by the volunteers, who have demanded executions instead.

In this instance, again, General Dulce acted humanely, at apparently great personal risk to himself.

* * * * * * * * *

On the evening of the 31st ultimo, numbers of volunteers collected in front of the hotel where he was supposed to be stopping, and gave vent to cries against him, which, on not finding him, they repeated in front of the palace, charging him with being a traitor and demanding that he be given up to them. The small regular cavalry patrol was at once placed on duty, and further disturbance for that night prevented.

The following day, however, it now appears, the excitement among the volunteers increased, and in the evening they commenced assembling, in large numbers, in the part of the city outside the walls. Here the larger portion of the force remained, while detachments proceeded to the palace, the custom-house, and other points, which latter remained occupied at daybreak.

The gathering and the excitement produced its work, and the cries now turned against the Captain General. The latter had meanwhile placed on guard at the palace the little body of some two hundred regulars, which, with the small cavalry force, was all he had to depend upon, and even these it appears, according to the accounts, refused to obey his orders when he instructed their colonel, as it is said, to fire upon the volunteers.

I am informed that all in the palace passed a sleepless night amidst the greatest alarm and excitement. A collision was only averted, it would appear, by the smallness of the regular force, and the refusal of their officers to fire upon the volunteers. During the night or early in the morning the action of the volunteers rose with their opportunity and took the form of demanding the immediate relinquishment by General Dulce of his command as Captain General, and his instant departure for Spain.

Reports add that a committee was formed composed of a number of the colonels and other officers of the volunteers, of which the captains were the organ, who waited upon the Captain General and presented their ultimatum. The struggle of the night was as to whether this demand be acceded to or not. It was necessarily ended but one way, and early in the morning General Dulce signed his resignation as Captain General in favor of the second in command, General Espinar, designated, it is stated, not from any special preference for him on the part of the volunteers, but from the desire of both parties to preserve, as far as possible the forms of legality.

* * * * * * * * *

About ten o'clock in the morning the result was announced to the companies of volunteers about the palace, who gave cheers and then quietly dispersed to their homes, the usual company resuming duty at the palace, as if nothing had happened.

The news was also communicated to the volunteers formed outside, who were then dismissed, and the city by noon presented no evidence that any event of more than usual importance had occurred.

Fortunately, so far as I have learned, not a single shot was fired, nor any act of personal violence committed. The odds were so overwhelming that a collision would have been madness. The naval force at hand could not have been resorted to except under the certainty of vastly complicating the situation for the Spanish interest, and it is stated on very good authority that the sailors on the Spanish men-of-war in port, who are frequently on shore, as also a considerable portion of the Spanish regular troops on the island, fraternize to such an extent with the volunteers as to render their services against them entirely unavailable.

At the same time I am informed that all of the colonels of the volunteers opposed the proceedings against General Dulce, but were obliged to yield to their men.

The foregoing, so far as I have gathered from the sources of information at my command, are the facts regarding the change that has taken place in the command of this island.

In the afternoon of the 2d there appeared in the Gazette the official notice of General Dulce's transfer of the command to General Espinar, which I have inclosed with my despatch No. 22.

On its face, General Dulce having power to so transfer his command, the transfer appears legal; but the facts are as I have stated, and in their light the importance of the event, in its effect upon the destinies of the island, can hardly be overestimated.

My own impression is, that the action of the volunteers in extorting the immediate resignation of General Dulce was not altogether premeditated; but there are many evidences of serious differences in the Spanish councils here, and there are doubtless influences opposed to the present order in Spain which are actively at work, as well as, on the other hand, some secretly favorable to the cause of the insurrection.

To the latter the event of the 2d is, even by some of the resident Spaniards, I am informed, admitted to be a great moral gain. They—the insurgents—rebel against all control of the mother country. The act of the 2d by the volunteers was the setting aside of a portion of the authority of the home government. The difference is not in kind, but in degree.

The tendency now must be to entire severance, on the part of the Spanish resident force, from the authority of the government at Madrid. Whether this may be with the object of favoring the restoration of the Bourbon dynasty in Spain, or simply for the purpose of local self-control, to secure the direction of affairs here in the hands of the Spanish resident population, the effect cannot but be to render the probability of the restoration of security and tranquillity on this island more remote.

No. 66.

Mr. Plumb to Mr. Fish.

No. 49.] HAVANA, *June* 24, 1869.

I beg to transmit to you herewith copy of a letter, under date of the 18th instant, which reached me yesterday from Mr. E. A. Phillips, acting United States consul at Santiago de Cuba, giving information of the summary execution at that place of a citizen of the United States.

The circumstances of the case, as also the situation of affairs at that place, are so graphically described in Mr. Phillips's letter, that it is not desirable I should attempt to recapitulate them here. I await such instructions as you may deem it necessary to give me in the premises.

* * * * * * * * *

Mr. Phillips to Mr. Plumb.

SANTIAGO DE CUBA, *June* 18, 1869.

I have the honor to inform you that a few days since the American schooner Grape Shot, from New York, landed men and munitions at Baitiquiri, near Guantanamo, and after a few days had an encounter with the Spanish troops; the Cubans, after sustaining themselves three hours, lost their commander, George Smith, a citizen of the United States, and retired into the interior, leaving a few Americans to the mercy of the Spanish troops. On Tuesday, the 13th, the English vice-consul sent me a note stating that an American prisoner had just passed his consulate for the city prison, and in a few minutes I received a dispatch from the governor, notifying me of the same. I immediately called upon this authority, who gave me a pass to the prison, where I could have a public or private interview with the prisoner. I called the fiscal (attorney general) and a captain of the volunteers, who understood English perfectly, and under oath to me made this declaration; he being unable to write from having had his arms so long pinioned as to have a partial paralysis of his hands. Stated that he was a native of Aurora, Indiana, being married and having a child four years of age. Left New York harbor in the schooner Grape Shot; signed the articles as a sailor, for Falmouth, Jamaica, in good faith, knowing nothing of the nature of the voyage save its legitimate object. After anchoring in the lower bay of New York, waiting for a tug to tow her to sea, which arrived at midnight, bringing some fifty armed Cubans, with a good supply of munitions of war, objected to continue the voyage, and desired to return to the city in the tug; the captain assured him that although he had taken the Cubans, he would not risk his vessel to run the Spanish blockade, but would proceed to Falmouth, land the men, and go for a cargo of cocoanuts. When off Cape Maysi, the Cubans took possession of the vessel, changed her course, run her inland and discharged.

He insisted upon continuing the voyage, but having had some difficulty with the captain, was left on shore under threat of shooting him if he attempted any resistance. After the subsequent engagement, in which he took no part, not being armed, he sought some place of safety, and finding two unarmed men, gave himself up and requested to be sent to the American consul; was bound and brought here, and, without judge or jury, sentenced to be shot on the following morning; protested against executioners, and declared that the vessel's register and mate's log-book would prove his capacity on board, and other evidence that he could procure from Jamaica would guarantee his innocence.

This declaration I read in English, and made a verbal translation to the fiscal, who had pronounced the sentence of death upon him. I immediately sent a copy to the governor, being 10 o'clock p. m., praying for a respite for a few days in order to procure proofs from Jamaica, and requested an immediate reply. I waited nearly all night in the office and received no reply. Early in the morning I visited him again and found the prisoner surrounded by the guards formed for his execution; he appeared calm and assured me he had no fear to die, and again assured me, as a dying man, of his innocence, and only begged for a day or two to furnish proofs. At that moment the English vice-consul kindly came in and offered to go with me to the governor. We found him still in bed; stated the urgency of the case, and asked in the name of mercy and of our countries for a respite, and assured him that the German man-of-war now lying in port would take the letter over. The governor seemed disposed to grant this request, but informed us of his superior instructions, and in order to wash his hands of the blood (in our opinion) of an innocent man, and had the debility to inform us of his impotence as the chief magistrate of this city. My troops will not obey; dissension prevails in the army; General Buceta, commanding officer of the forces, is a fugitive on board of a Spanish man-of-war; the Catalans, a few nights since, attempted to assassinate him, under the pretense of a serenade. General Camara was next selected, who, hearing of the plot, secreted soldiers in his house, which frustrated their plan. His death would have been the signal for a general uprising of the Catalans, and of sacking, plunder, and massacre of the Cubans.

Finding all hopes gone we retired, and in our exit met the governor's aide-de-camp, with whom we had some conversation; he assured us that anarchy prevailed; the mob rules; the governor is impotent and fears a counter-revolution. So the man was executed, leaving a letter for his wife and child, showing himself to be a man of good and fair education, proclaiming his innocence, and instructing her to sue the owners of the vessel for damages, having left her penniless. The English vice-consul writes the particulars to his consul general, and asks immediately for a man-of-war to protect himself and archives, as he sees the impending danger.

Such is the state of affairs at this place, and I have undeniable proofs that this place will be the theater of action, and in such cases you very well know that this consulate and the American citizens here will be left without protection, and the American flag dishonored, unless steps are taken to have a vessel of war in port, which I deem of the utmost importance. Had there been one, Speakman would not have been shot and hurled into eternity, and his mutilated remains dumped from an offal cart like an animal, at the so-called cemetery.

I send to-day, to the Secretary of State, an account of the proceedings, and also a copy of the letter of the deceased to his wife, which is painful to read, and hope such outrages will not be permitted to continue, and a suitable protection guaranteed to all citizens of the United States at this place.

The English vice-consul informs me that his letters have been opened. I inform you of this fact in order that your reply may come safe.

No. 67.

Mr. Phillips to Mr. Fish.

SANTIAGO DE CUBA, *June* 19, 1869.

I have the honor to inform you of the existing state of affairs in this city. A few days since two naturalized American citizens and a native of New Orleans, who formed part of the expedition on board of the steamer Peritt, were taken prisoners at Ramon, brought to this city, and within twelve hours, without any trial, publicly shot.

As I did not receive any communication from the authorities, and hearing the fact but too late, I requested the governor to inform in future eases, and allow me to visit the prisoners, in order to ascertain if they have just causes for such proceedings.

I received in due time a favorable and courteous reply.

Wednesday evening, June 16, the governor sent a note informing me that an American citizen had been brought in, taken prisoner at Baitiquiri, and forming part of the expedition which the American schooner Grape Shot had landed on the coast of Cuba, would, according to the laws of the nation, be shot as a pirate on the following morning at 9 o'clock.

Wishing to investigate his case I immediately called upon the governor and requested a pass for the prison, where I repaired, and in the presence of the fiscal, (attorney general,) and a captain of the volunteers, took down in writing the inclosed declaration made by prisoner.

On my return to the consulate I sent a copy to his excellency the governor, praying that before sentence of death be pronounced upon him to grant a respite of a few days in order to procure evidence of his innocence, and after waiting at the office nearly all night I received no reply.

Upon the following morning I again visited the prisoner, who was making an effort to write a farewell letter to his wife, which copy I have also the honor of inclosing, it being a true one. I assured him that all my efforts had been useless; he again protested against his execution, and begged for only a few days to furnish satisfactory proofs. At that moment the English vice-consul came in to offer his services in the matter, and proposed our calling on the governor; we did so, and owing to the early hour were admitted to his bedside, and used all endeavors to stay the proceeding, assuring him that we would request the captain of a Prussian man-of-war, now lying in port, to take over to Falmouth a letter from the prisoner. Our efforts were useless. His excellency gave us to understand that he was impotent in his position; dissension had broken out in the army, his troops reluctantly obeyed his orders, and had no confidence in his officers, and feared a counter-revolution, and was compelled to appease the wrath of the Catalans for his own safety. He further says that the commanding officer, General Buceta, was a fugitive on board of a Spanish man-of-war, for attempts had been made to assassinate him.

After our exit we met his excellency's aide-de-camp, who assured us that perfect anarchy prevailed; that another attempt had been made to assassinate, but this time it was General Camara who was to be the victim. In order to hide their traitorous intentions they went with music, under the pretense of serenading him. Their plot was frustrated, for the general, on hearing of it, stationed soldiers about his house. I have no doubt that it was a prudent measure, because under existing state of affairs a single shot would have been followed by a general plunder, massacre, and sacking of the defenceless inhabitants of this city.

The Spanish government, regarding the patriots of this unhappy country as rebels and traitors, apply the most rigorous and barbarous laws; that is the reason why this has become a war of extermination, which is shocking to every civilized nation. What seems more strange is that Spain having awakened from the lethargy in which her ignorant institutions and despotic kings had prostrated her, when they proclaim a liberal constitution, when they abolish capital punishment, and pardon the true rebels of Malaga and Cadiz, and the assassins of the governor of Burgos, they should grant the just demands of the Cuban people, which are only those granted to all civilized nations.

The country is in complete anarchy; the Catalonian volunteers do not allow the governor to render justice, and he cannot publicly resist them, as he has seen in the case of the unfortunate Speakman, as well as in other cases which have occurred in this jurisdiction. We cannot enjoy personal safety here until some foreign power interferes, and know no other who can have more influence here than the United States, whose citizens have much commercial interest on this island. I therefore consider it not only necessary but urgent that some vessel of war at this moment be stationed in this port to protect the archives of this consulate, and the lives and property of the American citizens in case that the republican patriots should come near the city, and have good reason to believe that they are preparing to do so, owing to their ranks being daily increased and becoming more disciplined, while desertion and sickness prevail in the Spanish army.

From my long residence in the island, and a thorough knowledge of the language and people, I am persuaded that in case of a conflict the archives of this consulate would fall into the hands of the Spanish volunteers unless means are taken to prevent. Under the existing state of political affairs I hope that some vessel of war may be sent to calm the anxiety of the American citizens residing here.

Declaration, under oath, of Charles Speakman, at the prison of Santiago de Cuba, Wednesday, June 16, *at* 9 *o'clock p. m.*

UNITED STATES CONSULATE,
Santiago de Cuba, June 17, 1869.

I, the undersigned, acting consul of the United States at this city, having been permitted by the civil governor to visit the above named prisoner at the city prison, and requested him to make a statement of his case in writing, replied that owing to his arms having been pinioned he could not write, and being sentenced to be shot on the following morning, at 9 o'clock, in the presence of Captain Francis O'Callaghan (of the volunteer corps) made the following declaration:

I, Charles Speakman, of the town of Aurora, State of Indiana, lately resident of Florida, thirty-three years of age, having a wife and child, the latter four years of age, left New York harbor on the last of April, on board of the American schooner Grape Shot, in capacity of sailor, bound, as stated in ship's register, for Falmouth, Jamaica. After dropping anchor at the lower bay, during the night a steam-tug came alongside and put on board of said schooner fifty armed Cubans; suspecting the object of the voyage to be an expedition for Cuba, protested, and requested the captain to be sent ashore, who assured me that he should not touch on the coast of Cuba, but land the men at Jamaica, and that the vessel would proceed for a cargo of cocoanuts; when off Cape Maysi, (eastern end of Cuba,) the captain keeping on his course, the Cubans took possession of the vessel, changed her course, and landed their men and her cargo at Bailiquiri, near Guantanamo; was compelled to assist in the landing, and when the captain went on board, refused to take me, under threat of shooting if I stepped into the boat. Being compelled to remain, I sauntered about the beach; a short time after they were attacked by the Spanish troops, and after a short encounter they retreated to the interior. Finding myself alone, sought a place of safety for the purpose of surrendering my person to the authorities, and being without arms for personal defense, found a rifle on the road, left by some fallen Cuban, took possession of the same, and upon meeting two unarmed men gave myself up, and in no case used the arms against the government, having never fired a single shot. Previous to the shipping I knew nothing of the expedition, nor did I receive any compensation, more than that of an ordinary seaman's wages. I have prayed for a respite to prove my innocence, which several prisoners before being shot declared and certified to, and offered to procure evidence by the vessel's log-book and by statements made at the custom-house at Jamaica. Having no fear of death, I still find it hard to die innocent, and do solemnly protest against my executioners; and I have demanded an opportunity to prove my innocence, having since my captivity had no time or chance to substantiate preceding facts.

Sworn to before me, in the presence of attorney general and Captain Francis O'Callaghan.

A. E. PHILLIPS,
Acting U. S. Consul.

SANTIAGO DE CUBA, *June* 17, 1869.

MY DEAR WIFE AND CHILD: These are the last lines you will ever receive from me. In four hours *I am to be shot*, having been captured by the Spaniards on the Island of Cuba, where the vessel ran instead of going to Falmouth, Jamaica, where I shipped to go. Now, Maggie, I have no money to leave you, and I am so sorry, darling, as I leave you penniless; but you may get some by getting a good lawyer to sue the owners of the vessel for damages; they have taken my life and deprived you of my support, and ought to support you.

There will be a statement sent to the government that he can see; there is also, I have been told, a contract in New York to land these men in Cuba, and if he can get hold of it, you can get big damages from them. The vessel's name was the Grape Shot, schooner, of New York; the owners' names are Henry Wall, a surveyor of New York, one Highdecker, a broker in the same place; one Slowmaker, a liquor dealer; all this can be found out in the New York custom-house. You can get a good deal of money if you get the right kind of a man to take hold of it, and enough to keep you for life. The time is getting short, darling, and if I could only see you and baby once more I could die happy. I have always loved you, darling, whatever you may think to the contrary; God knows it is true. For you and only you I have tried to get along and make you a good living. You have always been a good and true wife to me, and, darling, do forgive all the trouble I have ever given you, and meet me in heaven. Tell Smith that he must let you have some money to help you along; tell him, as a dying brother, I entreat him to take care of you and my little boy. I have one kind friend here, a Mr. O'Callaghan. Darling, I canno twrite more; my hand is sore. Tell cousin Fannie and Aunt Olden. May God Almighty bless you and keep you and baby, is my last and only prayer.

Tell baby his father's last prayer to him is, that he never drinks one drop, and be good to his mother.

After I am dead, Mr. O'Callaghan will cut a lock of my hair, and my handkerchief, and send it to you.

Good-by, darling; I command you to sue the owners; call a witness, one Wm. Craig, of Oliver street, New York, who was on the vessel with me.

God bless you.

Your affectionate and dying husband,

CHAS. SPEAKMAN.

MRS. MAGGIE C. SPEAKMAN,
Care of Captain J. W. Weaver, Aurora, Indiana, U. S.

No. 68.

Mr. Phillips to Mr. Fish.

SANTIAGO DE CUBA, *June* 25, 1869.

I have the honor to inform you that per Spanish steamer Dulce, which left this port for Philadelphia, I sent you a full account of the state of affairs at this city, and of the execution of Charles Speakman, which no doubt will have come to hand before you receive this. It is painful for me to inform you that on the 21st instant, at 9 o'clock a. m., Mr. Albert

Wyeth, of Chambersburg, Pennsylvania, lately residing at No. 24 Clinton Place, New York, and an operator at the telegraph office No. 145 Broadway, was also publicly shot, under such peculiar circumstances I feel it my duty to inform you of the facts. Being notified by the governor of his arrest and sentence to be shot, I repaired immediately to the city prison, where he made the declaration, a copy of which I have the honor to forward; also a certificate attesting the innocence of Mr. Speakman. The originals are on file at this office, corroborating my opinion respecting the same. After assuring the former that I would use all endeavors to save his life, I called upon the governor, the clergy, and some of the most influential citizens of this city, whose united efforts were unavailable.

The Catalans are so sanguine in their disposition that they could not in any way be prevailed upon to allow the governor to pardon the unfortunate victims of the Cuban revolution. It was truly painful, owing to his extreme youth, being but twenty years of age; his social position and fine education, being an invalid who sought a congenial climate and in no way (as represented) being privy to the nature of the expedition.

The arbitrary way in which the authorities treat those who are taken or give themselves up, owing to the manner in which they have been deceived by the revolutionary junta in the United States, are without parallel in history, and in view of the efforts I have used to procure a pardon in peculiar cases of this nature, has led to an order being issued that no more prisoners be brought to this city, but to shoot them without any form of trial or examination. Being convinced by the news that is in daily circulation that the patriots purpose an attack upon this city sooner or later, I fear very much that very little attention will be paid to the lives or property of the American citizens residing here, nor will a due respect be paid to the flag of this consulate, unless some protection be given by the presence of a man-of-war at this port, which is the most earnest wish of your most obedient servant.

P. S.—I inclose a copy of the morning papers, (Spanish organ,) containing a letter addressed to Charles S. Olden, esq., and signed by Francis O'Callaghan, and for want of time before the mail closes I do not send a translation. You will perceive that the authorities, conscious of the iniquity which they have committed in sending into eternity an honorable and innocent man, who protested against his executioners and demanded in the name of mercy an opportunity to send to Jamaica, assuring me of his innocence, without avail. It has been made to appear that the protest was made against the owners of the Grape Shot, yet I admit that he said "If he must die, the Cuban junta ought to take care of his wife and child, who were left penniless."

I have been called upon by a Spanish priest, a tool of the government, supplicating me to take no steps upon the matter, being better that our government knew nothing about it, and to allow the widow to remain in ignorance.

The Spanish press have made a good story for themselves, and is far from the facts of the case. I shall keep the department informed of the passing events as they appear, and shall send with quarterly reports, ending June 30, a full account of the political state of affairs at the eastern department.

Mr. Wyeth to Mr. Phillips.

SANTIAGO DE CUBA, *June* 20, 1869.

I, Albert Wyeth, citizen of the State of Pennsylvania, being out of health, left Hunter's Point, Long Island, in the State of New York, United States of North America, in the schooner Grape Shot, for a voyage to Falmouth, island of Jamaica, whither a certain Mr. Antonio A. Jimenez offered to take me free of charge. The schooner Grape Shot touched at Turk's Island, and after leaving that point they declared they were going to Cuba, when I energetically protested against taking part in the enterprise, and was told that if I attempted to desert them they would shoot me. I was forced to land with the rest on the Island of Cuba, under fear of death, and compelled to take arms on landing, which arms I threw away as soon as I could do so, without having used them at all, and presented myself in San Antonio to the Spanish authorities there. The above I have written of my own free will and accord, under no influence whatever, and is the truth, the whole truth, and nothing but the truth: so help me God.

Mr. Wyeth to Mr. Phillips.

SANTIAGO DE CUBA, *June* 20, 1869.

I, Albert Wyeth, certify that Charles Speakman, whom I learn has been shot in this city, was a sailor on board the schooner Grape Shot, bound from New York to Falmouth, in Jamaica, on which vessel I was a passenger, and to my knowledge was compelled to leave the vessel when it reached the island, by the captain, with whom he had a difficulty, under penalty of death if he remained on board, and was of his own accord in no way connected with the expedition.

No. 69.

Mr. Plumb to Mr. Fish.

No. 57.] HAVANA, *June* 29, 1866.

With my dispatch No. 49, I transmitted to you a copy of a letter from Mr. Phillips, late acting United States consul at Santiago de Cuba, giving an account of the summary execution of a citizen of the United States, one of the unfortunate victims of the Grape Shot expedition.

I have now to transmit herewith a further letter from Mr. Phillips, dated the 23d instant, received yesterday, in which he reports the execution at that place of another citizen of the United States, Albert Wyeth, of Chambersburg, Pennsylvania, taken prisoner with others of the expedition of the schooner Grape Shot.

Evidence given by Wyeth appears to confirm the statements made by the previous victim, Charles Speakman.

I beg to call your attention to the situation of affairs at Santiago de Cuba, as represented by Mr. Phillips, and to the request for instructions made at the close of his letter.

[Inclosure.]

Mr. Phillips to Mr. Plumb.

SANTIAGO DE CUBA, *June* 23, 1867.

I have the honor of informing you that I have forwarded to your address a letter bearing date 18th instant, manifesting the state of affairs at this city and giving you an account of the fate of the American citizen, Charles Speakman. Since which I have been under the painful duty of recording the unfortunate end of another American, whose declaration before me at the city prison is most painful.

Deposed, that being out of health, was invited by one Gimenz (who subsequently proved to be the originator of the Grape Shot expedition) to go to Falmouth, Jamaica, for the benefit of his health, and offered a passage free of expense; nothing occurred on the voyage to indicate its true object until they reached Turks' Island, where they declared their intentions, upon which the deceased protested energetically, and was informed that any desertion upon landing would be punished by death. Being compelled to land with arms and enter into service, he did so, but separated upon the first encounter, threw away his arms and presented himself to the Spanish authorities, who brought him to this city, and was shot without trial in company with five others.

The deceased deposed that he belonged to a very respectable and influential family at Chambersburg, Pennsylvania, and had been residing at 24 Clinton Place, New York, and an operator in the telegraph office, No. 145 Broadway.

After taking his deposition, I made every effort to save him, first by calling upon the governor and manifesting his extreme youth, being only twenty years of age, his social position, the circumstances in which he had been inveigled into the expedition, but to no purpose. I then brought the influence of the clergy and officers of the Catalanian volunteers, (the dread of the local authorities,) but could not save him. Also deposed, that Charles Speakman, to his knowledge, was in no way connected with the expedition, but forced to land under threat of being shot by the captain of the schooner, with whom he had some difficulty on the passage.

This corroborates my former opinion respecting Speakman's innocence. The Spanish government treating the patriots of this unhappy vicinity as rebels and traitors, apply the most vigorous and barbarous laws, and this applies both to Cubans and foreigners.

The mutilated remains, after being shot, are carted off in an offal cart to the so-called cemetery, and dumped into ditches like so many beasts, while those shot in combat are left to fester in the sun, a prey to the carrion birds and dogs. I am persuaded, from facts gathered from reliable sources, that preparations are being made for an attack, sooner or later, upon this city by the rebels. From the knowledge I have of the Catalanian volunteers, I fear that the archives of this consulate and the lives and property of the Americans residing here would fall a prey to the infuriated mob, unless some measures be taken to prevent it, by the presence of some naval force at this port, and unless some protection be given to me from our government, I do not feel disposed to continue in the capacity of acting consul, to be the laughing-stock of the community at large, having no power to interfere in such cases as those mentioned, whose lives could have been saved by the presence of a man-of-war in this port, or at least facilities would have been offered them to prove their innocence.

I have been informed by the officers of the Spanish government, that in future cases, owing to the active measures which I have taken in behalf of my countrymen, and to prevent them making any declaration, it is their determination to shoot all American prisoners immediately on the spot, in order that I may be prevented from communicating with them.

I hope, sir, you will represent these facts to Admiral Hoff, and manifest to him the necessity of looking in upon us, at least occasionally, in order to quiet the anxiety of our countrymen.

I shall also transmit to the department a copy of the proceedings, stated by the young man, Albert Wyeth. Please give me explicit instructions how to act in case that others be brought to this city, as it is painful and revolting to be persuaded of their innocence without power to assist them.

Please answer by first opportunity.

I am, most respectfully, your obedient servant,

A. E. PHILLIPS,
Acting United States Consul.

No. 70.

Mr. Davis to Mr. Plumb.

No. 20.]

DEPARTMENT OF STATE,
Washington, July 7, 1869.

* * * * * * *

I read your No. 49 (inclosing a copy of the report of the consul at Santiago de Cuba, upon the execution of Speakman) to the President, who immediately ordered a vessel of war to proceed to Santiago to investigate the case.

* * * * * * *

No. 71.

Mr. Fish to Gen. Sickles.

No. 9.] WASHINGTON, *August* 10, 1869.

On the third day of July last information was received at this department from Dr. Phillips, vice-consul of the United States at Santiago de Cuba, that Charles Speakman, a citizen of the United States, who had, against his will, been forced to accompany an expedition against Cuba in the Grape Shot, and had voluntarily surrendered himself to the Spanish authorities as a non-combatant, had been cruelly murdered, with a formality of trial that amounted only to a farce. The details of this are so fully set forth in the dispatch of Mr. Phillips, a copy of which is inclosed, that it is needless for me, in this connection, to do more than refer to it.

On the receipt of this information the President directed Admiral Hoff to proceed at once to Santiago de Cuba, and to investigate the case in person.

By direction of the President, Dr. Phillips's dispatch was also, on the same day, read to Mr. Roberts by Mr. Davis, and that gentleman, on hearing it, assured Mr. Davis that he would inquire into the case, and that a proper compensation should be made by the Spanish government to the family of Mr. Speakman.

A few days afterward another dispatch was received from Mr. Phillips, a copy of which is inclosed, containing an account of the execution of Albert Wyeth, another American citizen, under circumstances of equal barbarity and cruelty. For the details of this, also, I refer you to the consul's dispatch, confining myself in this connection to calling your attention to the fact that Mr. Wyeth's dying declarations fully confirm Mr. Speakman's assertions of his own innocence.

Admiral Hoff, upon the receipt of his instructions, sailed as soon as possible for Santiago de Cuba, and arrived there on the 11th of July, with the flag-ship, the steamship Gettysburg, and monitor Centaur. He proceeded at once to make a thorough investigation of these cases, and reported in detail to the Navy Department, with full enclosures, copies of all which are enclosed, in support of the conclusions to which he arrived.

Those conclusions are, "that these men were cruelly murdered, owing entirely to the weakness of the Spanish official at this city, (Santiago de Cuba,) in yielding to the demands of the Catalan volunteers, and in misconstruing or acting upon the cruel decree of the 24th of March, 1869."

In this opinion, and in the forcible language in which it is expressed, the President fully concurs. You are accordingly instructed to demand of the Spanish government full reparation to the families or representatives of Charles Speakman and of Albert Wyeth, for their murder by the Spanish authorities, so far as pecuniary compensation can make reparation therefor.

You will observe, also, that Admiral Hoff says that "Great Britain's laws of citizenship have enabled her to obtain from Spain the entire revocation of this proclamation, which fact seems to be known and observed by the Spaniards throughout the island, and certainly gives British subjects greater consideration when captured or wrecked upon the Cuban coast."

I do not know what peculiarity in the British laws Admiral Hoff refers to. You will, however, call the attention of the Spanish minister for foreign affairs to this fact, and will say that we shall expect citizens of the United States to be treated with as much consideration, and to enjoy as broad rights, as the citizens of any other country.

You will also, in the name of the President, solemnly protest against any longer carrying on this war in Cuba in this barbarous way. For now nearly a year the insurgents have maintained themselves against all the forces which Spain and the Catalan volunteers have been able to put into the field against them. In the judgment of the President, in which I believe the whole civilized world will coincide, the time has come when this struggle should be carried on in a more humane way. To shoot prisoners of war, simply because they are taken with arms in their hands, is not in accordance with the customs of the Christian world. This country is deeply interested in the proper solution of this question. Our relations with Cuba are so many and so intimate that we cannot regard this struggle, in all its details, with anything but intense interest. Our earnest wish has been and is to do our whole duty as a neutral nation toward Spain in this emergency. Feeling that we have done so; that under circumstances of peculiar difficulty we have enforced our laws and maintained our neutrality, we think that we have a right on our part to insist that Spain shall carry on this war hereafter in a manner more in accordance with the humane and Christian sentiment of the age.

No. 72.

General Sickles to Mr. Fish.

No. 15.] SEPTEMBER 8, 1869.

I have the honor to forward you a copy of my note to Mr. Becerra, the minister of state *ad interim*, in relation to Charles Speakman and Albert Wyeth, executed at Santiago de Cuba. In the further execution of your instructions No. 10, I have, in the same communication, formally protested against these deplorable excesses, demanding, in the name of humanity, that the war in Cuba, if prolonged, shall not be conducted in disregard of the customs and usages of Christian nations.

* * * * * * * * *

General Sickles to the Minister of State.

MADRID, *September* 6, 1869.

The undersigned, envoy extraordinary and minister plenipotentiary of the United States of America, in obedience to the instructions of his government, has the honor to request the attention of his excellency the minister of state to certain quite recent transactions at Santiago de Cuba, in which, by the orders of the governor of that place, two American citizens, who had committed no crime, and who had voluntarily sought the protection of the Spanish authorities, were put to death without trial.

On the third day of July last, the Department of State was informed by the American vice-consul at Santiago de Cuba that Charles Speakman, a citizen of the United States, who had voluntarily surrendered himself to the Spanish authorities as a non-combatant, had been executed by order of the governor after an *ex parte* proceeding, not to be called a trial.

On receipt of this information the President directed Admiral Hoff to proceed at once to Santiago de Cuba and to investigate the case in person.

By direction of the President the consul's dispatch was, on the same day, read to his excellency the Spanish minister at Washington by the acting Secretary of State, when Mr. Roberts assured Mr. Davis the matter should be investigated and a proper compensation made by the Spanish government to the family of the deceased.

A few days afterward the vice-consul at Santiago de Cuba reported to the Department of State the execution of Albert Wyeth, another American, under circumstances equally summary, groundless, and cruel.

Admiral Hoff, as soon as he had received his instructions, sailed for Santiago de Cuba, where he arrived on the 11th of July, and, after a thorough investigation, reported in detail all the material facts relating to both of these deplorable occurrences.

It appears from these official reports and the accompanying documents, that Charles Speakman, a citizen of the United States, residing in Aurora, Indiana, where he has a wife and child, being by occupation a sailor, about the end of April shipped as a seaman on board the schooner Grape Shot, of New York, signing articles for Falmouth, in Jamaica, in good faith, knowing nothing of the objects of the voyage. While lying in the lower bay of New York, the tug-boat which was to tow the Grape Shot to sea arrived at midnight, bringing some fifty armed Cubans, with a considerable supply of munitions of war. Speakman objected to continuing the voyage, and desired to return to the city in the propeller; but the captain assured him that, although he had taken the Cubans on board, he would not risk his vessel by attempting to run the Spanish blockade, but would proceed at once to Falmouth, land the Cubans, and go for a cargo of fruit. When off Cape Maysi the Cubans took charge of the vessel, ran her ashore, and disembarked.

Speakman, who had had a quarrel with the captain about the engagement, was forcibly put on shore with the Cubans. They were soon attacked by the Spanish troops, routed, and dispersed, Speakman taking no part in the fight. He took the first opportunity to give himself up to the Spanish authorities, and on the 16th of June was brought to Santiago, subjected to a private examination before the fiscal, in the presence of an interpreter, and condemned to death immediately. The consul of the United States made application to the governor of the place by letter to grant a reprieve of a few days, to enable Speakman to obtain from Jamaica the proofs necessary to establish his innocence. The letter of the consul was never answered. He then, in company with the English vice-consul, made a personal application to the governor. The governor replied that his orders were positive, alluding to Captain General Dulce's proclamation of the 24th of March, 1869, and added that, owing to the dissensions prevailing in the Spanish forces, the dissatisfaction of the Catalan volunteers, and the danger of a counter revolution against himself, it would be entirely impossible to grant even a short reprieve. Consequently Speakman was executed on the morning of the 17th June, within fourteen hours after he was brought to the city.

These facts are derived from the official reports of the acting United States consul, Dr. Phillips, Admiral Hoff, and the dying statements of Speakman, and of those who were executed with him, who united in declaring his innocence of all complicity in the objects of the expedition.

And it further appears that Albert Wyeth, of Pennsylvania, a young man of only twenty years of age, and very respectably connected, sailed in the same schooner Grapeshot for Falmouth, Jamaica, for the benefit of his health. On learning the real destination of the schooner he energetically protested against taking part in the enterprise. When the expedition disembarked he was forced to land with the Cubans, and took the first opportunity to surrender himself to the Spanish authorities. He was shot on the 21st of June, and, so far as can be ascertained, without even the pretense of a trial. The acting consul of the United States, in a personal interview with the governor, urged in vain the extreme youth of the prisoner, his respectable social standing, and his innocence of any criminal intent, as reasons for a commutation or reprieve of the sentence.

Admiral Hoff, in his report to the Navy Department, which is accompanied by all the evidence necessary to support his conclusions, declares that these men were sacrificed through "the weakness of the Spanish official at this city (Santiago de Cuba) in yielding to the demands of the Catalan volunteers, and in misconstruing or acting upon the cruel decree of the 24th day of March, 1869."

In this opinion and in the forcible language in which it is expressed the President fully concurs, and the undersigned is instructed to demand of the Spanish government full reparation to be made to the families or representatives of the said Charles Speakman and Albert Wyeth, in so far as pecuniary compensation can make reparation for these unjustifiable homicides.

It also appears by the report of Admiral Hoff that Great Britain has been enabled "to obtain from Spain the entire revocation of the proclamation of 24th March, 1869, which fact seems to be known and observed by the Spanish authorities throughout the island, and certainly gives British subjects greater consideration when captured or wrecked upon the Cuban coast." The undersigned, in bringing this circumstance to the notice of the minister of state, is instructed to say that the United States claim for their citizens the same consideration and the same rights enjoyed by the citizens or subjects of any other power.

The government of the United States has heretofore remonstrated against certain proclamations of the Captain General of Cuba, that threatened a mode of warfare at variance with the recognized customs of civilized nations. It has been the earnest hope of the President that these friendly representations would not be disregarded by

Spain. The United States, in dealing with a rebellion of vast proportions, which was not a struggle for self-government, emancipation, or ameliorated forms of administration, nevertheless accorded to the insurgents all the amenities of warfare. No life was sacrificed, not even among the conspicuous and responsible actors in the insurrection, unless in battle, and in accordance with the usages of war. Nor was any discrimination made between those citizens of the United States who took part in the insurrection and the citizens or subjects of foreign nations who joined the rebel standard; all, when captured, were treated alike as prisoners of war, and when non-combatants were accused of military offenses within the Union lines, and a trial by the ordinary tribunals was impracticable, they were arraigned before a military commission, in which all the safeguards essential to the administration of justice were carefully observed; the accused were allowed a reasonable time to prepare for trial, the privilege of counsel to assist in their defense, the attendance of witnesses as well as the right of cross-examination; and it was necessary to the validity of sentences pronounced by these tribunals, that the proceedings should be reviewed and sanctioned by superior authority.

It has been, and is now, the sincere wish of the United States to perform all their duties as a neutral nation towards Spain in this emergency. Under circumstances of peculiar difficulty, the United States have enforced their laws and maintained their neutrality throughout the contest. Their relations with Cuba are so many and so intimate, that they cannot but feel an intense interest in a struggle for independence which derives so much of its inspiration from the example of their own free institutions and the past intercourse between Cuba and the republic, not to speak of the recent illustration Spain herself has given of the love of liberty cherished by all Spaniards. For nearly a year the insurgents have maintained themselves against all the force Spain has been able to put into the field against them. In the judgment of the President, in which it is believed the whole civilized world will concur, the time has come when this struggle should be carried on in a more humane way. To shoot prisoners of war simply because they are taken with arms in their hands, is not in accordance with the customs of Christian nations. Hostilities so conducted, besides increasing the sympathy felt for the Cubans, can only aggravate and protract a contest involving questions in which the United States have interests too important to be disregarded.

In view of the foregoing facts and considerations, the undersigned is instructed to protest with all solemnity, in the name of the President of the United States, against the deplorable excesses which have thus far characterized the war in Cuba, and to insist, as the President believes he may rightfully insist, in the name of humanity, that hereafter, while hostilities are prolonged, the war shall be conducted in a manner more in accord with the humane and Christian sentiment of the age.

The undersigned avails himself of this occasion to renew to his excellency the minister of state the assurances of his most distinguished consideration.

D. E. SICKLES.

No. 73.

Gen. Sickles to Mr. Fish.

No. 17.] SEPTEMBER 14, 1869.

* * * * * * * * *

His excellency then informed me that a report from the Captain General of Cuba had been called for in relation to the cases of Speakman and Wyeth, and if the facts were as alleged, full reparation would be made to the families of the deceased; and he added that orders had been given to prevent such scenes of cruelty in the future conduct of the war.

* * * * * * * * *

No. 74.

Gen. Sickles to Mr. Fish.

MADRID, *November* 2, 1869.

I have the honor to transmit a translation of the note of the minister of state, Mr. Silvela, of the 10th of October, in reply to my note of the 6th of September, in relation to the Speakman and Wyeth murders, and a copy of my rejoinder, dated October 30th.

Mr. Silvela to Gen. Sickles.

[Translation.]

MADRID, *October* 11, 1869.

SIR: This ministry received in due time the note of your excellency, dated 6th of September, relating to two American citizens upon whom the penalty of death was inflicted in Santiago de Cuba, as you affirm, without their having committed any crime, and when they had voluntarily given themselves up to the authorities, asking for protection.

Circumstances and events which it is necessary to mention have caused some delay in my answer, but I believe no prejudice to the object of the note referred to has resulted from this, as, in the meanwhile, information has been received from the Captain General of the island of Cuba in regard to what took place in the case cited by your excellency.

One fact results from the documents belonging to the matter, to which I will, in the first place, call your attention, and this is, that in the cordial and frank interviews which Admiral Hoff held with the authorities of Santiago de Cuba, to inform himself, in accordance with the orders of his government, of the considerations which might have justified the punishment inflicted upon Charles Speakman, this officer of the American navy expressed himself, as it appears, satisfied with the explanations which he had received from the governor of Santiago without making any objection to the statements adduced by the latter in support of his conduct, and only when he was preparing to leave the island he directed to the above-mentioned governor a protest against his acts with respect to the American citizens in question.

This proceeding of Admiral Hoff permits the supposition that, in making a protest in that form, he yielded to other causes foreign to the subject rather than to his convictions of right, since, in the other case, he would at least have announced his purpose during the interview, contradicting the observations of the Spanish authority which so freely offered to furnish all the facts conducing to the manifestation of the justice with which he had acted.

The presumption favorable to the Spanish authority which arises from this is fully confirmed, if the facts are examined with care and impartiality.

A preliminary consideration necessary to be taken into account is the bloody character of the insurrection, and the cruelty and ferocity of its titular chiefs, who have gone so far as to openly order, as it appears from an edict of the leader Cespedes, arson, pillage, and murder. In this way was produced a just indignation among the government forces, and among the numerous islanders who assist them in the defense of the principle of authority against the felonious excesses of undisciplined bands, the desire was aroused among all to avenge injuries and insults which they had not provoked, and the civil war came to assume a character which the mother country deplores, and for which they are solely responsible, who, not contented with rushing to arms at a time when, more than ever, the way of realizing all legitimate aspirations was open to them, still sought to destroy their own country with fire and devastation.

Hence the necessity of rigorous measures, which, although they have subsequently been subjected to essential modifications in a lenient sense, could not be applied at that time, by the authorities, without distinction of natives and foreigners, even when in reality these last were much more culpable, taking an attitude of hostility to a government whose acts in no way affected them.

To these dispositions to which I allude, justified by the necessity of depriving the insurrection of the assistance which it received from abroad, the governor of Santiago had to conform in the case under discussion, being compelled to treat Speakman, taken with arms in his hands, as an enemy of Spain with regard to his nationality, which disappeared in presence of the crime for which he had made himself responsible. That the law was justly applied is shown by the confession of the accused, as appears from the letter which he addressed to his unfortunate family shortly before his death. I send you a copy of this document, and by reading it you will see that the unfortunate Speakman begins by declaring that he was captured by the Spanish forces, and this is sufficient, in my judgment, to remove all the force of the exculpation alleged in the supposition that Speakman had been forcibly landed in Cuba, and had afterward given himself up voluntarily to the authorities of the country. You will also observe that when about to suffer the final penalty, and when writing to his wife and child, Speakman makes no protest of his innocence, and only shows resentment against those who compromised him in the enterprise which cost him his life, whom he makes responsible for his misfortune, urging his family to institute proceedings against them.

In this connection I call your attention to the paragraph of the letter referred to, in which he says, literally, "claim damages of the ship-owners; they have taken my life, and have deprived you of my support, and they ought to aid you. There will be a statement here, which will go on to the government, and, by what I have been told, you will be able to see a contract between them and the Cuban Junta in New York to land these men in Cuba, and if you can obtain it you will recover large damages." These words need no comment. The victim himself indicates where the responsibility lies, and addressing himself at the last moment to the object of his greatest affection, completely exempts the Spanish government and accuses the ship-owners and the Cuban Junta, who have deprived him of his life, and mentions the contract to land those men in Cuba. The ship-owners and the Cuban Junta, whose mission is notorious, reside in the territory of the United States, and it is most just that that government, following the suggestion of the unfortunate Speakman, should endeavor to exact of them the responsibility which the last will of the accused throws upon them, and upon them exclusively. A case is impossible, therefore, in which the irresponsibility of the Spanish authorities could be more clearly proven. Still further it appears, as proof of his culpability, that Speakman was found armed with a gun when he came into the possession of the Spanish authorities; for if, victim of a deception as you affirm, he had wished to give himself up voluntarily, nothing obliged him to preserve in his hands the surest proof of his participation in the fight.

With this becomes inadmissible the exculpation which rests upon the supposition of a moral or material compulsion; because, if it were sufficient to allege such an exoneration to elude responsibility in cases like the present, the impunity of filibusterism would be almost absolute, it being always easy to declare one's self deceived or forced into taking part in filibustering expeditions.

In fine, it appears and is evident that Speakman formed part of a piratical expedition against Cuba, and that he disembarked in the island with re-enforcements en route for the insurrection, and that he was taken with arms in his hands; so that all the circumstances concur which are necessary to constitute the responsibility required by the law which was brought into action; and this being so, the charge which you make against the governor of Santiago, of a lack of energy to resist the animosity of the volunteers against the unfortunate Speakman, is destitute of foundation, as the officer in question only complied with an order, severe, if you please, but necessary to prevent the coming of foreigners, the principal element which keeps the insurrection alive, and which most contributes to the devastation of the Island of Cuba, whose ruin is to them entirely indifferent.

Referring to the observations of your excellency in respect to the character assumed by the fratricidal struggle which exists in that transatlantic province, I think proper to state that the government earnestly desires to establish all possible conditions of humanity in the struggle, in spite of the persistence of the insurgents in committing indescribable outrages; and if we have hitherto not seen realized our desire to mitigate the horrors of war, it is owing to the conduct of our enemies, who poison the minds of the many islanders who are attacked and injured in their families and their interests; the cause of the rigorous measures sometimes resorted to being also the just anxiety to prevent the coming of foreign re-enforcements, which have so much contributed and still contribute to prolong the insurrection.

As a proof of the humane disposition by which the government is actuated, I call your attention to the measures which, in accordance with this, have been already adopted. The first is (among others of less importance) the order given by the Captain General of the Island of Cuba, that in the cases of the imprisonment of a foreigner, the proper dispatch shall be drawn up at once to be sent to that official, if the case does not require to be submitted to the decision of a court-martial, and even then the necessary report must be sent for final action.

Among these measures figures also the circular of the 23d of September, emanating from the government, in which it is provided that the conquered enemy who surrenders under the faith which is pledged to respect his rights is a sacred object which Spain covers with her ægis, and it belongs to the tribunals alone to judge his conduct, without it being permitted to any one to invade the power of justice. It is also forbidden in all cases to employ reprisals against the barbarous devastation which, as a means of attaining an impossible victory, is resorted to by the rebels; and, in fine, mercy and humanity is generally recommended in the conduct of the war.

These are the sentiments which animate the Spanish government, which, representing in Spain the most liberal ideas for the government of a state, cannot represent in Cuba principles which would be the negative of these, and I therefore trust that your excellency, convinced of the loyalty of our views, and persuaded on the other hand of the justice with which the law has been applied in the case which was the occasion of your note to which this is a reply, will see that the subject in question shall not give rise to any misunderstanding.

I improve this opportunity to renew to your excellency the assurances of my most distinguished consideration.

MANUEL SILVELA.

Gen. Sickles to Mr. Silvela.

MADRID, *October* 30, 1869.

SIR: I have received your excellency's note of the 11th instant, in reply to mine of the 6th ultimo, demanding indemnity for the families of Charles Speakman and Albert Wyeth, two American citizens summarily put to death without cause by the Spanish authorities at Santiago de Cuba, in June last, and protesting against the repetition of such acts in the further prosecution of hostilities in Cuba.

My government will receive with due consideration the statement of your excellency that the Spanish government desires to establish all possible conditions of humanity in the fratricidal struggle which prevails in that island, and that, in proof of this humane disposition, the Captain General has ordered reports to be made to him of the imprisonment of foreigners, if the case does not require to be brought before a court-martial; that in such cases the proceedings are to be submitted to him for final action; that the circular of the 23d September ultimo, emanating from the Spanish government, has provided "that the conquered enemy who surrenders under the faith which is pledged to respect his rights is a sacred object which Spain covers with her ægis, and that it belongs to the tribunals alone to judge his conduct, without it being permitted to any one to invade that jurisdiction;" that acts of retaliation are forbidden in any case; that mercy and humanity are enjoined in the conduct of the war; and that the government which upholds in Spain the most liberal ideas cannot represent in Cuba principles in conflict with these.

Proceeding to the consideration of the particular cases to which I had the honor to invite the attention of the Spanish government, I cannot fail to observe that your excellency makes no allusion whatever to the case of Wyeth, from which I trust I may assume that the demand of my government in respect to him is admitted to be just.

It is not without regret that I note the avowal of your excellency that Speakman was executed in conformity with the law and the orders in force in Cuba; and that the fate of this unfortunate man was no other than had been decreed by competent authority against all enemies of Spain taken with arms in their hands; for, although the demand for indemnity in this case rests upon the ground that Speakman was innocent of any hostile act or intent against the Spanish authority, I must reject as repugnant to all the sentiments of our advanced civilization any assumption that appears to tolerate the indiscriminate slaughter of prisoners of war. I prefer, indeed, to discuss the question presented on the basis of the more benign code your excellency informs me has been lately adopted in Cuba.

Nor can I pass without emphatic dissent the inadmissible inference drawn from the courteous forbearance of Admiral Hoff in waiting until he had obtained all the testimony in relation to the execution of Speakman and Wyeth before addressing his formal protest to the authorities of Santiago de Cuba.

I must also note the significant omission of your excellency to affirm that Speakman was tried by a competent tribunal, and sentenced upon due proof of the commission of a capital crime. And although it is insisted that his offense consisted in the violation of a law, neither the tenor of the law, nor the authority sanctioning it, is mentioned. It may, however, be presumed that your excellency refers to the decree of the Captain General of Cuba, of the 24th of March, 1869, a copy of which was furnished to Admiral Hoff by the governor of Santiago de Cuba, as the authority under which he acted. It will be sufficient for me to repeat the purport of this decree as given to the consul of the United States by Mr. De la Torre, in his letter of the 13th of June last, in reply to inquiries made by the consul in relation to the fate of certain American citizens. The governor, quoting the words of the general commanding the department of the east, says that, "by the national laws, every foreigner setting foot in Spanish territory in attitude of war, and who is taken with arms in his hands, is liable to the penalty of death without process, *(sin formacion de causa;)* consequently the prisoners in question have suffered this punishment *without ascertainment of their nationality.*"

Your excellency, in the absence of any trial of the accused, relies upon the letter Speakman is represented to have written to his wife a few hours before he was shot, to prove that the law of Spain was regularly and justly applied to his case. It is a conclusive answer to any attempt to sustain the sentence by the contents of that letter, that it was written on the morning he was executed and after he had been condemned to death; so that, whatever might have been the force and effect of the testimony under other circumstances, it is impossible that the letter could have been in any way considered by the authorities in determining their action upon the case.

But I am quite prepared to maintain that Speakman's letter, so far from justifying the accusation against him, discloses a state of facts altogether inconsistent with any purpose of taking part in an expedition against Cuba. Your excellency cites the declaration of Speakman that "he had been captured by the Spaniards" as sufficient to remove all the force of the exculpation claimed in his behalf on the ground that he had been forcibly landed in Cuba, and had voluntarily given himself up to the authorities. I must observe that the actual declaration of Speakman, as contained in the copy of his letter sent to me with your excellency's note, differs materially from the words attributed to him, as the foundation of this argument. Speakman says: "I have been captured by the Spaniards on the Island of Cuba, *where the vessel went in*, instead of going to Falmouth, Jamaica, where I had shipped to go." It thus appears, beyond all question, by this accurate quotation from the very document so much depended upon by your excellency, that this unfortunate sailor was innocent of any intent to embark for Cuba, having expressly shipped for another destination.

Your excellency proceeds to make further deductions from another part of Speakman's letter, in which he says to his wife, "I am leaving you without a penny, but you will be able to recover something by getting a good lawyer to claim damages of the ship-owners. They have taken my life and deprived you of my support, and they ought to aid you. There will be a statement here which will go on to the government, and, *by what I have been told*, you will be able to see a contract between them and the Cuban Junta in New York, *to land these men in Cuba*, and, if you can obtain it, *you will recover large damages*." Before commenting on the observations made by your excellency on this part of the letter, I wish to invite attention to the force with which it repels the assumption of Speakman's culpability. It is plain that all his instructions are predicated upon his belief that having, as he declares, shipped to go to Falmouth, Jamaica, and having been deceived by the supposed collusion between the owners of the vessel and the parties who chartered her, his family will be entitled to recover damages for the injury suffered from the deceit thus practiced upon him. But, with what color of pretense could he have urged his family to claim damages, if, as your excellency contends in justifying his execution, Speakman voluntarily embarked in an expedition against Cuba, and landed on the island in conformity with the conditions on which he shipped for the voyage? How could he declare that "they," the ship-owners, "have taken my life," if he had himself engaged in the fatal enterprise? But his meaning is too plain to be misunderstood; he says, "by what I have been told you will be able to see a contract between them," the ship-owners, "and the Cuban Junta in New York, to land *these men* in Cuba." What men? Not the crew, of which he formed part; not the innocent passengers, like Wyeth, who was seeking a change of climate for his health; but the party who came aboard secretly, after the vessel cleared from New York, and who subsequently effected their landing in Cuba; and if anything could add to the force of these considerations, it is the appeal he makes in the last words of his letter, before invoking the Divine blessing on his family, to the testimony of William Craig, of New York, one of his shipmates, for the confirmation of his innocence of all complicity in the real objects of the voyage.

Your excellency gravely suggests that the United States government has mistaken its remedy in demanding indemnity from Spain. This point appears to be seriously urged, and I shall, therefore, treat it with respectful consideration. Whatever may be the liability of the parties in New York, in their relation to the voyage of the Grapeshot—whether it be to the government of the United States for a violation of the neutrality laws, or to individuals for deceit practiced upon the crew—these questions are completely distinct from the responsibility of the Spanish government for acts committed within its jurisdiction by its authorized agents. Spain is none the less bound to make indemnity in this case because there are other wrong-doers in the transaction. By the action of the authorities of Santiago de Cuba, now justified by the Spanish government, the innocent shared the fate of the guilty. If it be true that the ship-owners and the Cuban Junta, in New York, should be held responsible for offenses committed within the jurisdiction of the United States, it does not follow that Spain may escape her share of responsibility for the unjustifiable sacrifice within her lines of the unfortunate Speakman—victim as he was of fraud on the one hand and of outrage on the other.

Having shown, as I trust plainly, that the testimony relied upon by your excellency to prove the guilt of Speakman furnishes, in truth, the most satisfactory proof of his innocence, I proceed to examine the only additional consideration suggested by your excellency to establish his culpability. Your excellency states that it further appears that Speakman was found armed with a gun when he came into the hands of the Spanish authorities, and it is argued that if he had been deceived in shipping for the voyage or constrained to join the insurgents on landing, as has been affirmed, "nothing obliged him to preserve in his hands the surest proof of his participation in the fight." To this it may be fairly replied that nothing was easier to one who desired to conceal evidence of guilt than to throw away a gun; keeping his gun until he surrendered himself to the Spanish authorities, Speakman gave the surest pledge of his sincerity, and the most convincing proof of the truth of his representations. We are not left to conjecture to ascertain how it happened that Speakman had a gun in his possession. He explains this fact himself in his examination before the attorney general and the notary, which took place in the prison at Santiago de Cuba, the day before he was executed. In the course of this proceeding, the only prelude to his sentence and execution, the following question was put to the accused: "How is it you say you remained under arrest, and had refused to take arms, when you had a gun when you were captured?" To which

Speakman answered: "The gun he had when they took him prisoner was the one the captain of the ship, Mr. Welch, had." [In a note to the official copy of this document, furnished by the governor, it appears that Captain O'Callahan, the interpreter, stated this was a mistake for the "captain of the expedition, G. B. Smith."]

It is a recognized principle of the law of evidence that a party is bound by the testimony of the witness he produces; another maxim not less imperative requires that all the declarations of a witness must be taken together, for it is not permitted to a party to avail himself of so much only as benefits his case and reject the remainder. I must therefore remind your excellency of the testimony of Speakman in his formal examination already mentioned. In this examination Speakman stated that "he shipped as a sailor;" "the number of men disembarked was some five and thirty, more or less;" that he "staid on shore because they stove the boat they landed in;" and after a quarrel with the captain "they put him under arrest and he remained under arrest seven or eight days; he saw two men, to whom he gave himself up, delivering also the gun which he had." This testimony is not contradicted; it is consistent with all the declarations of Speakman himself, and is confirmed by the dying declarations of Wyeth, and others who were on board the Grape Shot. The American and British vice-consuls, satisfied of the innocence of Speakman, appealed in vain to the governor to grant a respite of three days, to obtain from Falmouth, Jamaica, conclusive testimony of the innocence of the accused. Refusing to postpone the execution of the sentence, which swiftly followed the accusation, and was pronounced without any opportunity afforded the accused to exculpate himself, the Spanish authorities have imposed upon themselves the obligation to establish indisputably the guilt of Speakman, at once their victim and in the world could pronounce a sentence of death on the meager testimony produced their witness; and failing in this, his bloodis upon their heads. No judicial tribunal against this man.

The enlightened statesmen who now administer the government of Spain have themselves denounced the summary and sanguinary code which consigns to instant death a prisoner of war, taken with arms in his hands. Regarded with the most lenient disposition toward the Spanish authorities, the case presents no feature of mitigation to screen them from denunciation. Concede all that is alleged against Speakman, and he was a prisoner of war put to death by his captors in obedience to a decree of the Captain General, against which the United States government had not alone remonstrated, as contrary to the usages of nations; a brief respite of the sentence was refused to the consul of the United States; the same appeal from the British consul made in the name of humanity was impeded; no mercy was accorded in consideration of a voluntary surrender; instantly shot in cold blood, the mutilated remains of this sacrifice to a code of war not recognized by any civilized nation, were refused a decent burial.

In conclusion, dismissing from the discussion all that is irrelevant, it is enough to recapitulate the facts as they are derived from official sources. The United States consul at Santiago de Cuba, in a dispatch to the Secretary of State of June 18, 1869, immediately after the occurrence, reports the whole transaction fully and circumstantially; and in this testimony I rest the case presented on the part of the United States to the government of Spain; he says:

"On Tuesday, 13th, the English vice-consul sent me a note stating that an American prisoner had just passed his consulate for the city prison, and in a few minutes I received a dispatch from the governor notifying me of the same. I immediately called upon this authority, who gave me a pass to the prison where I could have a public or private interview with the prisoner. I called the fiscal (attorney general) and a captain of the volunteers, who understood English perfectly, and under oath to me the prisoner made this declaration, he being unable to write from having his arms so long pinioned as to leave a partial paralysis of his hands: stated that he was a native of Aurora, Indiana, being married, and having a child four years of age; left New York Harbor in the schooner Grape Shot; signed the articles as a sailor for Falmouth, Jamaica, in good faith, knowing nothing of the nature of the voyage save its legitimate object. After anchoring in the Lower Bay of New York, waiting for a tug to tow her out to sea, which arrived at midnight, bringing some fifty armed Cubans with a good supply of munitions of war, objected to continue the voyage and desired to return to the city in the tug. The captain assured him that although he had taken the Cubans, he would not risk his vessel to run the Spanish blockade, but would proceed to Falmouth, land the men, and go for a cargo of cocoanuts. When off Cape Maysi the Cubans took possession of the vessel, changed her course, ran her to land, and discharged.

"He insisted upon continuing the voyage, but, having had some difficulty with the captain, was left on shore under threat of shooting him if he attempted any resistance. After the subsequent engagement, in which he took no part, not being armed, he sought some place of safety, and finding the unarmed men, gave himself up and requested to be sent to the American consul; was bound and brought here, and, without judge or jury, sentenced to be shot on the following morning; protested against his executioners, and declared that the vessel's register and mate's log-book would prove his capacity on board, and other evidence that he could procure from Jamaica would guarantee his innocence.

"This declaration I read in English and made a verbal translation to the fiscal, who had pronounced the sentence of death upon him. I immediately sent a copy to the governor, being 10 o'clock p. m., praying for a respite for a few days, in order to procure proofs from Jamaica, and requested an immediate reply. I waited nearly all night in the office, and received no reply. Early in the morning I visited him again and found the prisoner surrounded by the guards formed for his execution. He appeared calm, and assured me had no fear to die, and again assured me, as a dying man, of his innocence, and only begged for a day or two to furnish proofs. At that moment the English vice-consul kindly came in and offered to go with me to the governor. We found him still in bed, stated the urgency of the case, and asked, in the name of mercy and of our countries, for a respite, and assured him that the German man-of-war, now lying in port, would take the letter over. The governor seemed disposed to grant this request, but informed us of his superior instructions, and in order to wash his hands of the blood (in our opinion) of an innocent man, had the debility to inform us of his impotence as the chief magistrate of this city. 'My troops will not obey; dissention prevails in the army; General Buceta, commanding officer of the forces, is a fugitive on board of a Spanish man-of-war. The Catalans, a few nights since, attempted to assassinate him under the pretence of a serenade. General Camara was next selected, who, hearing of the plot, secreted soldiers in his house, which frustrated their plan. His death would have been the signal for a general uprising of the Catalans, and of sacking, plunder, and massacre of Cubans.'

"Finding all hopes gone we retired, and in our exit met the governor's aide-de-camp, with whom we had some conversation. He assured us that anarchy prevailed; the mob rules; the governor is impotent and fears a counter-revolution.

"So the man was executed, leaving a letter for his wife and child, showing himself to be a man of good and fair education, proclaiming his innocence, and instructing her to sue the owners of the vessel for damages, having left her penniless."

This evidence, which is not contradicted in a material statement by any testimony which has been produced, presents so plain a case for indemnity that I trust the Spanish government will not fail to respond without delay to the just demand made in my note of the 6th ultimo, and which is now repeated.

I avail myself of this occasion to renew to your excellency assurances of my most distinguished consideration.

D. E. SICKLES.

No. 75.

Mr. Plumb to Mr. Fish.

No. 56.] HAVANA, *June* 29, 1869.

Inclosed herewith I transmit copy of a letter, under date of 26th instant, received yesterday from Mr. Price, consular agent at Nuevitas, giving an account of the progress of events in that vicinity.

The capture by the insurgents of a detachment of upwards of one hundred Spanish regular troops, guarding the railroad between Nuevitas and Puerto Principe, at a point some seven miles from the latter place, as reported by Mr. Price, appears to be fully confirmed, and is commented on with some degree of frankness by the papers published in this city.

Mr. Price to Mr. Plumb.

NUEVITAS, *June* 26, 1869.

Since mine of the 10th, 11th, and 16th instant, I have none of your favors to refer to. The train due here on Tuesday last did not arrive as was expected, which gave cause to the circulating of a great many false rumors. But on the 23d instant the train arrived here safely. The following account will explain the delay. This train left here last Sunday morning and arrived within seven miles of Puerto Principe without any mishap. At this point found an encampment of regular troops entirely abandoned, the huts burned to the ground, dead horses lying about, the bodies of dead soldiers sticking halfway up from under the ground, as if buried in haste, and signs of general desolation. Those in charge of the train not knowing what had happened, and fearing danger ahead, returned to the Minas, and passed the night at the station.

Monday morning the train left the Minas again for Puerto Principe; arriving near the point from whence they returned the day before, they were met by a column, at the head of which was General Letona.

It seems the insurgents had surprised, early Sunday morning before daylight, the detachment composed of seventy-one regulars of the battalion La Reyna, commanded by a captain and two lieutenants, thirty Lancers del Rey, commanded by a captain, encamped within seven miles of Puerto Principe, on the railroad, in an open sebana or large plain.

Only one soldier of all these made good his escape; the rest were all made prisoners; the sentinels were killed at their posts.

The soldier who escaped arrived at Puerto Principe to relate, in an exaggerated manner, what had happened.

This is what brought General Letona out with a column, only to find the remains above mentioned.

This reverse has been sorely felt. Their natural pride is highly offended. They cannot realize the possibility of a detachment of regular Spanish infantry and cavalry being overpowered by the insurgents, to whom they deny all valor.

Besides the above, there have recently been several skirmishes along the railroad and in the vicinity of Puerto Principe; the number of casualties is not stated. In one of them along the road the Spaniards lost six soldiers and an officer. Many arbitrary arrests are being made.

All such Cubans as are able are leaving the country.

On the 24th instant the Spanish gunboat Andaluza returned from Puerto Padre, bringing the battalion La Union, which had been sent last week to re enforce the column of Brigadier Ferrer.

There has been very little fighting in that vicinity since my last.

The last convoy lost three carts loaded with provisions.

The cholera is thinning the ranks of Ferrer's brigade faster than the bullets of the insurgents.

The cholera has decreased in this port, and but few cases present themselves; the disease so far has not been of an epidemic character.

The Atalonja estate, owned by Colonel Francisco Acosta, situated across the bay, was burned by the insurgents yesterday. The fire could be seen plainly from here. The buildings on this estate were valued at over $60,000.

Mrs. Polhamus is waiting here to get to the United States. I hope some of our war vessels may touch here soon.

No. 76.

Mr. Plumb to Mr. Fish.

No. 66.] HAVANA, *July* 8, 1869.

In his dispatch No. 17, of the 27th of March last, my predecessor, Mr. Hall, transmitted to the department copy of a decree issued on the 24th of that month by Captain General Dulce "relative to the vessels approaching this island with hostile intentions, having men, arms, or munitions of war on board."

I have now the honor to transmit to you herewith copy and translation of a decree published in the Gazette of last evening, issued by Captain General Caballero de Rodas, under date of the 7th instant, in substitution for the said decree of the 24th of March last, and of three other decrees, of prior date, pertinent to the same subject, and relating to the ports and coasts of this island, and communication therewith.

In an interview with General Caballero de Rodas to-day, the hope was expressed by him that the present decree would be found satisfactory by the government of the United States.

[Translation.]

FIRST SECTION—GENERAL SUPERIOR OFFICES—SUPERIOR POLITICAL GOVERNMENT OF THE PROVINCE OF CUBA.

HAVANA, *July* 7, 1869.

The custody and vigilance of the coasts of this island, adjacent keys, and territorial waters, being of the utmost importance in order to put an end to the parties of insurgents, which have been sustained by exterior aid, determined to give a vigorous impulse to their prosecution, and in order to explain certain doubts which have occurred to our cruisers as to the genuine interpretation of the decrees published by this superior political government under date of the 9th of November, 1868, and 18th and 26th of February, and 24th of March of the present year, I have determined to unite and amplify in this all of the said dispositions, which therefor remain substituted by the present, and making use of the faculties with which I am invested by the government of the nation, I decree:

ARTICLE 1. There shall continue closed to import and export trade, as well for vessels in foreign commerce as also those in the coasting trade, all the ports situated from Cayo Bahia de Cadiz to Punta Mayso, on the north, and from Punta Mayso to Cienfuegos on the south, with the exception of those of Sagua la Grande, Caibarien, Neuvitas, Gibara, Baracoa, Guantanamo, Santiago de Cuba, Manzanillo, Santa Cruz, Zara, Casildo, or Trinidad, and Cienfuegos, in which there are established custom-houses or collection offices.

Those who attempt to enter the closed ports or to hold communication with the coast shall be pursued, and, on being apprehended, prosecuted as infractors of the laws.

ART. 2. In accordance with the same there shall also be prosecuted vessels carrying powder, arms, or military supplies.

ART. 3. The transportation of individuals for the service of the insurrection is much more grave than that of contraband, and will be considered as an act decidedly hostile, being proceeded against in such case as an enemy, the vessel and its crew.

ART. 4. If the individuals to which the preceding article refers come armed, they will afford proof in fact of their intentions, and will be tried as pirates the same as the crew of the vessel.

ART. 5. There shall also be held to be pirates, in conformity with law, vessels which may be seized bearing a flag not recognized, whether the same be armed or not as vessels of war.

ART. 6. On the high seas contiguous to those of this island the cruisers shall confine themselves to exercise over such vessels as may be denounced, or those that by their proceedings excite suspicion, the rights stipulated in the treaties signed by Spain with the United States in 1795, with Great Britain in 1835, and with other nations subsequently, and if in the exercise of these rights vessels should be found recognized as enemies of the integrity of the territory, they shall be brought into port for the corresponding legal investigation and trial.

CABALLERO DE RODAS.

No. 77.

Mr. Fish to Mr. Lopez Roberts.

WASHINGTON, *July* 16, 1869.

The undersigned, Secretary of State of the United States, has the honor to enclose to Mr. Roberts, envoy extraordinary and minister plenipotentiary of Spain, a translation of a decree which he has received, published in the Gaceta de la Habana, (*parte official,*) under date of July 7, 1869, purporting to be signed by General Caballero de Rodas, the Captain General of the Island of Cuba, to which the undersigned desires to call the attention of Mr. Roberts, as it may in its possible operation involve serious complications between the government of Spain and that of the United States. It purports to be issued in order to put an end to an insurrection in the Island of Cuba, which the United States have hitherto treated only as a civil commotion within the dominions of Spain, that did not give rise to what are understood as belligerent rights on the part of either party to the conflict. But the decree of the Captain General de Rodas assumes powers and rights over the trade and commerce of other peoples, inconsistent with a state of peace, and which the United States can be expected to allow their vessels to be subjected to only when Spain avows herself to be in a state of war, or shall be manifestly exercising the rights conceded only to belligerents in the time of war.

The first article of the decree proposes to close certain ports, embracing a large extent of the Island of Cuba, against the peaceful commerce of foreign countries. Without contesting the right of a government in time of peace to exclude from its ports the trade and commerce of a friendly people, the undersigned assumes that the exercise of this power is to be understood purely as a municipal act, to be executed and enforced wholly within the recognized exclusive jurisdiction of Spain, and only as to ports which are in the possession of the Spanish authorities. In case the success of the insurrectionary party should put any of the ports, declared to be closed, in their possession, the United States, as a maritime nation, will regard an effective blockade to be necessary to the exclusion of their commerce.

The second article of the decree is vague in the absence of the limits within which it proposes to prohibit the carrying of powder, arms, or military supplies.

The transportation on the high seas, in time of peace, of articles commonly known as contraband of war, is a legitimate traffic and commerce which cannot be interfered with or denounced unless by a power at war with a third party in the admitted exercise of the recognized rights of a belligerent. The freedom of the ocean can nowhere and under no circumstances be yielded by the United States. The high seas contiguous to those of the island of Cuba are a direct pathway of a large part of the purely domestic trade of the United States. Their vessels trading between their ports in the Gulf of Mexico and those of the Atlantic coast pass necessarily through these waters. The greater part of the trade between the ports of the United States on the eastern side of the continent and those on the Pacific slope, of necessity, passes in sight of the Island of Cuba. The United States cannot, then, be indifferent or silent under a decree which, by the vagueness of its terms, may be construed to allow their vessels on the high seas, whatever may be their cargo, to be embarrassed or interfered with. If Spain be at war with Cuba, the United States will submit to those rights which public law concedes to belligerents. But while Spain disclaims a state of belligerency, or until the United States may find it necessary to recognize her as a belligerent, the government of the United States cannot fail to look with solicitude upon a decree which, if enforced against any vessel of the United States on the high seas, cannot but be regarded as a violation of their rights that may lead to serious complications.

The sixth article of the decree refers to certain rights claimed to be stipulated by the treaty entered into between Spain and the United States in 1795.

The undersigned desires to call the attention of Mr. Roberts and of the government of Spain to the fact that the treaty of 1795 confers upon neither of the contracting parties any rights on the high seas over the vessels of the other in time of peace.

The articles of the treaty of 1795 from I to XI, inclusive, define and regulate the reciprocal relations and obligations of the parties without reference to either party being engaged in war. The portion of the treaty from the XIIth article to the XVIIIth, contemplates exclusively their relations as neutrals, the duties and powers of each toward the other, when one or the other may be engaged in war with a third party. The eighteenth section recognizes and regulates the right of visit or of approach in time of war, for the inspection of the passport and the identification of the nationality of a vessel of commerce by the vessels of war, or by any privateer of the nation which shall be at war. It confers no right; it limits and prescribes the manner of exercising a belligerent right when such may exist. The clear object and intent of this provision of the treaty is the avoidance of dissension and annoyance, and the prevention of abuse or indiscretion in the exercise of a belligerent right. Its location in the treaty, the recognition of the right of a privateer (who has no existence except in war) as having the same power and right in the particular referred to with a national vessel of war, and the whole scope and aim of the XVIIIth article of the treaty established beyond possibility of question that it refers only to the rights which one of the parties may have by reason of being in a state of war.

The treaty authorizes nothing but the inspection of the passport of the vessel of trade met with, while the 6th article of the decree of General de Rodas contemplates a search as to the character of the vessel beyond the limitation fixed by the treaty.

If Spain be engaged in war, it is essential to the rights as well as to the definition of the duties of the people of the United States that they be publicly and authoritatively advised thereof, and admonished as to their obligations and liabilities in their new relation with a friendly power. And such admonition admits of no avoidable delay in view of the vast commerce that will thus be subjected to restriction, limitation, and possible detention.

The undersigned, therefore, respectfully desires to be informed by Mr. Roberts, at the earliest practicable moment, whether, in the issuance of this decree, it is to be understood by the United States that Spain recognizes that she is in a state of war, and claims the right of a belligerent.

The undersigned has the honor further to say to Mr Roberts, that the government of the United States cannot fail to regard the continuance of the decree referred to, or any exercise on the high seas near the Island of Cuba, by any vessel of war or privateer of Spain, of the right to visit or board any vessel of the United States, under color of the provisions of the treaty of 1795, as involving the logical conclusion of a recognition by Spain of a state of war with Cuba.

Before concluding, the undersigned begs to call Mr. Roberts's attention to the very grave complication which might ensue from any interference with a vessel of the United States engaged in a lawful voyage, passing near the Island of Cuba. The United States maintain the right of their flag to cover and protect their ships on the high seas.

In conclusion, the undersigned expresses the hope that Mr. Roberts will speedily be at liberty to announce the formal abrogation of a decree which causes so much serious apprehension to the government of the United States, and against which this government feels bound, most earnestly, to remonstrate.

For inclosure, see Mr. Plumb's dispatch to Mr. Fish of July 8, 1869.

No. 78.

Mr. Plumb to Mr. Fish.

No. 83.] HAVANA, *July* 21, 1869.

With my dispatch No. 66 of the 8th instant, I had the honor to transmit to you a copy of an important maritime decree issued by Captain General Caballero de Rodas on the 7th of this month.

I have now the honor to transmit to you herewith a copy and translation of a decree issued under date of the 18th instant, published in the Official Gazette of last evening, modifying the decree of the 7th instant, by the suppression from it of the last or 6th article.

* * * * * *

[From the Official Gazette, Havana, July 20, 1869.—Translation.]

SUPERIOR POLITICAL GOVERNMENT OF THE PROVINCE OF CUBA.

In view of the determinations adopted by the government of the United States of America, as reported by his excellency the minister of Spain in Washington, under date of the 15th instant, and which were published in the Official Gazette of the following day, and in order, at the same time, to relieve legitimate commerce from all unnecessary interference, in use of the facilities which are conferred upon me by the supreme government of the nation, I have determined to modify my decree of the 7th instant, leaving the same reduced to the first five and essential articles.

CABALLERO DE RODAS.

HAVANA, *July* 18, 1869.

No. 79.

Mr. Plumb to Mr. Fish.

No. 75.] JULY 13, 1869.

* * * * * *

I have the honor to transmit to you herewith copy and translation of an important general order issued by the Captain General on the 8th instant, which appears published in the papers here of the 11th.

* * * * * *

[Translation.]

COMMANDING GENERAL *of the District of Matanzas:*

His excellency the Captain General communicates to me through a circular of yesterday's date the following:

[Circular.]

CAPTAIN GENERALSHIP OF THE EVER-FAITHFUL ISLAND OF CUBA,
Chief-of-staff's Office, Fifth Section.

The extraordinary circumstances through which we are passing, the necessity of correcting certain abuses, which, perhaps, through a badly-understood zeal, are committed, rendering more difficult the work of pacification which I have proposed, and the desire that all who exercise an independent command shall conform to a common criterion, impel me to fix certain rules in which are condensed my ideas and the line of conduct I propose to follow.

Wars are always very lamentable, but when they are civil wars they are too apt to take a character of unlimited ferocity, while on the part of the strongest there should be always generosity, indulgence, and nobility.

It may happen that some, who, up to the present time, have been hallucinated, and are found among the insurgents, may present themselves to the chiefs of columns or authorities of the government. In such case, they shall be religiously respected in their persons and interests, and I shall exact the most strict responsibility from those who tolerate that they be annoyed or insulted.

The conditions of this war of insurrection against the common country demand speedy and exemplary punishments, and therefore my predecessors have justly imposed capital punishment for those who may be apprehended with arms in hand.

Civilization and the prestige of Spain, before the judgment of other nations, impose, nevertheless, the obligation of being as sparing as possible in the shedding of blood, and this painful extreme should only be resorted to with leaders, or men against whom there have been proved crimes of incendiarism or assassination, remitting the prisoners in other cases subject to my disposition.

All functionaries who depend upon my authority will cause to be respected the lives, houses, and properties of all the inhabitants without distinction, punishing with rigor those who act in a contrary manner.

No one shall be imprisoned upon mere suspicion and without having proof of the offense, and in case of arrest an examination shall immediately be had.

The greatest care shall be taken that in proceeding in any manner against foreigners no legal requisite shall be omitted, for the just consideration that is due to their nations.

From a consideration not well construed, acts of notorious cowardice are sought to be concealed. On this point I shall be inexorable, and I shall exact strict account from the officer who tolerates the slightest fault, and does not bring it to my knowledge, at the same time adopting himself such measures as the case may require, as arrest, suspension from position, &c., of those who may be guilty.

The greater portion of the defeats and reverses which are experienced in war are due to carelessness, want of experience, lack of vigilance, or of punctuality. It is to be understood that all shall be tried by court-martial who may be surprised, who may lose more men than necessary in battle by their bad dispositions, or who allow part or the whole of a convoy to be taken from them without proving that they have made every effort within the limits of possibility to save it.

Lack of discipline shall be punished with all rigor, employing, when the case requires, the proceedings of verbal courts-martial, in the understanding that I shall be inexorable with officers lukewarm in maintaining subordination, it being understood that all dispositions now in force upon this subject remain in full effect.

The chiefs should watch over the maintenance of their troops in order to prevent the lack of clothes, shoes, munitions, and useful armament.

The troops who consume much ammunition show almost always cowardice. Let the soldier be accustomed to shoot little and well.

Reports should always be true, and without containing more details than necessary for the exact cognizance of the facts.

Finally, let those who perform acts of bravery be recommended, laying aside friendships and compaternity, in the assurance that true merit will be recompensed, and the just aspirations of the chiefs, officers, and troops who distinguish themselves.

I recommend to you to circulate these instructions to all the authorities dependent upon your jurisdiction and commanders of columns, in order that they may have the greater publicity, with the understanding that I shall always exact the greatest responsibility in their compliance.

God preserve your honor many years.

CABALLERO.

HAVANA, *July* 8, 1869.

And the same is made known for the general intelligence and exact compliance.

The Colonel Commandant General,
DOMINGO DE LEON.

MATANZAS, *July* 9, 1869.

No. 80.

General Sickles to Mr. Fish.

No. 4.] MADRID, *August* 12, 1869.

* * * * * * *

The minister interrupting me, as if he thought I had gone quite far enough, for the present at least, acknowledged the sincere and loyal manner in which the government of the United States had fulfilled its international duties in regard to the Cuban insurrection.

* * * * * * *

In former days, when the pro-slavery party held the reins of power, there was some anxiety from time to time lest the recklessness of filibusters should involve the two nations in difficulty; but that since the victory of the national cause in the great war, the liberal people of Spain had come to regard the United States as their natural friend.

The Cuban question was one of the utmost gravity and delicacy. It was the intention of the Spanish liberals who planned and executed the revolutionary movements which have given to Spain its new political life, to make, at the earliest moment, provision for granting self-government to Cuba. But this fatal insurrection broke out at the very moment when it was becoming possible to give to Cuba all the rights she desired. The cry of "Death to Spaniards" was heard in Spain, and it became impossible, in the face of civil war, to carry out the beneficent plan that had been formed. The liberal party in Spain finds itself, to its own infinite regret, forced into a seeming sympathy with the reactionary party in Cuba, and the liberals of Cuba, who ought to be its firm friends, are converted, by the fatality of the situation, into its bitterest enemies. There is no sentiment dearer to the hearts of the liberal leaders than that of freedom to all men, yet they stand before the world, in this Cuban conflict, as opposed to self-government and resisting the abolition of slavery. He considered the insurrection as a most deplorable misfortune and mistake, both for Cuba and for Spain.

If a way could be found to settle all these questions in such a manner as to do justice to Cuba, without infringing upon the honor of Spain, the government would be greatly gratified. There is no intention or desire among the liberals of Spain ever again to work *(exploiter)* the island of Cuba on the old selfish system. It has been their constant hope and wish to grant to the Cubans the administration of their own affairs, and the full fruits of their own labor, preserving their commercial connections and some shadow of their political relations.

* * * * * * *

No. 81.

Mr. Plumb to Mr. Davis.

No. 115.] HAVANA, *August* 18, 1869.

* * * * * * *

As there appears to be a systematic effort to represent the situation of the insurrection on this island in an invariably favorable light, in certain accounts from Washington, which are spread very extensively through the press in the United States, which leads to the belief that these efforts may be used also in other ways, it may be my duty to state, that so far as all the information that reaches me here—and I have some means of learning the situation in all parts of the island—the accounts I have referred to are so grossly exaggerated as, it appears to me, to be entirely unworthy of credit.

While I have very definite ideas as to what must be the inevitable final result of the struggle here, I do not believe a cause is usually well advanced by exaggeration, and I am very far from believing that the relative strength of the combatants is yet even approximate to what would be inferred from the statements to which I have made reference.

* * * * * * *

No. 82.

General Sickles to Mr. Fish.

No. 6.] MADRID, *August* 14, 1869.

* * * * * * *

Mr. Silvela then entered upon a very full analysis of article 108 of the Spanish constitution, showing that it had two distinct and opposite phases in its relation to the present question; that while by its terms it precluded the government from making any definitive arrangement in regard to Cuba until the Cuban representatives shall have taken their seats in the Cortes, on the other hand it authorizes the government to make any arrangement that might seem expedient after the Cuban deputies arrive. * * * * *

Inclosed will be found * * * a copy of article 108 of the constitution of Spain.

* * * * * *

CONSTITUTION OF THE SPANISH MONARCHY.

SECTION 10.—*Of the Transmarine Provinces.*

ARTICLE 108. The Cortes constituents shall reform the present system of government in the transmarine provinces, when the deputies of Cuba or Porto Rico shall have taken their seats, in order to extend to the same, with the modifications which shall be deemed necessary, the privileges set forth in the constitution.

No. 83.

General Sickles to Mr. Fish.

No. 9.] MADRID, *August* 20, 1869.

* * * * * *

To these and like amplifications of the argument, he (General Prim) replied with great earnestness and emphasis, "Let the United States be assured of the good faith and the good disposition of Spain. * * * Formidable as the insurrection in Cuba may become, it has not yet approached the proportions of any of those conflicts in which governments have found themselves constrained to treat during hostilities. The Cuban insurgents hold no city or fortresses; they have no port, no ships; they have no army that presumes to offer or accept battle; and now, before the period arrives for active operations, when Spain will send the ample re-enforcements she holds in readiness, it is only necessary for the Cubans to accept the assurance of the United States, given on the faith of Spain, that they may have their independence by laying down their arms, electing their deputies, and declaring their wish to be free by a vote of the people."

* * * * * *

No. 84.

General Sickles to Mr. Fish.

No. 10.] MADRID, *August* 21, 1869.

* * * * * *

The president of the council said: "There is a vast difference between the present insurrection in Cuba and those revolutionary movements by which the republics of the Western Continent gained their independence. In those examples, negotiation was resorted to after campaigns had been fought, and battles lost and gained; they had armies in the field and organized governments supporting them. We see nothing of this in Cuba; only mere roving bands, who fly when they are pursued, and who have never been found in numbers sufficient to give or accept battle. It is very possible that in the lapse of time the insurrection may become more formidable; it may raise armies; it may take cities and fortified places; it may demonstrate what has not yet been in any way demonstrated, that it is supported by the majority of the population. In that case Spain will have something tangible to treat with. But we hope to avoid all this bloodshed, disaster, and ruin, by making some amicable arrangement now."

* * * * * *

No. 85.

General Sickles to Mr. Fish.

No. 12.] MADRID, *August* 24, 1869.

* * * * * *

In general, I find less susceptibility to the idea of a transfer of the island to the United States than to the concession of the independence of Cuba.

There is an apprehension that the persons and property of Spaniards in Cuba would not be safe under Cuban control. This impression, I hear, prevails in Catalonia.

* * * * * *

No. 86.

Mr. Plumb to Mr. Davis.

No. 119.] HAVANA, *August* 21, 1869.

In the absence of any communication from the acting United States consul at Santiago de Cuba, relating thereto, which may have failed to reach me, I transmit to you the herewith unofficial information, received yesterday, regarding the reported murder of certain prominent citizens of that place and their friends and attendants, numbering upward of twenty persons in all, by order, it is stated, of a subordinate officer of the Spanish army, on the 7th instant, while being conveyed as political prisoners, at or near a place called Jiguani, the chief town of the district of that name, situated seven leagues from the town of Bayamo, the headquarters of Count Valmaseda, the commander-in-chief of the eastern department of this island.

The absence yesterday and to-day of the Captain General and political secretary, on a visit to Matanzas, prevents me from making an inquiry before the departure of to-day's (Saturday's) mail, but which I shall make on Monday, first, in the name of humanity, whether this report is true; and secondly, whether, as is stated, one of the persons so murdered is a citizen of the United States; and if this be true, what steps have been taken for the due and immediate punishment of the guilty officer or officers, and for the prevention of the recurrence of such acts in the future.

* * * * * *

[Inclosure.]

Mr. Hall to Mr. Plumb.

MATANZAS, *August* 18, 1869.

From a very reliable source I have received the following statement, and although you have probably been informed already in regard to the affair to which it refers, I have concluded to transmit it to you for communication to the department should you deem it of sufficient importance. My informant could not state whether the executions were by order of General Count Valmaseda or another of those acts of insubordination of the volunteers; he is under the impression, however, that they are to be attributed to the latter.

"On the 4th July, ultimo, the following gentlemen, heads of families and well known in St. Jago, were imprisoned at that place, viz: Gonzalo Villar, lawyer; José Antonio Perez, physician, said to be a French citizen; Manuel Espin, physician, said to be a citizen of the United States; Salvador Benitez, merchant; the brothers Brune and José Antonio Collaro, merchants; Miguel Ascensio, employé of the city government; Antonio Villasana, notary public; Manuel Fresnada, notary public.

"The judicial investigation to which they were subjected resulted in their being set at liberty on the 25th. Within a day or two thereafter they were summoned to appear before General Count Valmaseda, and were again arrested and imprisoned on the 28th, to be sent to Bayamo. Their wives and friends, belonging to the most respectable families residing at St. Jago, demanded of the governor, General de la Torre, some guarantee for the personal safety and good treatment of the prisoners, and it is said that such assurance was given by the governor to the consular corps of that place, as also to the families and friends of the prisoners.

"On the 30th they were embarked on board of the Villaclara (steamer) for Manzanillo, and thence proceeded to Bayamo, accompanied by several of their friends and servants, ten of the former and two of the latter. At Bayamo they were asked no questions, were treated with great consideration, and thence sent to Jiguani. At Jiguani they were received by the commandant of the place, and two hundred troops forming a square.

"The party, *i. e.*, the before-named persons, their friends and servants, among them Don Manuel Benitez, brother of Salvador, a merchant of Jiguaní, but a native of St. Jago, numbering in all upward of twenty persons, were ordered to the centre of the hollow square, where they were forthwith indiscriminately shot down."

Since the foregoing was written I have seen a letter from St. Jago, dated the 13th, which in the main corroborates the foregoing statement, but charges the act upon Colonel Palacios, of the regular regiment of Antequera, who, it seems, acted entirely upon his own responsibility and without orders from any one.

* * * * * * *

[Inclosure.—Translation.]

SANTIAGO DE CUBA, *August* 13, 1869.

* * * * * *

I write you to advise of the horrible news that has spread through the town since the return of the Villaclara, which will take this letter.

The facts are that on account of the departure of the prisoners Espin and Perez, physicians, Salvador Benitez, jr., Ascencio, the two Collaros, one of the Villasana, beside some intimate friends and relatives, and a son of one of the Benitez, called Lico, by the same steamer for Bayamo, where, it was said, the prisoners were to be confronted with an individual who accused them of being in correspondence with the insurgents, no guilt having been discovered in the proceedings previously instituted in this city; a large number of persons went to the wharf to meet the steamer, it having also been rumored that she would bring back the prisoners. I leave you to imagine their horror when they witnessed the landing of the escort and its commander and heard the report of the latter, that the prisoners had been shot between Jiguani and an encampment called Lorma de Piedra, by order of a colonel called Palacios, of the regiment of Antequera, without authority of any source whatsoever. He also had shot, according to report, the persons who accompanied the prisoners; they were Sinforiano Alvarez, Manuel Fresnada, Lico Benitez, a mulatto servant of Perez, and even the horses that they rode.

* * * * * *

Let us proceed with the news: Firstly, it was given by some of the passengers who came in the steamer from Manzanillo, as follows: That it was said at Manzanillo, and even by the commander of the escort and the soldiers composing it, the commander adding that he had left them at Bayamo in good health, and had brought with him a testimonial letter signed by all of them; that on the following day they were to proceed to Jiguani, and that after his return to Manzanillo he heard the news of the massacre, as before related, and of the truth of which there can be no doubt whatever.

It appears that they were shot on the 7th instant. I have seen a letter of Lico Benitez to his wife, dated August 5, at Jiguani, in which he states that they had all arrived safely and that the prisoners had been lodged in the municipal buildings. Afterward one of our merchants received a letter dated the 8th from Manzanillo, from a brother, who states that he had been prompted to abandon Jiguani and his interests at that place because the lives of men were not respected there; that Colonel Palacios has had a Spaniard by the name of Estrada shot without the semblance of a trial, also a Spanish sub-lieutenant, who interposed to prevent the perpetration of such a crime; the colonel's secretary, it appears, also shared the same fate for his officious interference; and finally that all the prisoners sent there from Santiago de Cuba had been deliberately massacred.

* * * * * *

Thus far it appears that no official report has been received here in regard to the affair at Jiguani, and many persist in maintaining that it is too monstrously barbarous for belief.

No. 87.

Mr. Plumb to Mr. Davis.

No. 123.] HAVANA, *August* 24, 1869.

Referring to my dispatch No. 119, of the 21st instant, and the account therewith transmitted of the reported murder of a number of prominent citizens of Santiago de Cuba, and their friends and attendants, by order of an officer of the Spanish army, while being conveyed as political prisoners, at a point a short distance from the headquarters of General Valmaseda, the commander-in-chief of the eastern department of this island, I beg now to state that, as indicated in that dispatch, I have had an interview to day with the Captain General for the purpose of making inquiries with reference to this occurrence. I regret to say that I find that the report, to use his own words, of such assassination, proves to be true.

These prisoners were taken from Santiaga de Cuba to Bayamo, the headquarters of General Valmaseda, and from there were sent by him to Jiguani, near which place they and their friends and attendants, in all to the number of upwards of twenty persons, were, while under the escort of a Colonel Palacios, all shot to death by the force under his command.

Upon stating to the Captain General the object of my visit he informed me that, so far as he knew, no citizen of the United States was among those who had been so executed; that the news of this event had been to him the most painful occurrence that had happened to him since his arrival here, and had caused him the most regret; that he had been informed from Santiago de Cuba, after the second arrest of the individuals referred to, that there were apprehensions for their safety if sent to Bayamo, either there or on the road, and that he had immediately, on the 5th instant, sent orders that they should not be removed from Santiago de Cuba, and to Manzanillo; that if they had reached that point they should at once be sent back to Santiago de Cuba, but these orders had unfortunately been too late; that the first information that reached him was that the escort had been attacked by insurgents, and that in the encounter the prisoners attempting to escape had been shot; that while such information was all that was in his possession, Colonel Palacios had arrived here and left by the steamer for Cadiz of the 15th instant.

Subsequently information, still not official, had been received that not merely the prisoners had been shot but also their friends and attendants accompanying them, and that there was reason to believe no attack upon the escort by the insurgents had been made, as was first reported. Upon this information, the Captain General added, he had already telegraphed to Spain requesting the apprehension of Colonel Palacios on his arrival there and his immediate return to this island for due trial and punishment. He had also sent an engineer officer of his confidence to fully investigate this affair with the most terminant orders and full powers. He could not express to me, he said, the regret and displeasure this affair had occasioned him.

I stated to the Captain General that upon hearing of this occurrence I had felt it to be my duty, as the representative upon this island of the government of the United States, to call upon him for such information as he might be willing or able to furnish with regard to an act of a character so calculated necessarily to influence the judgment not only of the government of the United States but of all nations, with regard to the struggle now in progress here; but that I had felt confident from the judgment of his character my intercourse with him had led me to form, that so deplorable an occurrence could neither have had his previous knowledge nor the slightest sanction in any orders he had issued, and that it could not but meet with his highest indignation, and would receive at his hands prompt and severe punishment. I also added that the judgment of the world would be very much influenced with regard to this affair by the character of the proclamation issued by General Valmaseda in April last, which everywhere received such strong condemnation.

The manifestations made by General Caballero de Rodas in my interview with him were so unreserved and his expressions of regret so strong that I should do him injustice if I failed especially to mention this; at the same time I fear that, under the circumstances now existing here, there is little hope that due punishment will reach the really guilty parties, or that any adequate security can be provided, however strong and well-intentioned may be the orders and purposes of the Captain General, that such occurrences, under the excited passions that have now been aroused on both sides in this struggle, may not be repeated by the acts of subordinate commanders.

As yet no official information regarding this affair appears to have reached here. I cannot but think the acting consul at Santiago de Cuba must have written to me, but no letter from him later than the 7th instant has reached me.

The French consul general and the acting English consul general both have received private letters from their consular officers at Santiago de Cuba, giving an account of the affair, but no official advices. They have communicated information of the occurrence to their governments.

* * * * * * *

No. 88.

Mr. Plumb to Mr. Davis.

No. 127.] HAVANA, *August* 26, 1869.

* * * * * * *

This first circular of General Dulce, explanatory of the policy he felt called upon to adopt, was accompanied by the publication of an order directing the embargo of the property of Morales Lemus, and others, whose names were mentioned, which had been issued on the first of that month.

This was followed by the publication, on the following day, of a decree, dated the 1st of April, requiring that all contracts for the sale of movable and immovable property, before being carried into effect, should be presented for the revision of the government, and declaring null all contracts made without such revision. This was afterward followed by two circulars relating to the formalities of revision, and extending the same also to mortgages.

In the case of movable property under the above circular, such approval or disapproval was to be given within twenty-four hours, and in the case of real estate within four days. I do not find that any complaint is made on the part of the merchants here with reference to the operation of this order, as regards the sales of the products of the country, but, on the contrary, the action of the government being prompt, an official character and countenance is thus given to the transaction, which, in these times, the merchants, as I am informed, consider undesirable.

A decree was then issued on the 17th of April, creating an administrative council for the custody and management of embargoed property, which was endowed with full powers in the premises. At the same time the members of this commission were named, and the governor of the city, Dionesio Lopez Roberts, was appointed president of the board.

By a decree issued by General Caballero de Rodas on the 24th instant, Governor Roberts has been relieved from this charge, and the Captain General has assumed to himself the presidency of the council, and has appointed as vice-president the general intendant of the treasury of this island, an officer who has very recently arrived here from Spain.

But the most important of the measures of embargo is the circular issued by General Dulce, on the 20th of April, which in its first article declares comprehended in the circular of the 15th of that month, with reference to the embargo of the property of José Morales Lemus, and others, all individuals against whom it may be proved that they have taken part in the insurrection, either within or without the island, and whether with arms in the hand, or aiding it with arms, munitions, money and articles of subsistence.

Article second excepts from the preceding provisions those who have been amnestied or pardoned.

Article third prescribes that the individuals comprehended in article first shall remain deprived of the political and civil rights which they have enjoyed under the laws, and that this resolution shall take effect from the 10th of October last, when the insurrection commenced at Yara, or from the date when it may appear that they took part in the preparations for the insurrection.

And article four requires that all contracts made by said individuals from the dates above indicated, shall be presented for the revision of the government within three days subsequent to the publication of the circular.

In this circular it is provided that separate proceedings shall be formed against each individual, and that only when proof is shown of the culpability of the delinquent shall the embargo of his property be declared. The formalities of embargo are also prescribed in this circular. Article twenty-two states that the embargoed property shall be responsible, in the first place, for the necessary expenses of its preservation and working, including the current and over-due taxes; and in the second place, for the payment of the debts contracted by the owne before the dates referred to in article three, that is, of his complicity with the insurrection.

In article twenty-three it is provided that when the creditor is not himself a person subject to embargo he shall prove his claims before the governor or lieutenant governor, who shall give account to the president of the administrative council, in order that directions may be issued for payment to be proceeded with.

The avowed purpose of these measures of embargo is to prevent the use, for insurgent purposes, during the continuance of the insurrection, of the income, products, or avails of any property situated within the control of the Spanish government.

The embargo, it is claimed, is not laid unless there is, in each instance, proof that the person against whom the measure is had has taken part in favor of the insurrection.

And the Captain General has informed me, if it can be shown in any case that such evidence is not well grounded, the embargo will be raised, and any income or proceeds of property received will be returned by the government. It is also claimed that while the embargo may be the occupation of the revenue or the proceeds of property, it is not the confiscation of the property itself, which, in the case of real estate, by descent would still freely pass to innocent heirs; and that it is not designed to affect the interests of any innocent third party.

But while the circular of the 20th of April is in some respects retroactive, there is also ground for the belief that practically its dispositions in many instances amount to confiscation.

This is shown by the order of the Captain General of the 3d instant, authorizing a new loan of six millions of dollars from the Spanish bank,

* * * * * * *

which, in addition to the war tax and export duties, pledged as a guarantee for the previous loan of eight millions of dollars, now pledges "the proceeds of the property embargoed of those hostilely disaffected to the national integrity."

* * * * * * *

No. 89.

Mr. Plumb to Mr. Davis.

No. 129.] HAVANA, *August* 27, 1869.

For some time past the information has been increasing that as a political measure in the struggle in progress upon this island, the burning and destruction of property, and especially of houses and sugar estates, has been deliberately resolved upon. It now appears probable that this plan may very soon be extended to the richest and most largely producing districts.

I need not call the attention of the department, by whom this subject, so far as it relates to the government and to the interests of the citizens of the United States, has doubtless already been considered, to the immense loss that by such a system of warfare will be inflicted not only upon peaceful industrial interests upon this island, and upon the wealth and importance of the island itself, but also upon the vested and extensive commercial interests here of all nations.

* * * * * * *

No. 90.

Mr. Plumb to Mr. Davis.

No. 135.] HAVANA, *August* 31, 1869.

The newspapers of last evening and this morning have published a document, said to have been found among the papers of a captured insurgent leader, purporting to be a communication addressed by the chief insurgent authority to their different military leaders, under date of the 4th of May last, containing a general basis of administration, and recommending certain plans for the prosecution of the insurrection, among which the most notable points are the destruction of towns as a system, and the instigation of risings on the part of the blacks and Asiatics.

* * * * * * *

[From the Diario de la Marina, Havana, August 30, 1869.—Translation.]

We publish below one of the documents taken from the rebel leader Callejas:

No. 132.] OFFICE OF THE SECRETARY OF STATE.

On the 12th day of March the citizen C. M. de Cespedes, now President of the Republic, and then general-in-chief of the liberating army of Cuba, and provisional governor, addressed a communication to the Central Revolutionary Junta of Havana, which contained the following:

1. The territory extending from the dividing line between Camagüey and Sancti Spiritus to Cape St. Antonio, shall be divided into three military districts, each one under the command of a general directing operations, who shall have the privilege of appointing a second in command, and such other subalterns as he may require, submitting said appointments to my approval.

The first shall be called Trinidad, and shall comprise the territory between the said limits and the line dividing Cienfuegos from Colon. The second shall be called the Havana district, and shall extend to the line dividing Guanajay from San Cristobal; and the third shall be called the district of Pinar del Rio, and shall extend from the said line to Cape San Antonio.

2. These generals shall report to me directly all operations undertaken by them, besides communicating with the Central Revolutionary Junta of Havana for whatever may be necessary. They shall propose to me the districts in which it may seem proper to divide their departments, and likewise the persons whom they may select to take command of the same, in capacity of commandants or deputy governors, also giving information thereof to the said central junta, lest the latter might have some objection to make.

3. The commandants will receive instructions from the said junta with regard to all matters relating to their administration, and the junta will report its determinations to me. In case communication with that body should be cut off, they will communicate with me directly, and should this not be possible, with the chief of operations to whose district they belong.

4. In each district there shall be appointed a quartermaster dependent upon the quartermaster general, to whom (*i. e.*, the quartermaster general) the central junta shall report in order that he may inform me of the communications of these functionaries, who shall be in direct communication with the central junta aforesaid.

The quartermasters shall appoint officers, collectors, commissaries of war, and purveyors in the manner and for the purposes for which provision has been made, obeying the orders issued by the quartermaster general, barring the exceptions which may be specially required by each locality.

5. A postal system shall be organized, postmasters shall be appointed, and the necessary post offices established.

6. A judicial and municipal government shall likewise be organized wherever it may be possible.

7. A police system shall likewise receive due attention.

8. The system of the extinct Spanish government shall be everywhere observed, it being interpreted in the most liberal sense possible, until some other determination be reached for the future government of the Cuban Republic.

9. The central junta shall represent this provisional government, and shall make the appointments belonging to it, subject to my approval, until the meeting of a congress, representing the people of the island in proportion to the number of inhabitants.

10. From this time forward all liberties are established in their widest sense, subject, however, to the state of war in which the public now is.

All appointments now made shall be merely provisional, and shall impart no character and give no claim to any compensation until congress shall have decided upon what it may think proper.

Now the C. (citizen) President Carlos M. de Cespedes, in his new capacity, considering it exceedingly important to have that state governed in all branches of administration in a manner similar to the one observed in the rest of the republic, has determined to modify the preceding rules with reference to Las Villas (villas—literally, chartered towns) limiting their number to eight, introducing in them the changes given below.

In the first the military district shall be called the district of Las Villas, and not of Trinidad, and shall consist of six military divisions, entitled:

Moron and Sancti Spiritus.
Remedios.
Cienfuegos.
Trinidad.
Sagua.
Villaclara.

The general-chief of operations shall have the privilege of appointing a second in command, a chief of staff, and such other subalterns as he may require, submitting these appointments to the approval of the executive.

2. The chief of operations shall no longer be required to report to the central junta of Havana, the said chief reporting, instead, all military matters to the secretary of war and to the general-in-chief of the liberating army. The chiefs of division shall make reports to the chief of operations, and shall receive them from their subalterns, requiring them if they be not made.

Instead of a commandant, a governor of the state has been chosen; instead of deputy governors, there shall be prefects; and instead of district captains, sub-perfects. Where there are perfects, the chief of operations shall appoint military commanders; the former shall attend to political (civil) and the latter to military matters. In like manner the governor shall attend to civil and the chief of operations to military affairs.

The governor shall appoint the prefectures and sub-prefectures into which it may be proper to divide the country; and as the saving of time is important, the system shall be inaugurated without delay, and the appointees shall discharge their functions, their appointments being subsequently referred to the President for his approval.

3. This is hereby declared null and void.

4. There shall be appointed, not a quartermaster, but a director of finance, who shall communicate with and receive his instructions from the secretary of finance only; and until his appointment the civil governor of the State shall perform his duties. The latter, or the director of finance in his stead, shall appoint officers, collectors, commissaries of war, and purveyors, in the manner indicated by the article, making a report of the same to the proper office, with the understanding that the department of finance is in no way connected with that of military affairs.

The commissaries of war are appointed solely that they may be the channel through which in all cases the military chiefs may ask of the department of finance what they may require for the army.

5. The postal service shall be organized by the appointment of a postmaster general, subject to the secretary of the interior. He shall select his employés and establish the necessary offices, and report everything to said secretary of the interior.

6, 7, and 8 remain unchanged.

9 is declared null and void.

10 remains unchanged.

By this latter, martial law is declared in force, which notice is printed in order that it may be punctually observed, since we are driven to this extreme by the barbarous enemy whom we are fighting.

The rules which are preserved bear the same numbers as those which have been suppressed.

For the fulfillment of these orders the President has appointed as chief of operations C. Juan Villegas; as chief of the division of Moron y Sancti Spiritus, C. Honorato Castillo; of Remedios, C. Mateo Casanova; of Cienfuegos, C. Adolpho Cavada; of Trinidad, C. (C.=citizen) Frederico Cavada; of Villaclara, C. Salome Hernandez; of Sagua, C. Fernando Callejas.

These individuals shall continue to occupy the rank which they have hitherto held in the liberating army, with the exception of Callejas, on whom the executive has conferred the rank of colonel; and when the army shall be definitively organized, their proper positions shall be assigned them.

The C. Joaquin Morales has been chosen governor of the State, and the C. President confirms this appointment.

The chief of operations is required to forward to me at once an exact statement of all the forces of the district, and of their arms, munitions, and clothing; taking care, as is done by the chiefs of division, to organize his troops in battalions, companies, &c., and to obtain good drill-masters to instruct them when their services are not otherwise required.

We are assured that Remedios is without any Spanish force. The C. Casanova will judge whether by an energetic movement it is possible to seize this place, in order to cause it to disappear (*i. e.*, destroy it) entirely, after having put to good use all that it contains, as must be done with all the towns that fall into our power, since we cannot hold them for lack of means, and since the enemy uses these centers as strongholds whence to resist and persecute us.

It is very necessary to hasten the operations of the war, that our enemies may effect no concentration here, as they intend, and that they may be divided; for when they are divided, and thereby weakened, their annihilation and total destruction will be more easy.

Let not only towns, but also strong country houses, where the enemy may desire to seek shelter, be destroyed with fire and the pickaxe.

Thus the enemy will never occupy the republic, and the persecution which has been commenced against families therein sheltered, while he (*i. e.*, the enemy) carefully avoids all contact with our soldiers, will be accomplished with much greater difficulty. Let the arms be collected which are hidden, under whatever pretext, by private individuals or chiefs, for the persons holding them, who are not fit for military service, can be otherwise employed. Let the laborers on estates be encouraged to rise; let serviceable freedmen remain in Las Villas for military service, and let others be sent to Camaguey, so that their former masters may lose all hope of recovering them. The person sending them need only communicate this fact to the chief of operations, and the latter to the governor of the State.

Asiatic laborers should also be taken.

The director of finance, and now in his stead the governor of the State, is requested to collect all sorts of supplies, both of money and provisions, to aid the revolution and encourage the contraband trade on our coasts, without neglecting due vigilance, in order that the enemy may not learn through this trade the position of those places, and thus cause us injury.

Let each chief aid the others; let them maintain fraternal harmony among themselves; let them keep up a constant correspondence; let them report everything; let them pass from one jurisdiction (*i. e.*, district) to another, when the interest of the cause requires it; and let them fulfill all orders in obedience to the present general plan, and in cases for which provision is not made let them use the discretionary powers with which they are invested by the executive.

I send this to the Captain General, and hope you will be pleased to acknowledge his receipt of the same.

P. and L. Patria y libertad! Our country and liberty!

BERROCAL.

May 4, 1869. In the absence of the secretary,

THE SECRETARY OF FINANCE.

To the C. Colonel FERNANDO CALLEJAS.

No. 91.

Mr. Plumb to Mr. Davis.

No. 139.] HAVANA, *September* 1, 1869.

I beg to transmit to you, herewith, a copy of a letter under date of 28th ultimo, received to-day from the acting United States consular agent at Manzanillo.

It contains some general information of interest, and is confirmatory of the assassination of the unfortunate prisoners from Santiago de Cuba, and their friends at Jiguani.

* * * * * *

Mr. Bithorn to Mr. Plumb.

MANZANILLO, CUBA, *August* 28, 1869.

* * * * * * * *

I am sorry to say that the political condition of this town and district remains in the same confused state, much to the detriment of commerce and agriculture, and with the great mortality among the Spanish forces, rainy weather, and bad roads, which impede all military operations, as well as a reluctance of the natives to show open fight, this unfortunate struggle, without mightier interference, threatens the utter ruin of the country.

There is very little, if any, information, to be gained of military proceedings in the interior, although I have heard of acts of violence and barbarity, such as the massacre of captives without any trial, some of which came from Santiago to undergo their trial at Jiguani, and, as is stated, were shot, even with those who accompanied them, particulars of which no doubt you will have learned through the United States acting consul at Santiago, who, I am told, together with the representatives of other nations, interfered in their behalf.

* * * * * * * *

No. 92.

Mr. Lopez Roberts to Mr. Fish.

[Translation.]

WASHINGTON, *September* 18, 1869.

The undersigned, envoy extraordinary and minister plenipotentiary of Spain, to-day addresses the honorable Secretary of State of the United States, with the design of submitting to his judgment certain important considerations relative to the declaration of belligerent rights which, as it appears, it is intended to grant to the insurgents of Cuba. * * * He should fail to perform his duty as the representative of Spain in this republic, he would be unmindful of the great liberal cause for the triumph of which his government is now fighting, unmindful of the traditional friendship which, since 1789 until now, has united Spain to the United States, if he kept silence at the announcement of so important a resolution.

I do not flatter myself, on taking up this subject, to be able to present to your consideration any arguments which shall be new and hitherto unknown to you; for my object it is more than sufficient for me to have recourse to those arguments furnished me by the history of North American politics themselves. The honorable Secretary of State is doubtless not ignorant of the favorable opinion which the world entertains of American neutrality, commenced by those great men Washington and Hamilton, during the war of the French Revolution, which neutrality was continued afterward by Presidents Madison and Monroe, at the time of the struggle between Spain and her insurgent American possessions, and which, still later, was seen confirmed with great brilliancy in the recent diplomatic controversy with England, in which the Hon. William H. Seward, his immediate predecessor to the Hon. Charles Francis Adams, minister of the United States at London, and the Hon. Charles Sumner, chairman of the Committee on Foreign Affairs in the Senate, did, with great intelligence and with force equal to that of the first-named statesmen, sustain the principles of that neutrality.

What is the doctrine constantly defended and expounded by these illustrious authorities? I cannot define it better than in the following words of Mr. Charles Francis Adams. (See the original words of Mr. Adams at the end of of the Spanish document.)

The doctrine set forth in these lines by Mr. Charles Francis Adams is that of all the principal statesmen of America; all believe belligerence is a fact, and not a principle; and in support of this they say: "That it must be proved that the causes for making such declaration exist and are visible; it (belligerence) can therefore neither be imagined nor guessed at nor invented; its existence must be a fact, and be recognized as such by the world, or at least it must be of such a nature that it may be considered as a fact." And the same authorities add: "That it cannot be inferred from the fact that belligerence exists on land that it also exists at sea." "Such is the rule," says Mr. Sumner, "so simple, clear, and intelligible, as it has been established by Mr. Canning." Thus, then, the proof with regard to the facts of the causes for a declaration of belligerent rights must always precede the declaration; belligerent rights are not made on presumption; their existence must be proved. Again, considering the whole American doctrine on this important question, Mr. Richard H. Dana has defined in the following manner the conditions which must precede a declaration of belligerent rights. (See original texts at the end; extract from the Elements of International Law, by H. Wheaton.)

And why all these precautions? The same writers on international law, and the most illustrious American statesmen, both tell us in the following terms: "If a single one of those guarantees of impartiality fails to exist, the element foreign to the struggle is that which should take part in the cause of the insurgents and give them aid."

If belligerence is a question of fact, and not of principle, how can an American statesman at once renounce his country's traditions of the policy of neutrality in the matter of the insurgents of Cuba?

I am not ignorant of the fact that their agents and emissaries in the United States publicly declare the existence of an established government. But has the truth of this assertion been investigated? Has an attempt even been made to do so? And if it has been done, if other documents are possessed which do not proceed from a suspicious source, why are they not published in the United States? In this way it would be possible to enlighten the opinion of the rest of the world, which is now in the most complete darkness with respect to the matter. It is certainly not in treating with the descendants of those who signed the declaration of their country's independence, and conquered their freedom at the price of so much blood, that I must longer insist upon the conditions which a new government just establishing itself requires.

The bands of rebels roaming throughout the eastern department of the Island of Cuba have not a single line of communication with the sea. Where, then, are their ports, or their ships, or their prize court? The fertile imagination of their agents in the United States has as yet furnished no reply to these questions.

I must now compare the policy pursued in 1861 by the Spanish government toward the United States with that which the government of this republic now appears inclined to put into practice with respect to Spain. At the outbreak of the civil war in this country, England and France took the initiative, granting belligerent rights to the so-called confederates, whom they considered as being organized. Prussia made the same declaration on the 13th of June. Spain could not, by reason of her geographical and maritime situation, longer abstain from making a similar concession, without exposing herself to the gravest complications; but she declared, in doing so, that she desired to maintain the mutual sentiments of friendship prevailing between Spain and the republic, these sympathies being clearly shown by the subsequent acts of the

Spanish government, which proved that its policy recognized as its base the most friendly feeling toward the cabinet at Washington. This conduct was so manifest that its proof is found in the diplomatic correspondence published by the federal government.

Mr. Perry wrote from Madrid, June 19, 1861, to the Honorable Mr. Seward, as follows: (See original at the end of the Spanish paper.)

Mr. Schurz, United States minister at Madrid, shortly afterward wrote to Señor Calderon Collantes, the Spanish minister of state, (July 31 of the same year,) as follows: (See original which accompanies the Spanish paper.)

If the present Spanish government is, to a certain extent, responsible for the political acts of the one which it replaces, much less can the honorable Secrétary of State disregard the declarations made by his predecessor in the name of President Lincoln, and excuse to-day, by that course then appreciated in a manner so favorable for the United States by the President and Secretary of State, so grave a political act as the one in question, which cannot be explained, much less justified by the actual situation of Cuba. Nor can any distinction be made between an insurrection breaking out in an integral part of the national territory, and in a colony. Those publicists who have written upon this international point admit nothing of the kind; all adhere to the doctrine expressed by Vattel in the following form:

"When a nation," says he, "takes possession of a distant territory and establishes a colony there, this country, although separated from the mother country, forms a part of the state equally with its former possessions."

Therefore, neither can the American doctrine of neutrality, nor the precedents found in the federal policy, nor the situation of the Island of Cuba, nor the course pursued by Spain toward the United States, justify a resolution of this serious character, viz: the accordance of belligerent rights to the roving bands of insurgents in Cuba.

Whence arises, then, the resolution which the federal government is apparently on the eve of adopting? These are questions which, with all due delicacy, I will take the liberty of answering in the following terms:

First. Certain malcontent Cubans have established themselves in the United States, especially in New York, and these are endeavoring by every means in their power, not to conquer their independence by their own efforts, but to gain at present the sympathies of the American people in order afterward to seek the aid of this government for their cause. The history of what has taken place in the last few months is the clearest proof of this. In a state of peace, it has been seen with astonishment that associations were publicly organized in many ports belonging to a friendly nation, said associations being composed of the agents of the insurgents, with no other object than that of directing their attacks against Spain. Enlistments of men have also taken place during whole weeks, as if the object were to form expeditions authorized by law, and consequently with the consent of the authorities. These emissaries have carried their spirit of speculation so far as to take advantage of the good faith of emigrants from Europe, sending them to fight in Cuba under command of the so-called General Jordan, and other officers who fought on the side of the South in the civil war. Hostile demonstrations have likewise been suffered to take place against a nation which in 1861 had not even allowed (in order not to wound the susceptibility of the United States) the title of belligerents to be given to an insurgent population numbering six or seven millions of whites, who occupied a third of the territory of the republic, and were in possession of such resources that they were only conquered by prodigies of valor, military talent, and heroic perseverance; and, after having seen the departure of various filibustering expeditions in broad day-light, and unmolested, from New York and other federal ports, the minister of Spain finally found himself obliged, by the incomprehensible apathy of the authorities, to take the initiative in order to prevent these repeated infractions of the neutrality laws; but he will not now insist on these facts, to which at the proper time he will call the attention of the honorable Secretary of State.

Secondly. If the duties of every foreign power, with respect to a rebellion carried on against a regular and legitimate government, oblige said power to abstain from all participation in such rebellion, as was so aptly said by the Hon. Charles Francis Adams, avoiding in this manner the exercising of any influence on the result by the element foreign to the struggle, the honorable Secretary of State must have deeply regretted the extravagant demonstrations which have been seen in a large portion of the country, and which have been echoed by the press. He will also sincerely regret that the Cuban emissaries have gone so far as to compromise the reputation for impartiality (without doubt well deserved) of persons holding high official positions, boasting, doubtless without any reason, of being in possession of important confidential information with regard to political affairs, and to have knowledge of plans, the accomplishment of which they predicted with great confidence. With this view, I take the liberty of calling your attention to a letter from Mr. Dallas, (May 2, 1861,) then minister of the United States in London, to Mr. Seward. (See original texts for what is designated above, and for Mr. Seward's reply.)

Thirdly. Finally I am about to treat of the question of belligerent rights, which is the most important matter of these observations. Why do the Cuban agents solicit these with so much urgency? Why do they not hesitate to employ calumny in order to compromise the government of the United States in favor of their cause? Why do they not recoil (so that they may accomplish their object) at the danger of employing means which are punished by the laws? The reply to these questions is, that the Cuban agents stand in the most pressing need of the aid of the United States; that what they seek and require is the moral participation, at least, of the American Union in their struggle with Spain; which, hitherto, has attained no proportions save those given it by the reports of victories of the Cuban insurgents, manufactured at Key West and in New York, and which, under pretext of obtaining the title of belligerents, only tend to cause the United States to abandon that policy, the strict observance of which is dictated by the law of nations as taught and practiced by themselves. Thus, then, before closing these considerations relative to the announcement of the concession of belligerent rights to the insurgents of Cuba by the United States, it seems fitting to me to copy, in addition, the words addressed, September 18, 1865, by Mr. Charles Francis Adams, minister of this republic in London, to Lord John Russell. (See end of Spanish document.)

The undersigned avails himself of this opportunity to reiterate to the honorable Secretary of State the assurances of highest consideration.

MAURICIO LOPEZ ROBERTS.

Hon. SECRETARY OF STATE *of the United States.*

[Inclosure.]

Extract from the correspondence of the Hon. C. F. Adams, envoy extraordinary and minister plenipotentiary of the United States, with Lord Russell, minister for foreign affairs of England, respecting the Alabama, on September 18, 1865.

Page 155. "Whenever an insurrection against the established government of a country takes place, the duty of governments under obligations to maintain peace and friendship with it appears to be at first to *abstain carefully from any step that may have the smallest influence in affecting the result.*" Whenever facts occur of which it is necessary to take notice, either because they involve a necessity of protecting personal interests at home, or avoiding an implication in the struggle, then it appears to be just and right to provide for the emergency by specific *measures precisely to the extent that may be required, but no further.* It is, then, facts alone, and not appearances or presumptions, that justify action. *But even these are not to be dealt with further than the occasion demands. A rigid neutrality in whatever may be done is of course understood.*

* * * * * * * * * * *

Such appears to me to have been the course rigidly adhered to by the government which I have the honor to represent in the long struggle that took place between Spain and her colonies in South America. On which side of it the sympathies of the people were, cannot admit of a doubt, yet the respective dates which your lordship has been kind enough to search out and record in your note, sufficiently established the fact how carefully all precipitation was avoided in judging of the issue in regard to the mother country.

Extract from the Elements of International Law, by Henry Wheaton, LL. D.

PART 1.—NATIONS AND SOVEREIGN STATES.

Page 23. It is certain that the state of things between the parent state and insurgents must amount in fact to a *war in the sense of international law*—that is, powers and *rights* of war *must be* in actual exercise—otherwise the recognition is falsified, for the *recognition* is a *fact.* The tests to determine the question are various.

* * * * * * * * * * *

Among the tests are the existence of a *de facto* political organization of the insurgents, sufficient in character, population, and resources, to constitute it, if left to itself, a state among the nations, reasonably capable of discharging the duties of a state; the actual employment of *military forces* on *each side, acting in accordance with the rules and customs of war, such as the use of flags of truce, cartels, exchange of prisoners,* and the treatment of captured insurgents by the parent state as prisoners of war.

* * * * * * * * * *

Extract of a note written by Mr. Perry to Mr. Seward, dated Legation of the United States, Madrid, June 17, 1861.

The minister of state has to-day, while acknowledging that its provisions are in great part taken from the French decree, drawn my attention to the fact that he has avoided the use of the expression *belligerents* as far as possible, or any other which could be considered as prejudging the question of right in any manner.

* * * * * * * * * * *

Extract from a note of Mr. Schurz to Señor Calderon Collantes, dated Legation of the United States, Madrid, July 31, 1861.

SIR: Yesterday I received a dispatch from the Secretary of State of the United States, informing me that the President has read with the greatest satisfaction the proclamation of her Catholic Majesty's concerning the unfortunate troubles that have arisen in the United States, and it affords me the sincerest pleasure to express to your excellency the *high sense* which the President entertains of her Majesty's prompt decision and friendly action upon this occasion.

* * * * * * * * * *

Extract from a note of Mr. Dallas to Mr. Seward, dated Legation of the United States, London, May 2, 1861.

He (Lord Russell) told me that the three representatives of the southern confederacy were here; that he had not seen them, but was not unwilling to do so unofficially.

* * * * * * * * * * *

Extract from a note of Mr. Seward to Mr. Adams, dated Department of State, Washington, May 21, 1861.

The President regrets that Mr. Dallas did not protest against the proposed unofficial intercourse *between the British government and the missionaries* of the insurgents.

* * * * * * * * * * *

Intercourse of any kind with the so-called *commissioners* is liable to be construed as a recognition of the authority which appointed them. Such intercourse would be none the less hurtful to us for being called *unofficial, and it might be even more injurious,* because we should have no means of knowing what points might be resolved by it.

* * * * * * * * * * *

You will in any event desist from all intercourse whatever, unofficial as well as official, with the British government, so long as it shall continue intercourse of either kind with the domestic enemies of this country.

Extract from the correspondence between the Hon. Mr. C. F. Adams, American minister, and Earl Russell, Minister for Foreign Affairs of England, respecting the Alabama, dated Legation of the United States, London, September 18, 1865.

* * * * * * * * * * *

But entertaining as I do a strong impression that in the matter now at issue is *involved a question of international comity based upon grave principles of morals of universal application, the decision upon which is likely to have a very wide bearing upon the future relations of all civilized nations,* and especially those most frequenting the high seas, I feel myself under the necessity of placing upon record the views of it held by the government which I have the honor to represent.

No. 93.

Mr. Fish to Mr. Lopez Roberts.

WASHINGTON, *October* 13, 1869.

The undersigned, Secretary of State of the United States, has the honor to acknowledge the receipt of the note of Mr. Roberts, envoy extraordinary and minister plenipotentiary of Spain, under date of 18th September, which was received on the 25th of that month, on which day the undersigned left Washington for a temporary absence.

Mr. Roberts states the object of his note to be the submission of "certain important considerations relative to the declaration of belligerent rights which, as it appears, it is intended to grant to the insurgents of Cuba."

Mr. Roberts does not state how or whence appears the intention, which in various parts of his note, with more or less force of expression, but always with equal and entire absence of proof, or of facts in support thereof, he assumes to be formed, and attributes to this government.

It might be a sufficient answer to say, that no intention to grant belligerent rights to the insurgents of Cuba has been announced by this government. It is a more perfect answer to say that no such intention has been reached by this government.

The undersigned has read with interest the "important considerations" submitted by Mr. Roberts, and observes with great satisfaction the appreciation by that gentleman of the strict observance by this government of its international obligations of neutrality; and he notices further with equal satisfaction, that Mr. Roberts draws the most of his authority in favor of the observance of those neutral obligations from the precedent furnished by this government, and from the diplomatic correspondence of this department and its representatives.

Mr. Roberts, in various parts of his note, attributes to this government an intention which is not warranted by any declaration or act of the government, and which is justified only by Mr. Roberts's appreciation of the demands made upon it, or by the unduly excited hopes of some and apprehensions of other persons.

In this view he compares the policy pursued by Spain in 1861 with that which he assumes this government now appears inclined to put in practice with respect to Spain.

The undersigned would have desired not to draw any comparisons; but if one is to be drawn, it should be between the policy actually pursued by the respective governments, and not between that which has been adopted by Spain and that which Mr. Roberts imagines the United States may be inclined to put in practice.

Referring to the concession of belligerent rights by Spain to the southern insurgents during the recent civil war in the United States, Mr. Roberts says it had been preceded by a similar concession on the part of Great Britain, France, and Prussia, and that "Spain could not by reason of her geographical and maritime situation longer abstain from making."

This concession was made by Spain on the 17th day of June, 1861, only sixty-six days after the assault on Fort Sumter, the outbreak of the rebellion, and which was the only combat or conflict of arms of which any account had reached Europe at the date of Spain's action in the matter; a single and a bloodless combat, an attack upon a handful of half-starved men, being the extent of war on which Spain based the "fact of belligerency."

It is true that Great Britain and France may have been more precipitate even than Spain in their haste to grant belligerent rights to the insurgents of the United States; and the example of these monarchies of the Old World may be pleaded by the Republics of Peru, Chili, and Bolivia, in the New, in their proceeding towards Cuba, with the difference in favor of the latter, that they waited for months, instead of days, and until scores of conflicts had been fought, and the slain were numbered by thousands.

The United States have not followed these or any similar precedents. When Mr. Roberts alludes to the "geographical and maritime situation of Spain" as presenting the necessity for her action in June, 1861, the undersigned is forced to admit that the geopraphical and maritime situation of a neutral power may become a controlling consideration in deciding its attitude toward parties engaged in a civil conflict, within the limits of another power. The United States have felt and still feel the force of this consideration, in its bearing upon the pending conflict in Cuba. But in this connection the undersigned is compelled to ask himself the question, whether the scene of conflict in the southern States was nearer to the possessions of Spain, in 1861, than the scene of the present conflict is to the territory of the United States; and he fails to see that the maritime situation of Spain was as intimately affected by the civil war in the United States, as the maritime situation of the

United States is affected by that which rages in the neighboring Island of Cuba.

The civil war in Cuba has continued for a year; battle after battle has been fought, thousands of lives have been sacrificed, and the result is still in suspense. But the United States have hitherto resisted the considerations which, in 1861, controlled the action of Spain, and determined her to act upon the occurrence of a single bloodless conflict of arms and within sixty-six days from its date.

Riquelme, one of the ablest modern writers on international law, (one for whom the world is indebted to Spain,) says "that foreign intervention in civil wars may be excusable when the interest of humanity evidently requires it, or when the essential interests of a state are injured by the civil war of a neighboring power." No claims of humanity were alleged as calling for intervention in the civil war in the United States; on the contrary, humanity called for the repression of a rebellion whose avowed object was the enslavement and oppression of a race.

The undersigned has not now to remind Mr. Roberts of the frequency with which, in the interest of humanity, he has been obliged to remonstrate against the atrocities and the cruelties which have attended the conflict in Cuba for the past year; and if these cruelties and this inhumanity have not been confined to one party to the conflict, the force of the justification for intervention assigned by the eminent Spanish authority referred to has been so much the more pressing.

The United States have not acted on this justification assigned by Riquelme, nor by that other of neighborhood, although the scene of strife lies at their very threshold, but have acted upon their early established policy, under which, in the beginning of their history, in the absence of any municipal enactments on the subject, and in advance of other nations, they set the example of repressing violations of neutrality to the prejudice of nations with whom they were at peace. This proud feature in their history, and their strict adherence to it during subsequent years when Spain was engaged in war with her revolted provinces, are candidly admitted by Mr. Roberts.

This principle has controlled their proceedings with regard to the war in Cuba. It does not, however, admit the indefinite protraction of a conflict in a contiguous territory, such as that which has existed for the past year in that island—a conflict marked with cruelties and destruction and devastation without parallel in modern civilized warfare. To quote again the language of Riquelme, "Humanity and the essential interests of other powers may at length compel their action."

The friendship of the government of the United States for Spain, unbroken during its existence as a nation, has led it to hope for a different solution to the difficulties with which its ancient ally now finds herself involved. It still hopes and will continue to hope for such solution. It must, however, reserve for the future its independent action as a sovereign power. The future of the contest, and of its conduct, will determine the future course of this government.

The undersigned cannot close this note without the expression of regret that a part of Mr. Roberts's note seems to have been written under a misapprehension of facts that have occurred, as well as of the spirit and operations of a government founded upon liberal principles, and acting under constitutional and limited powers.

The United States freely offer an asylum to the oppressed of all nationalities; many of the subjects of Spain have availed themselves of that asylum; and if, as Mr. Roberts alleges, they, or some of them, have abused the hospitality extended alike to all, this is not the fault of the United States.

This government allows freedom of speech and of action to all, citizens or strangers, restricted only to the observance of the rights of others, and of the public peace. The Constitution of the United States secures to the people the right peacefully to assemble, and also to keep and bear arms; it secures them in their persons against unreasonable search and seizure, and provides that no warrant shall issue but upon probable cause, supported by oath or affirmation, and that no person shall be deprived of life, liberty, or property without due process of law.

If certain malcontent Cubans (subjects of Spain) have misconstrued and abused the privileges thus accorded by a liberal government, the undersigned need not remind Mr. Roberts what the occurrences daily reported from across the ocean are showing—that governments cannot always restrain their malcontent subjects or residents. Laws will be broken at times; and happy is that form of government that can control the tendency of evil minds, and restrain, by its peaceful agencies, the violence of evil passions.

The undersigned is forced to admit, with regret, that an unlawful expedition did succeed in stealthily escaping from the United States, and landing on the shores of Cuba. It escaped from the United States without having attracted any notice or suspicion on the part of the government or its officers or agents, and, as the undersigned believes, without any suspicion on the part of the agents of the Spanish government. Previous to its departure, Mr. Roberts had been frequently informed that this government would act upon any information or suggestion which it could obtain through its own agents, or that might be furnished by the Spanish authorities or their agents.

The undersigned has, on several occasions, caused proceedings to be adopted on information received from Mr. Roberts, which information proved to be totally unfounded. In no single instance where any information was received, either from the representative or the agents of Spain, or from the offiers of this government, or from any other source, indicating the probability of any unlawful enterprise against Spain or her possessions, has this government failed in arresting and defeating the objects of such enterprise.

No. 94.

General Sickles to Mr. Fish.

No. 19.] MADRID, *September* 19, 1869.

I inclose with this dispatch a decree organizing a commission to consider and propose within thirty days a plan of political and administrative reform for Porto Rico, including the abolition of slavery. It is preceded by a decree dissolving a former commission, and establishing another to prepare and submit forthwith the necessary changes in the penal code of the peninsula to make it applicable to the colonies. The report of the colonial minister preceding the decree in relation to Porto Rico is not without interest in its recognition of the cogent reasons demanding radical changes in Spanish colonial government, and thorough reforms in colonial administration. Other decrees are foreshadowed establishing freedom of worship in Cuba, and providing for the election of deputies to the Cortes; although several times announced semi-officially as forthcoming, they have not yet appeared.

I am assured by the President of the Cortes, that among the first subjects brought before that body, will be the cruel and vindictive manner in which the war in Cuba is prosecuted, and he feels confident the Cortes will require the most energetic measures to be taken by the government to prevent hereafter the outrages which have been so justly denounced by the United States. Captain General Concha, Marquis of Duro, has likewise expressed to me his abhorrence of the treatment of prisoners of war and other captives in Cuba, and will move actively in the matter on the assembling of the Cortes, where his high military reputation and personal character will exercise their just influence. Other prominent personages have given me similar assurance.

* * * * * * * *

[Translation.]

MINISTRY OF TRANSMARINE AFFAIRS, *i. e.*, AFFAIRS OF THE SPANISH TRANSMARINE POSSESSIONS.

STATEMENT.

SIR: By a decree of September 29, 1866, a commission was appointed, whose duty it was to "examine and propose a reform of the penal laws in force in our transmarine possessions," and also to propose "the principles and rules whereby judgments in criminal cases shall be governed" in those territories.

This commission taking as its basis the penal code which is in force in the peninsula, and accepting as its object the application of said code in our transmarine possessions, has labored to facilitate the same by means of some reforms in the text. But these labors do not embrace the whole code, nor do they refer to the enforcement of the penal code, which was, and justly so, one of the principal ends for which the commission was appointed.

It is important to carry out this intention, and it would be a matter of great regret, if, by reason of its being unduly extended, any obstacle should be placed in the way of its speedy accomplishment. Hence the undersigned minister is of opinion that the duties of the aforesaid commission being considered at an end, another should be appointed to examine and propose the various reforms and modifications whereby our penal code may be applied to our various transmarine territories, and at the same time to prepare a provisional law for the application of the code, deferring the elaborate preparation of a law for judicial procedure until some future time.

In this manner, limiting its task to the examinatien of the common penal law and to the form of its immediate application, the committee will be able to accomplish this as speedily as the government of your highness and our brethren beyond the sea desire and need.

With these considerations, the undersigned minister has the honor to submit to the approval of your highness the accompanying plan of a decree.

The Minister of Transmarine Affairs,
MANUEL BECERRA.

MADRID, *September* 10, 1869.

DECREE.

In accordance with the suggestion of the minister of transmarine affairs, made with the approval of the council of ministers, I decree as follows:

ARTICLE 1. The commission which was appointed by the decree of September 29, 1866, to examine and propose reforms in the penal laws in force in the transmarine possessions in Spain, is hereby dissolved.

ART. 2. Another commission is appointed in its stead, to consist of a president, five voting members, and a secretary, who shall have the right to vote, and it shall be the duty of said commission: first, to propose as speedily as possible such alterations as may be necessary in the penal code now in force in the peninsula, in order to apply the same to the various Spanish territories lying beyond the sea; secondly, to prepare likewise, with all speed, a provisional law for the application of the same code; thirdly, to examine and propose the basis of a law for judicial procedure in criminal cases for the said territories.

ART. 3. The ministry of the transmarine affairs will furnish the commission with the data and information which it possesses, and will further give the necessary orders for the execution of this decree.

Done at Madrid, September 10, 1869.

FRANCIS. SERRANO.

The Minister of Transmarine Affairs,
MANUEL BECERRA.

STATEMENT.

SIR: The day being at hand for our legislative body to renew its labors, and the legitimate representatives of Porto Rico being now present in the metropolis, the time has arrived for the fulfillment of the just duty and of the solemn obligation imposed upon us by the September revolution toward the Spaniards beyond the sea.

Spain is not limited to the peninsula which is bounded by the Mediterranean and the Atlantic. The community of race and traditions, which is manifested by a common language and a glorious history never tarnished by disloyalty, clearly shows that nations are made principally by means of moral bonds of union far stronger than misfortune and errors. If governments that distrusted the national spirit by which they disdained to be actuated, hoped more from the always doubtful efficacy of external and violent means than from the attractive virtue of national solidity, never appealed to in vain among our people, it is now time to seek in the free manifestations of the aspirations of all that potent union and that dauntless courage whereby we may recover the position which history claims for us, and which of right belongs to us in the council and assembly of enlightened nations. Sovereign Spain cannot deprive any of her members of that portion of sovereignty which is their due.

The revolutionary mevement, therefore, was very soon made in our transmarine possessions, and gave rise to legitimate as well as encouraging hopes. But in an unfortunate hour, by reason of inveterate feelings of distrust; by reason of the excessive exaggeration of past offenses; perhaps, also, by reason of inordinate aspirations, this movement, which ought to have been as measured as regular, and as productive of good as in the peninsula, stepped beyond the limits within which it should have confined itself, raising the *flag of rebellion* in Cuba to violate the sacred integrity of the Spanish nation.

In presence of such a danger, the honor of the country, the duty of the government, the vital interests of the revolution, peremptorily demanded the defense of the territory, and as a *consequence of the state of hostilities*, the much to be regretted but necessary postponement of reforms, so that these might not be confounded with timorous and arbitrary reforms of past times, nor fail to appear solemnly consecrated by the action and free consent of all interested in them, thus strengthening with firmer bonds than those of force—the lasting union of Cuba and Spain.

But if such invincible obstacles temporarily prevent the Spanish revolution from exercising its political influence in the most precious of our Antilles, this is not the case in Port Rico, and the government being free from the well-founded apprehension which the state of affairs in Cuba causes it to entertain with respect to that island, when the question is to radically change the political and social system there prevailing, it is proper to show how energetic, honest, and sincere is its desire to admit the colonies to the full enjoyment of their rights, and to an untrammeled participation in the great conquests of modern civilization.

A deplorable and pertinacious tradition of despotism, which if it could ever be justified, is without a shadow of reason at the present time, intrusted the direction and management of our colonial establishment to the agents of the metropolis, destroying by their dominant and exclusive authority the vital energies of the country, and the creative and productive activity of free individuals.

And although the system may now have improved in some of its details, the domineering action of the authorities being less felt, it still appears full of the original error, which is upheld by the force of tradition, and the necessary influence of interests created under their protection, (*i. e.* that of the authorities,) which doubtless are deserving of respect so far as they are reconcilable with the requirements of justice, with the common welfare, and with the principles on which every liberal system should be founded.

A change of system, political as well as administrative, is therefore imperatively demanded. To declare and respect the inalienable rights of persons, municipalities and provinces, to seek to bring about administrative centralization, allowing the widest freedom of action to municipal boards and provincial deputations, as legitimate, immediate, and direct organs and representatives of the people electing them; to simplify the complicated mechanism of the superior administration, restoring to those natural centers the powers which of right belong to them, and as a political guarantee of still greater importance, firmly to establish the public representation at one time near the colonial government, at another near that of the metropolis, or in both at once, if it should be possible and necessary—such is, in brief, the general intention of the undersigned minister.

But in order that these intentions may be duly fulfilled and that these results may be felt by all alike, it is indispensable to solve one of the most difficult social problems at once the danger and the glory of our epoch. Errors arising from a false view of life sacrificed, for more than three centuries, the personal liberty of thousands of beings to the idea of preparing for them a greater degree of happiness after death. Mistaken notions of economy were joined to these, seeking in forced labor that wealth and production which are found far more abundantly on free labor. But neither do the eternal laws of morality, which permit not even a good end to be attained through unjust means, nor does the mission of the state, which as the supreme organ of right ought to respect it (*i. e.*, right) under all circumstances and above all interests, permit the existence of slavery, with its horrors and dangers, to continue any longer without an act of immorality and injustice. This was recognized by the commissioners appointed to propose political, social, and economical reforms in Cuba and Porto Rico, without for this reason forgetting, as the undersigned likewise will not forget, the just respect due to material interests, created under the protection of ancient institutions and laws. No progress, no advancement of humanity, is ever accomplished by an absolute disregard of a previously existing state of things, unjust though this may have been, for notwithstanding its unjustice, it has given rise to human relations, the consideration of which it is neither right nor prudent, much less politic, to lay aside, thereby reaching a solution which will only be productive of lasting disturbances.

Besides this, the serious difficulties presented by every social change; the discretion with which liberty should be accorded to persons whom it was considered a crime to call human beings, and for whom labor has been a permanent sign of servitude, disappear almost entirely where the white and civilized population is much more numerous than the colored, and where the majority of the latter have been able to earn a subsistence, and even competence and wealth, by free labor, which experience as well as the teachings of economical science has shown to be the most beneficial and productive.

In order happily and speedily to effect these important changes, which notwithstanding the urgent call for them must receive serious and conscientious study, the undersigned proposes to your highness the appointment of a commission composed of persons of high character and having a knowledge of the real necessities of the country, who in a brief and determinate space of time, but not sufficient for those who must already have formed their opinions, shall propose such reforms and plans as may be necessary to harmonize the social political, and administrative situation of the island of Porto Rico, with the imperative demands of justice and morality, and, as far as possible, with the principles laid down in the democratic constitution of the Spanish nation, which ought to be applied as soon as possible to those remote countries.

With the foregoing considerations the undersigned has the honor to submit to the approval of your highness the accompanying plan of a decree.

MANUEL BECERRA,
Minister of Transmarine Affairs.

MADRID, *September* 10, 1869.

DECREE.

In view of the statements made by the minister of transmarine affairs, with the approval of the council of ministers, I decree as follows:

ARTICLE 1. A commission is hereby appointed, whose duty it shall be to discuss and propose to the minister of transmarine affairs the principles in accordance with which shall be made all plans of laws for political and administrative reform and for the abolition of slavery in the island of Port Rico.

ART. 2. The commission shall consist of a president, (and the minister of transmarine affairs shall act in this capacity,) of fifteen voting members, and the under-secretary of the ministry, who shall act as secretary, with voice and vote. The voting members shall elect the vice-president.

ART. 3. The commission shall remain in office for thirty days precisely from the moment of entering upon the discharge of its duties, which shall take place three days after the publication of the present decree.

ART. 4. The ministry of transmarine affairs will furnish to the commission such data and information as it may possess, and the necessary orders will be given for the execution of this decree.

Done at Madrid, September 10, 1869.

FRANCISCO SERRANO.

The Minister of Transmarine Affairs,
MANUEL BECERRA.

No 95.

Mr. Plumb to Mr. Fish.

HAVANA, *September* 16, 1869.

* * * * * * *

I find that there was published here in the "Diario de la Marina," of the 14th of July last, the only version of the insurgent constitution which I have seen or known of appearing in the Spanish papers of the island.

* * * * * * * *

In this constitution, as so published, it appears by article 24 that "All the inhabitants of the republic are entirely free," and so is in harmony with the previous proclamations referred to in Mr. Hall's and Mr. La Reintrie's dispatches. It does not appear to me to be likely that any other copies than that I now send of the constitution, and those sent by Mr. La Reintrie and Mr. Hall of the proclamations issued, can have been published here, that are any differently worded with reference to slavery; for these, in the manner in which they have been procured, appear to have been designed for circulation on the island rather than especially to be sent abroad.

[Diario de la Marina, Havana, July 14, 1869.—Translation.]

The Bandera Española, of Santiago de Cuba, publishes a curious document, which is said to have been found in Del Gallo street, copied on a half sheet of paper, torn at the creases where it had been folded, dirty and greasy. It is nothing less than the "Constitution of the Cuban Republic," and is as follows:

"CUBAN REPUBLIC.

"*Political constitution which shall remain in force during the war of independence.*

"ARTICLE 1. The legislative power shall reside in a house of representatives.

"ART. 2. Each of the four States into which the island is henceforth divided shall be equally represented in this house.

"ART. 3. These States are: Oriente, Camagney, Las Villas, and Occidente.

"ART. 4. Only citizens of the republic, above twenty years of age, can be representatives.

"ART. 5. No representative can hold any other office under the republic.

"ART. 6. When a vacancy shall occur in the representation of any State the executive of the same shall prescribe measures for a new election.

"ART. 7. The house of representatives shall appoint the president, vested with the executive power, the general-in-chief, the president of the sessions, and its other officers. The general-in-chief is subordinate to the executive, and must make reports to him of his operations.

"ART. 8. The following persons shall be impeached before the house of representatives, if occasion therefor arise: The president of the republic, the general-in-chief, and the members of the house. This impeachment may be made by any citizen; if the house find it worthy of attention it shall submit the party impeached to the judicial power.

"ART. 9. The house of representatives may depose at pleasure the functionaries whose appointment belongs to it.

"ART. 10. The legislative enactments of the house require, in order to become valid, the sanction of the president.

"ART. 11. If they do not obtain it they shall be returned to the house for further deliberation, when the objections presented by the president shall be considered.

"ART. 12. The president is obliged to give or refuse his approval to any law which shall be proposed within ten days.

"ART. 13. Any resolution (law) having been passed by the house a second time, the president shall be obliged to sanction it.

"ART. 14. The following shall always be matters to be settled by law: Taxes, public loans, the ratification of treaties, the declaration and conclusion of war, the authorization of the president to grant letters of marque and reprisal, the raising and maintaining of troops, the providing and sustaining of a fleet, and the declaration of reprisals against an enemy.

"ART. 15. The house of representatives declares itself in permanent session from the moment when the representatives of the people shall ratify this fundamental law until the close of the war.

"ART. 16. The executive power shall reside in the president of the republic.

"ART. 17. Any one, in order to be president, must be at least thirty years of age and have been born in the island of Cuba.

"ART. 18. The president may make treaties, with the ratification of the house, (*i. e.*, subject to the ratification of the house.)

"ART. 19. He shall appoint ambassadors, public ministers, and consuls of the republic in foreign countries.

"ART. 20. He shall receive ambassadors, take care that the laws be faithfully executed, and send his dispatches to all officers of the republic.

"ART. 21. The secretaries of the government (of state, &c.) shall be nominated by the president and appointed by the house.

"ART. 22. The judicial power is independent, its organization shall be the object of a special law.

"ART. 23. In order to become an elector the same conditions are required as in order to be elected.

"ART. 24. All inhabitants of the island are entirely free.

"ART. 25. All citizens of the republic are considered as soldiers of the liberating army.

"ART. 26. The republic recognizes no dignities, special honors, or privileges.

"ART. 27. Citizens of the republic shall receive no honors or distinctions from a foreign country.

"ART. 28. The house cannot assail religious liberty, the freedom of the press, the right of petition, nor any other inalienable right of the people.

"ART. 29. This constitution may be amended whenever the house shall unanimously so determine.

"This constitution was voted for in the free town of Gúaimaro, on the 10th of April, 1869, by the citizens Cárlos M. de Céspedes, president of the constituent assembly, and the citizen deputies, Salvador, Cisneros, Betancourt, Francisco Sanchez, Miguel Betancourt Guerra, Ignacio Agramonte Ceiman, Antonio Zambrana, Jesus Rodriguez, Antonio Alcalá, José Izaguirre, Honorato Castillo, Miguel Géronimo Gutierrez, Avendio Garcia, Tranquilino Valdés, Antonio Lorda, and Edwardo Machado Gómez."

The Bandera Española adds:

"It is said to have been voted for by the citizen Cárlos M. de Céspedes, (the Most Excellent is here wanting; what irreverence!) and the citizen deputies, &c. We are not informed, however, nor do we know, nor does any one know, where, when, or how the voting took place in the various towns of the island, in order to elect these gentlemen, who, as the constitution says, are called deputies. Of what districts, of what departments, of what towns are these citizen deputies the representatives? Who elected them? Who gave them the right or authority to palm themselves off upon the country as representing the opinion of the majority? Heaven help us! Everything done by our revolutionists must be something absurd and ridiculous."

No. 96.

Mr. Plumb to Mr. Fish.

No. 156.] HAVANA, *September* 20, 1869.

During the past few weeks much popular interest has been manifested here in the formation of a volunteer reserve corps, to embrace all who are not now enrolled in the existing organization of volunteers, and especially those men of position whose action in taking a stand or refraining from doing so is calculated to influence public sentiment, and whose adherence usually weighs largely in the moral determination of any cause.

There is much expression, also, of the feeling that the time has now come when all must define their position, and must take sides one way or the other; that those who are not now openly and fully for the preservation of this island to Spain are to be classed with the adherents of the insurrection, and are to be treated accordingly.

A memorial, embracing the projected organization of this reserve corps and the preliminary steps regarding it, has been addressed to the Captain General, and has received and is now receiving the signatures of a large class of influential men, whose names have not before appeared on one side or the other, but who now, whether willingly or not, commit themselves to the side of the maintenance of Spanish authority.

No. 97.

Mr. Plumb to Mr. Fish.

No. 159.] HAVANA, *September* 21, 1869.

There are some signs of the times which attract the eye of the careful observer here, which are deserving of more than a passing notice. One of the most notable is that the people of this island—and to a great extent Havana is to the island what Paris is to France—the people, especially of Havana, now read the newspapers; they therefore think upon current events.

There are ten thousand young men and of middle life, in this city alone, enrolled and armed as volunteers. They feel now that they are a part of the body politic, and they want to know what is said about that, about themselves. They, therefore, now read the newspapers. Reading gives rise to discussion and to thinking, and thinking will some day lead to action.

It is therefore important to know what ideas are thus daily read, what is permitted to be read here, for heretofore there has been a rigid, and there still is a government censorship.

The popular organ of the volunteers is the Voz de Cuba. That paper in its issue of yesterday told its readers, and it was permitted to do so, that it is now not alone the newspapers of the United States that urge the cession to the United States by Spain of one of its most important provinces, nor yet the Times of London, La France, and La Patrie of Paris, nor is it alone the republican papers of Madrid, accustomed to overlook all in their realization of their exaggerated theories, but it is also thoroughly Spanish, and at the same time conservative publications of high standing, and which exercise a great influence over public opinion, organs of parties, and even as it is said of entire provinces that have immense interests in the island of Cuba, that now counsel Spain to the sale or cession of this island to the United States.

It then proceeds to refer to the Diario de Barcelona, which, it states, from its age, its influence, the moderation and practical good sense which distinguishes it, is read with interest in all the Catalan provinces, in much of the rest of Spain, and also abroad, where it has reason to know it is highly appreciated—and it states that this paper in a recent article emits the following conclusion:

"In our judgment no other resource remains to us but to open negotiations with the United States for the cession to them of our Antilles."

The Voz de Cuba, of course, proceeds to combat this view, which it characterizes as absurd; but the notable fact is that the publication of such an opinion as this and its open comment has now been reached in Cuba.

* * * * * * *

No. 98.

General Sickles to Mr. Fish.

No. 22.] MADRID, *September* 25, 1869.

* * * * * * *

In answer to my question about the volunteers, he (General Prim) said that the government did not propose to have a repetition of the scenes which took place in the time of General Dulce.

I expressed my gratification at this information, and hoped that the government had also taken measures to prevent those barbarous and cruel executions that had hitherto marked the progress of the war. This was one of the causes that most embarrassed the government of the United States, as the sufferers in these outrages were not only the Cuban insurgents but also Americans, and, in many instances, persons entirely innocent of any participation in the insurrection.

General Prim stated that he had given very severe and positive orders on that subject to the Captain General, that these scandalous scenes should be prevented at all hazards; and that General de Rodas had answered, avowing his intention of putting a stop to such occurrences, and of resorting to the punishment of death, if necessary, to accomplish this.

I said I would beg to commend to the consideration of the Spanish government the propriety of adopting the system of cartel, and treatment of prisoners according to the rules of ordinary warfare; that this would at once divest the war of its savage character, and make more practicable the projects of pacification which the government entertained.

General Prim said that it was necessary to proceed gradually and surely. The government was now occupied with various decrees carrying its liberal policy into effect in Cuba. A decree would soon be issued initiating the gradual abolition of slavery, by giving freedom to all negroes born after date. The government would also soon announce a plan of administration and municipal reform for Cuba; all this without waiting for the termination of the war. * * *

No. 99.

[Telegram.]

General Sickles to Mr. Fish.

MADRID, *September* 25, 1869.

* * * * * * *

Measures already taken to disarm volunteers simultaneously with cessation of hostilities. Severe and positive orders given to stop the scandalous execution of captives, and like cruelties. General de Rodas promises to do so at all hazards.

A decree will be promulgated forthwith for the gradual abolition of slavery. Government will proceed with liberal reforms, without waiting for termination of war. * * * *

No. 100.

[Confidential.]

Mr. Davis to Mr. Plumb.

No. 46.] WASHINGTON, *September* 28, 1869.

We get information from Madrid that measures have already been taken there to disarm the volunteers in Cuba simultaneously with a proposed cessation of hostilities, and that severe and positive orders have been given to stop the scandalous execution of captives, and like cruelties, and it is further said that General de Rodas promises to do so at all hazards. The same day that this information came by cable, a dispatch was received from you announcing the promotion of General Valmaseda, the perpetrator of the worst of the cruelties, and the information contained in your No. 156, also, would seem to indicate that the information from Madrid may be correct.

We are also informed from Madrid that a decree will be projected forthwith for the immediate abolition of slavery, while the general tenor of the information from Cuba is the other way.

It is of great importance that the department should know at an early date how far the news from Madrid can be depended on. You will, therefore, please ascertain, so far as you can do so without exciting suspicion, whether the purposes of the cabinet at Madrid in these important respects are known in Cuba, and whether they are, or can be, carried out. I need not point out to you how delicate an investigation this is; how sensitive the Spanish authorities may be at even the instigation of an inquiry; how important it may be for them that the matter should be kept a profound secret until they are ready to act; nor how cautiously you must move in taking any steps under these instructions. Indeed I should hardly feel justified in giving you any instructions on so delicate a subject, were it not that the late public news from Cuba—later than any dispatches from you—seems to indicate that there is some movement going on under the surface, which has not yet been made public. * * * * * *

No. 101.

Mr. Plumb to Mr. Davis.

[Confidential.]

No. 193.] HAVANA, *October* 21, 1869.

I had the honor to receive on the 6th instant your dispatch, No. 46, of the 28th ultimo, marked confidential.

Since its receipt I have endeavored, so far as has been practicable, to obtain further information in addition to that previously derived from my intercourse with officials here and from other sources upon the several points with regard to which you make inquiry.

What I can now say in reply must necessarily be in the form of my general conclusions based upon such information, and upon a careful study of the situation here.

With regard to the first point of your inquiry, the disarmament of the volunteers, I have no hesitation in saying that, whatever may be the desire that to some extent may naturally be entertained by the existing government of Spain in that regard, the execution of such a measure is at present impracticable, and is, I think, so regarded by all the representatives here of Spanish authority; and there are many reasons to believe that no time will arrive, while this island shall remain connected with Spain, when such a measure will become practicable.

That organization appears now to be a permanent power in this island, and has to be taken into account in any political calculations regarding it.

In the deposition of General Dulce, it was disloyal to the authority of the home government. To-day it is devotedly loyal to the preservation of the connection between the island and Spain; and there is little doubt it is due to the presence of this organization, in the early part of the present year, and since, that the island has been saved to the mother country. This organization now numbers probably upward of forty thousand men, well organized, armed, and equipped, and now considerably accustomed to the exercise of arms. They hold all the ports and all the towns, and they have a stake and interest to defend, for they are residents here; they are connected with the commerce and industry of the island, and they expect and desire to remain here. They are not government employés. Their officers are generally men of some position and wealth, as are also very many in the ranks. They have no idea of submitting to, or being ruled by, the Cuban portion of the population. It may be doubted whether all the Cubans in arms within the island number half as many; nor have they the means, the organization, or the arms of the volunteers.

The entire government force that will be here, should all the promised re-enforcements arrive, will not be equal in numbers to the volunteers, and the former soon fraternize with the latter. To attempt to disarm them, therefore, might inaugurate another civil war. The government in Spain must rely either upon the Cubans or upon the Spanish residents. It is hardly probable it would now leave the latter to unite with the former. Under more liberal institutions, after the insurrection shall have been put down, it is believed that both may again be united.

To the power of the volunteers, as an armed force, there is now added, co-operating with it, another species of organization, ostensibly for purely patriotic, that is Spanish, purposes, which is known in this city as the "Casino Español," or Spanish Club; in the city of Matanzas by that of "the National Conservative Committee of Matanzas," and in other towns by similar local names. These organizations are as potent in their sphere as were our loyal Union leagues during the war. If they are not now, they may at any time become, powerful political organizations.

The expenses of the very re-enforcements now being sent to the island from Spain are borne, in great part, by voluntary contributions from here, toward the raising of which, those who compose these organizations have largely contributed.

Under these circumstances, I do not well see how the design referred to can be entertained by the government of Madrid, except as a desired and remote possibility, and that to the Captain General here it must be irksome to feel that he has constantly to defer, or hold in account the prejudices and the power of the volunteers, especially as affects his action in the remoter points and interior of the island. Any one in his place—any successor of a Captain General deposed by that influence—must feel, as well as the government whose representative was so set aside, a desire to draw the reins upon an organization become so powerful. But whether this can be done, and when, are questions that certainly have to give place to the first and more immediate issue—that of putting down the insurrection.

With regard to a simultaneous proposed cessation of hostilities, the point has evidently to be considered only in its latter aspect.

I cannot learn that any such intention is entertained here, nor is there anything in the nature of the situation that appears to render such a measure probable or practicable.

There is some reason to believe that considerable numbers of the insurgents are submitting, and I think it is believed that the time is near at hand when the insurgents will have to be dealt with mainly in that light, and, except with reference to the leaders, there appears to be a disposition to observe a policy of clemency. Any idea of a cessation of hostilities, looking to any other end than the submission of the insurgents, would, apparently, be scouted under the present circumstances, and might be dangerous.

That the enlightened and liberal men who are now at the head of the government of Spain are sincere in wishing well to this island; are willing to concede to it all desirable reforms, and that the instructions which have been issued to the representative here seek to stay the effusion of blood, I most sincerely believe, and I also believe that General Caballero de Rodas, and those who are now more immediately associated with him in the government of this island, second these desires, and will endeavor to carry them out, but much must be left to their discretion, and the full character of all the peculiar and exceptional circumstances now existing here can hardly be appreciated at Madrid, or elsewhere abroad.

I have had no occasion whatever to doubt the good intentions of General Rodas, but the circumstances with which he has to deal may in some cases be stronger than his present power to overcome them.

A communication from the minister of ultramar addressed to the Captain General of this island, containing instructions relating to the conduct of the war here, in the sense of the information received by the department, appears to have been published in Madrid since the date of your dispatch, and has doubtless been communicated to the department by the legation there.

I do not doubt General Rodas's entire willingness to act in accordance with such instructions.

With reference to the question of slavery, I have found but one opinion here, and that is, that its abolition is now a question only of whether it shall be immediate, or extend over a period of, say, five or more years. I think the opinion is almost universal that it would be safer for all interests that the measure should be made gradual, freeing at once all born hereafter, and, by a system of regulated labor, accomplishing total emancipation within a brief term of years.

There is also opposition to the question being touched until the deputies from this island can be heard in the Cortes regarding it, and therefore a belief that it should be deferred until the insurrection shall have been put down.

One of the largest, if not the largest, slaveholder on the island, in conversation with me some time since, stated that he would be entirely willing to accept abolition effected in a term of five years, and I have met no one yet who does not admit the measure, if accomplished in this manner, to be not only necessary but desirable.

But I do not find any expression of belief in official quarters that a leclaration of immediate, total abolition would be practicable, and I can hardly think the government of Spain designs to treat the question in that way.

With tranquillity here, and as a measure to be accomplished within a period of five or eight years, I do not think the question of the abolition of slavery on this island would present any serious difficulties, nor would it in this manner be attended, it is believed, with any great disturbance of the labor or the production of the island.

There certainly does not exist here now any extended belief in the possibility of the preservation of the institution, and the character of the present government of Spain would appear to render its early termination certain, so far as may depend upon action from that quarter. By immediate abolition, as referred to in your dispatch, may be meant the freedom of all born after the date of the decree, as also, perhaps, total emancipation within a brief period. Instantaneous abolition, while it might, if there is tranquillity, not be so destructive to labor here as it is elsewhere, would yet, it is believed, create great apprehension and disorganization, as also political dissatisfaction.

* * * * * *

On that occasion I inquired of General La Torre, putting the question to him directly, how many foreigners, from all the sources of information he had had, he thought there now were in the ranks of the insurgents within the eastern department. He replied, without any hesitation, that he did not believe the number exceeded ninety or one hundred.

All of the information I have received tends to confirm the correctness of this statement. I doubt if the total number within the island exceeds one hundred and fifty.

* * * * * *

No. 102.

Mr. Plumb to Mr. Fish.

No. 167.] HAVANA, *September* 27, 1869.

Mr. Hall, United States consul at Matanzas, has transmitted to me what purports to be a copy of a circular issued on the 10th instant by the governor of Matanzas to the commanders of the different corps of volunteers within that jurisdiction, relating to the arrests made, and other unauthorized powers assumed by the volunteers from which there is too much reason to believe there is resulting a most undesirable state of affairs, not only in the vicinity of Matanzas, but in many other localities on the island.

I beg to inclose to you a translation of this document as so received herewith.

As illustrative of these violent and unauthorized proceedings, I further transmit to you herewith, a copy in English, which I have also received from Mr. Hall, of what purports to be a detailed narrative of the action of the volunteers in the special case referred to by the governor of Matanzas.

CIRCULAR OF THE GOVERNOR OF MATANZAS TO THE DIFFERENT COMMANDERS OF THE CORPS OF VOLUNTEERS.

[Translation.]

On assuming charge, on my return to this city, of the dispatch of the affairs of the commandancy general, I have found a legal process, already decided, instituted to examine the antecedents of a certain Don Francisco Rodriguez, who was arrested on the night of the 1st instant, by the volunteers of company two of the third battalion—Don Matias Maroto and Don Vicente Clarens.

I have examined with the same care with which I customarily examine this class of proceedings, and it appears to be proved that the civilian Rodriguez is an inoffensive old man, without any antecedents which appear to his prejudice.

It is also proved that the individuals who arrested him proceeded to do so of their own volition, without the knowledge of the authorities, without the presence of any agent of the same, and upon mere presumption, and there are even witnesses who testify that they used the name of the police when they made the apprehension, and appealed to that of the authority to effect the encarcelacion.

By the declaration of the volunteers, Maroto and Clarens, it appears that these individuals proceeded without malice, violating the orders and laws in force through ignorance as to the responsibility they assumed; but as I observe that an abusive and punishable system has been adopted, some being prompted by an exaggerated zeal, and others from a want of knowledge of the penalties to be imposed for their conduct, I believe it is desirable to make some remarks of admonition to you in order to prevent the illegal and unnecessary course adopted by several parties which tends to disturb the public peace, and to create a want of confidence among families, and, perhaps, to gratify personal vengeance.

Well known to all is my firm resolution of pursuing and bringing the full force of the law to bear upon those against whom it be proven that they directly or indirectly contribute toward aiding in fomenting the insurrection, and the moment that there is a conviction of this fact the people of all classes and conditions should place confidence in the authority, and call upon the same at any hour, and upon the functionaries who depend upon the same, in order to notify them and communicate what they know, and to make the remarks they deem proper, and they may rest assured that I shall not neglect any means which may contribute to the discovery of the offense wherever I am informed it exists, and I shall adopt active and prompt measures for the chastisement of the same.

The volunteer force, as also all who bear arms, is nothing less, in cases where there is a necessity of a warrant for the searching of a house, than an auxiliary of the authorities charged with carrying the same into effect; any other proceeding is illegal, prenicious, and fruitless, and gives room to reckless acts to which I cannot consent, nor can the majority of the individuals who compose the corps whose officers I now address consent to the same; and I say reckless acts, because such are those when, while shielded with the uniform of volunteers, some few persons dare to assume upon themselves certain attributes for which they are not competent; inasmuch as there exist zealous, active, and intelligent public functionaries, charged with obtaining the same results without altering the legal course established by the laws. Those who commit said offenses incur, likewise, in the crimes of *riots, violent force, and searching of houses*, prescribed in the ordinances of war—in note 9, title 30, book 4, and the laws 1, 2, 3, 8, and 9, title 10, part 7, book 8, of the new collection of statutes—which punish them with severe penalties, according to the circumstances of the case, it being well to observe that judgment in these cases belongs to those who exercise common law jurisdiction, without their being able to allege any privilege which exempts them from the same, as appears by the stipulations of laws 4 and 5, title 11, book 12, of the new collection of statutes before cited.

In consequence, I trust that you, as commander-in-chief of this corps of volunteers, calling together the officers and members of the same and reading to them this communication, will endeavor to diffuse among all of them doctrines of order, and these provisions of the law of which some are ignorant, in order to avoid personal conflicts, which would be occasioned by their non-observance; and to state to them that they can with all confidence call upon my authority, upon the chief of public protection and security, or on the inspectors or constables, in cases when they may have any affair or incident of interest to denounce, and that these will proceed to act in obedience to the laws and of right; and so justice will be done and the crime shall not be unpunished.

God keep you many years. Matanzas, September 10, 1869.

The Colonel Commandant General,
RAMON FAJARDO.

The LIEUTENANT COLONEL,
First in command of the battalion of volunteers of this city.

DETAILED NARRATIVE OF THE PROCEEDINGS OF THE VOLUNTEERS IN THE CASE REFERRED TO IN THE PRECEDING CIRCULAR.

Don José Francisco Rodriguez, brother to Don Agustin Rodriguez, who rose in Jaguey Grande several months ago, a resident of Macuriges, where he owned a grazing farm, aged sixty-five years, with wife, two daughters, (one of which insane,) and seven grand-children, the youngest of which is two months old, lately left his house to escort to the "Guira," a village station on the Matanzas railway, his sister-in-law, and wife of Don Agustin, who had been ordered or advised to quit the jurisdiction of Colon. Arriving at the Guira, of the rail on the "Jutia," he immediately returned per rail to the station Torriente, where he found the teacher of his grandchildren waiting for him with a led horse, and was informed that his son-in-law, a near relative of Don Jórge Rodriguez, resident at his father-in-law's, had been arrested by Don José Menendez, a native of the Canary Islands, and commander of a party of volunteers, and taken to Jaguey to give a declaration, and that there was a rumor of his having been shot on the way, as is the practice. The teacher was sent early next morning to Jaguey to inquire, and returned with the tidings that Mr. Jórge Rodriguez, aged forty-four, and a man exclusively dedicated to the care of his family, had been shot on reaching the public square of Jaguey. Don Francisco then broke the news to his widowed daughter, and determined to remove his family to Matanzas, but first passed on to Colon to notify the lieutenant governor of what had happened, and solicit a "pasé de domicilio" for himself and family. On the first point the answer was that he could do nothing, and the "pasé" was refused. Don Francisco, however, provided with "cedulas" of transit, came to Matanzas, and took house in New Town, in the street called Espiritu Santo, which extends from the cavalry barracks westward to and through the waste common called the Palmar de Junco. On Saturday, the 4th September, he was arrested in his house, at midnight, by two volunteers, who pretended to act by authority, and marched off in the center and in single file, one volunteer before him and the other behind. The march being in the direction of the common, on arriving at the first waste, and the rear rank summoning the front to join him, Don Francisco stopped and declared that he would proceed no further, expressing his desire to be shot there, in preference to going any further. One of the men answered that *all* should die, when a watchman came up and said that they should retrace their steps and take their prisoner to the cavalry barracks, whence they should deliver him to the chief of police, who was there at that moment. They obeyed, and on their way another watchman came running up and ordered them to stop, as the chief of police was already coming up. This functionary arrived and put several questions to Don Francisco, as to name, whence he came, &c., and Don Francisco then announced to him that he would not consent, in any way, to remain in custody of volunteers, as he presumed that they sought his life. The chief of police then took him to the police barracks, where he remained thirty-six hours, and was decently treated. At liberty he received a letter from the "mayoral" or overseer of his farm, informing him that the celebrated Durante, at the head of his command, the volunteers, "Tiradores de la muerte," had made a descent on the farm and carried away thirty head of horned cattle and three horses, and on leaving declared that not even a flower should be extracted from the place, as everything was "embargoed" by himself. The overseer had furthermore sent a fat hog to Durante, in obedience to his order, as appeared by a letter he had received from Durante, and which he enclosed as a voucher for the missing fat hog. Don Francisco Rodriguez, now thoroughly alarmed, called on his old friend and neighbor planter, Du Cosme Torriente, colonel of the volunteers at Matanzas, who recommended immediately his case to his friend, M. Cardenal, assessor to the mercantile tribunal, and influential member of the "comité nacional conservador," who took him to his own house to sleep, out of harm's way, and next day accompanied him to the governor's, to whom Mr. Cardenal stated the case in all its details, and requested the governor to ask a "pasé de domicilio" for Mr. Rodriguez from the lieutenant governor of Colon, in order to avoid any pretext for murder on the part of the volunteers. Governor Farjardo requested Mr. Rodriguez to hand him, and leave him, Durante's letter, which he would forward to the lieutenant governor of Colon for his information, and that he might inquire with what authority Durante had embargoed and extracted cattle, &c. Governor Fajardo likewise gave order to the police to respect Mr. Rodriguez as an honest person and peaceful citizen, and to provide him with a certificate to that effect, in which it should be stated that he was, for a moment, unprovided with a "pasé de domicilio" for himself, family, and servants, which would shortly arrive from Colon.

The chief of police provided Mr. Rodriguez with said document. It is even whispered that the governor gave out a secret circular, almost a dignified one, which had been confidentially read to all the volunteers, censuring the act of the two patriotic members of their corps who had waylaid Mr. R. This I cannot vouch for, although it is universally admitted sub rosa; however, Mr. R. breathed more freely, and Mr. Cardenal bestirred himself in his behalf, and promised that he would see him through and have his property restored to him.

Mr. Rodriguez then moved to Matanzas proper, No. 84 Velarde street, having fallen sick from despondency and grief and with symptoms of low fever, such as a sensation of cold and much vomiting; was ordered quinine by a physician called in. This happened on the first day of his moving to his new home, and on the second day, which was the 18th instant, Mr. R. was again imprisoned, it is said, by order coming from Colon, and passed feverish to the hospital, where he was closely confined in the dungeon, (calabozo;) a peninsular who has been in his service called on Sunday at the hospital, where he was refused intercourse with Mr. Rodriguez, as the gentleman was "incommunicado," and, besides, senseless, as it was supposed from congestion of the brain.

The widowed daughter of Mr. Rodriguez called upon Governor Fajardo, beseeching him to permit her father to be conveyed as a prisoner to his own house, that he might be assisted by his family. Her persistent supplications at last extorted from the governor a promise that he would give orders that the old gentleman should be conveyed to his home.

It appears that the governor gave the order, as the volunteers took the body of Mr Rodriguez at 5 o'clock of Tuesday morning to the house, where it was received by the frenzied family that rushed to meet the husband, the father and the grandfather. The body was conveyed in a dirty hospital coffin. The immediate cause of death I ignore, as no value can be scientifically given to the answer on that point, given by the volunteer sentinel: "Murió de rabia carajo!"

No. 103.

Mr. Plumb to Mr. Davis.

No. 181.] HAVANA, *October* 15, 1869.

On the 28th ultimo, a decree, of which I inclose a copy and translation herewith, was issued by the Captain General, relating to passengers embarking and vessels carrying passengers from the ports of this island.

The objectionable character of some of the provisions of this decree has led me to confer with the authorities here upon the subject, and I have pleasure in now being able to transmit to you herewith a copy and translation of regulations under which the decree is to be executed, which have in consequence been issued, and were published in the Gazette of yesterday, which very materially modify the character of the original decree.

I have found in this matter a liberal disposition on the part of the Captain General and other authorities, when once their attention was called to the objectionable features of the decree as first issued.

Most of the steamers under the flag of the United States leaving this port are in transit from one port of the United States to another, or from a Mexican port to a port in the United States, and *vice versa.*

These vessels have passengers on board without passports, making the voyage between such ports.

There is no evidence relating to their character except the passenger list of the steamer and the declarations of the officers.

It is obviously impossible to permit such passengers to be at the discretion of any officer in a foreign port to distinguish between them and those who may have embarked clandestinely in this harbor.

I am assured by the authorities here that the officers intrusted with the execution of this decree will be so instructed that no case can arise of molestation to such passengers in transit.

[Translation.]

SUPERIOR POLITICAL GOVERNMENT OF THE PROVINCE OF CUBA.

DECREE.

Owing to the abuse which is being practiced by masters of steamships and sailing vessels that daily leave the ports of the island admitting on board persons who are not provided with the necessary passports, I have deemed proper to resolve the following:

1st. In future all steam or sailing vessels that depart from whatever port of the island and admit passengers shall be searched, after weighing anchor, by the employé of the police designated for that purpose, who will compare the passports delivered to him by the captain with the number of passengers, as also the description of both, and if any one is found without that document he will be taken from on board.

Every person found in this case shall pay a fine of two hundred dollars or shall suffer the same number of days imprisonment.

The captain of the vessel shall pay a fine of two hundred dollars for every such person, which shall be paid before leaving, unless the consignee obliges himself to make the payment.

2d. Consignees who issue passage tickets without the presentation of a passport shall pay a fine of two hundred dollars.

The captains of the ports are charged to see to the compliance with this decree.

CABALLERO DE RODAS.

HAVANA, *September* 28, 1869.

[From the Official Gazette, Havana, October 14, 1869.—Translation.]

SUPERIOR POLITICAL GOVERNMENT OF THE PROVINCE OF CUBA, OFFICE OF THE SECRETARY.

His excellency, the superior political governor, has been pleased to sanction the following regulations, which are to be observed by the functionaries who are to execute the decree of the 28th of September, relating to passengers who leave this island:

1st. The employés of the police will be advised as to the hour of sailing of vessels carrying passengers, and, in conformity therewith, will proceed to the examination ordered, with the necessary anticipation, in order not to delay nor to hinder the movements of the vessel.

2d. Said examination must be terminated before, and not after, weighing the anchor, as erroneously appears in the decree referred to; nevertheless, the employés for this purpose shall remain on board until the vessel shall have arrived alongside the guard-ship, or at the point designated for her dismissal.

3d. The employés of the police shall perform the operations of examinations with that urbanity and the good manners which on all occasions are recommended to them.

4th. They shall, upon application, obtain assistance of the captains of the port, should the same be necessary.

5th. The fines which are prescribed for passengers without passports, and to the consignees who become liable to the same, will be paid with stamped paper of the usual class, giving the interested parties a proper receipt.

6th. It is to be understood that the fine prescribed for the captains of vessels shall not be imposed if they have not had knowledge of the entrance on board of such infractors, and they declare the same in writing and over their signature.

The Secretary,

CESAREO FERNANDEZ.

HAVANA, *October* 13, 1869.

No. 104.

Mr. Fish to Mr. Plumb.

No. 63.] WASHINGTON, *October* 25, 1869.

Your dispatch No. 181 of the 15th instant has been received. The decree which accompanied it, relative to passengers embarking and vessels carrying passengers from the ports of Cuba, has been taken into consideration in connection with the rules for the execution of the decree, which you say are the result of your conference with the authorities upon the subject. It is apprehended that the decree, even if faithfully and impartially carried into effect, pursuant to those rules, may still lead to abuses of the just rights of citizens of the United States, which it is now especially desirable for both governments to anticipate and avoid.

The first article of the decree provides that if any one is found without a passport on board a vessel about to start from a Cuban port, that person shall be liable to a fine of one hundred dollars and the master of the vessel to a fine of two hundred dollars.

There can be no objection to this provision so far as it may relate to any person who may have been charged with an offense against Spanish law, or to Spanish subjects who may not have been so charged. This government, however, cannot acquiesce in the application of the decree to citizens of the United States, especially to those who may be passengers on board vessels which may merely touch at Havana, on their way to some other port. The application of the decree to passengers on board the steamers which may ply between New York and New Orleans would be particularly offensive. It is probable that passengers, by the latter steamers especially, seldom take passports. To require them so to do merely for the privilege of entering the port of Havana, probably without any intention of landing there, and to exact the fine for an omission to comply with the requirement, seems to be a useless and irritating exercise of power.

This government has no disposition to screen from Spanish authority any person who may have committed or may contemplate the commission of an offense against that authority. It also acknowledges the right and the duty of that authority, especially at this juncture, to adopt extraordinary precautions for self-defense. We are aware of the necessity for this from having been compelled to take a similar course during our late civil war. We, however, endeavored to respect the freedom of well-meaning foreigners, and certainly never adopted or carried into effect any measure as objectionable as the decree referred to. You will, consequently, with firmness, but with courtesy, protest against the indiscriminate execution of that decree.

A copy of this instruction will be communicated to Mr. Roberts, the envoy extraordinary and minister plenipotentiary of Spain here, in order that he may make known to the proper authorities the views of this government on the subject.

No. 105.

Mr. Plumb to Mr. Fish.

No. 225.] HAVANA, *November* 17, 1869.

I had the honor to receive, on the 3d instant, your dispatch No. 63, of the 25th ultimo, upon the subject of the decree issued by the Captain General of this island on the 28th of September last, relating to passengers embarking and vessels carrying passengers from the ports of Cuba, which decree was transmitted to the department with my dispatch No. 181, of the 15th of October.

By the same mail that brought me your dispatch, there was received here, as I have learned, from the Spanish minister at Washington, a transcript of the same, as communicated to him by the department, in order that he might make known to the proper authorities the views of the government of the United States upon the subject of the said decree. I further learn that a reply to his communication was made by General Carbo, acting in the temporary absence of General Rodas, and was forwarded by the mail of the 13th instant.

Deeming it best to await the return of General Rodas and the political secretary, Mr. Fernandez, before acting under the instruction contained in your dispatch, I have, in an interview with them to-day, stated that I had received your instructions to protest against the indiscriminate execution of the decree referred to.

The Captain General assured me that the decree in question was not intended to apply to passengers in transit, and would not be so applied, and that if any modification in this respect of the decree and regulations, as issued, was necessary, to remove misapprehension, it would immediately be made.

I understood modifications to this effect will be issued and published in the Gazette, possibly in time to send by this mail.

It is proper I should state that no case has yet been brought to my notice of difficulty experienced by any citizen of the United States arising from the operations of the said decree, as thus far executed.

No. 106.

Mr. Plumb to Mr. Fish.

No. 230.] HAVANA, *November* 20, 1869.

* * * * * * *

Referring to my dispatch No. 225, of the 17th instant, I have now the honor to transmit herewith a copy of an order published in the Official Gazette of last evening, explanatory of the decree of the 28th of September last, relating to passengers embarking and vessels carrying passengers from the ports of this island, and declaring that the said decree does not apply to passengers in transit.

[Translation.]

SUPERIOR POLITICAL GOVERNMENT OF CUBA, OFFICE OF THE SECRETARY.

Doubts having arisen with regard to the first article of the decree of the 28th of September last, notwithstanding the instructions published on the 13th of October for its execution, his excellency the superior political governor has seen fit to declare, in order to avoid further misunderstanding, and although this is distinctly stated in the said article, that it only applies to passengers embarking in the ports of this island, and not to those arriving in transit; which is published for the information of whom it may concern.

Havana, November 19, 1869.

The Secretary,

CASAREO FERNANDEZ.

No. 107.

General Sickles to Mr. Fish.

No. 26.] MADRID, *October* 16, 1869.

I have the honor to transmit herewith a copy * * * * and translation of his (Mr. Silvela's) reply, dated the 8th instant; also a copy of the decree concerning liberty of worship in the Island of Cuba, and the circular of the minister of ultramar, referred to in Mr. Silvela's note, taken from the Official Gazette of the 28th September.

Mr. Silvela to General Sickles.

[Translation.]

OCTOBER 8.

* * * * * * * * *

Your excellency observes that while the President of the republic reserves his liberty of action, he will be happy if he can contribute in anything to the pacification of Cuba, a result equally advantageous to the interests of America and of Spain.

This frank and noble declaration is extremely satisfactory, and I beg that your excellency will present to the President the thanks of the Spanish government. At the same time, I venture to indicate two acts which it is in his power to accomplish, and which will serve as an illustration of these loyal and friendly purposes toward Spain.

The first is to exercise all his natural influence upon those who, having taken refuge in American territory, foment the rebellion, to the end that they, following the generous initiative of the Spanish government, contained in the Gazette of the 28th of September, may induce their followers to abstain from giving a savage character to the conflict, with the outrages and ferocious crimes with which they have been hitherto stained.

The Spanish government having manifested its purpose to confine the contest within the limits prescribed by modern civilization, orders having been given to the authorities to proceed with all the moderation required by humanity, it would be truly monstrous if the insurgents should continue the barbarous conflict which they have begun, and should keep on perpetrating the excesses which outrage the consciences of honorable men, rendering themselves wholly unworthy of the generous hospitality which the republic dispenses to those who, under the name of the Cuban Junta, stand forth as promoters of the insurrection. The Spanish government having spontaneously set this example, and being resolved to act in a civilizing and humanitarian sense, a wide field is opened to the United States to show their sympathies and their good will toward a government and a nation which proceeds in this manner, notwithstanding the conduct of the rebels.

The second act, which may illustrate the sincerity of the President's offers, is in regard to the gunboats constructed in the United States by the order and at the expense of Spain, not to go against Peru, nor even to fight the insurgents of Cuba, but to defend our coasts against the aggressions of filibusters and pirates.

The strongest argument which your excellency has used on various occasions to endeavor to demonstrate the importance of the insurrection has been the extent of its duration; but this argument will have no weight while the insurrection receives continual increase and nutriment from abroad; while it does not remain isolated and without other partisans and champions than the Cubans themselves. Only when the insurrection persists in this manner can it be urged that it is rooted in the country; that the majority of the Cubans desire to be independent, and even that they are worthy to be so, and are possessed of sufficient means, vigor, and energy to form a nationality and a separate state. At this time, in the present state of things on that island, Spain cannot believe nor admit that the majority of the Cubans incline to separation from the mother country, but that a turbulent and blind minority, excited and aided by adventurers and speculators of other countries, by filibusters and pirates guided by evil passions and not by patriotic purposes, aspire to overcome the general will of their own countrymen, and that this is the sole cause of the discord which we deplore. At this time Spain does not and cannot see in Cuba the profound sentiment and true capacity of independence, and therefore, if she should consent to a separation from that rich and ancient colony, she would not have the great consolation of thinking that she was giving existence to a new nation, but the deep remorse of weakly abandoning her own children—of leaving unprotected a people of her own language and race to miserably perish and disappear.

* * * * * * * * *

No. 108.

Mr. Plumb to Mr. Davis.

No. 195.] HAVANA, *October* 26, 1869.

I have the honor to inclose to you herewith a copy of a decree published in the Official Gazette of this city, on Sunday, the 24th instant, establishing freedom of religion in this island.

This great step of progress in a country so closely connected with us as is the Island of Cuba, I have deemed should receive some notice on the part of the representative here of the United States, and I have therefore to-day called upon the Captain General, and have presented to him, in that character, my congratulations upon the adoption of this most important measure, in which I assured him the people and the government of the United States could not but feel a deep interest, forming, as the principle of religious liberty does, one of the cardinal bases of our institutions.

General Rodas said it was a source of great satisfaction to him to have the privilege of placing his signature to a measure of this character.

[Translation—Official.]

SUPERIOR POLITICAL GOVERNMENT OF THE PROVINCE OF CUBA—REGENCY OF THE KINGDOM—MINISTRY OF ULTRAMAR.

SIR: One of the most sacred rights possessed by the human race, religious liberty unanimously demanded by popular assemblies, has, at length, been legitimately consecrated by the Spanish democratic constitution, in which it is expressly declared that the State, as an institution called to accomplish one great end of life, can neither penetrate into the recesses of the spirits of man, and should not impede manifestations which are foreign to it. The natural limits which separate the domain of religion from that of politics being thus distinctly drawn, the pious man will no longer fear lest a foreign authority dictate to the conscience laws which, right though they may be, carry with them a denial of the religion which they pretend to aid, tacitly supposing that it has not within itself reasons to exist, and capable, at most, of disguising inward indifference with the rigor or the ostentation of the most scrupulous practices. Nor will the state view with fear a power which, recognizing no authority among men, and uniting all powers in its own hand, might, perhaps, think again to raise pretensions to guardianship and political power, which, if they deserved to exist in former times, would now involve the condemnation of science and history.

Spain could not stand remote from the general movement of Europe and the world. It would have been useless and impolitic to try to sustain, by artificial means as a universal creed, what does not seem equally acceptable to the intelligence of all Spaniards, and experience admonished us to prevent struggles for power, which are almost always precursors of lamentable catastrophes. These considerations become, if possible, more weighty when applied to the inhabitants of the Spanish Antilles. Very near to a continent where religious liberty is a universal fact; close to a powerful republic, whose most free constitution has none like it in Europe, except that of Spain; needing emigrants to people their fertile though abandoned fields, and open, by reason of their insular position, to contact with all nations, it would be unjust to deny to foreigners who, by their intelligence, labor, and capital, contribute to their (*i. e.*, that of the Antilles) enviable prosperity, the privilege of openly holding religious creeds which are certainly deserving of respect; and would likewise be dangerous, and especially inopportune, to alienate from us, by useless and unjustifiable intolerance, the sympathies of the friendly nations, and vain and illusory to maintain legal barriers which the necessities of commerce, that relentless destroyer of all exclusiveness, must constantly pass. And as to the Spaniards who were born in the territories, our course would be most illogical were we to deny them a right which, on the mere consideration that they are men, we accord to natives of the peninsula; we should thus oppose the irresistible tendency of the age, which directly conducts to the fraternal union of nations. The government, which is the guardian of the unity of the state, must defend, even by force, the integrity of its territory, which is but another expression of said unity; but it is determined, aided by the will of a people whose courage and energy increase in proportion to the difficulties that arise, to spare, for the attainment of this object, neither efforts nor sacrifices. It must also (and it has given many proofs of its firm intention to do so) inaugurate the necessary reforms, in order that our brethren beyond the sea may enter upon the life of liberty and justice which Spain, by the revolution of September, has conquered for all her sons. For these reasons the undersigned minister has the honor to propose to your highness the following plan of a decree.

The Minister of Ultramar,

MANUEL BECERRA.

MADRID, *September* 20, 1869.

DECREE.

In accordance with the suggestion of the minister of ultramar, (*i. e.*, of the Spanish transmarine possessions,) with the approval of the council of ministers, I decree as follows:

ARTICLE I. The public and private exercise of the religion which they may profess is guaranteed to all inhabitants of the Spanish Antilles, without any limitations, save the universal rules of propriety and law.

ART. II. The obtainment and discharge of all public functions, as well as the acquisition and exercise of civil and political rights, are independent of creeds.

ART. III. The government will give due notice to the Cortes of the present decree.

Done at Madrid, September 26, 1869.

FRANCISCO SERRANO.

The Minister of Ultramar,

MANUEL BECERRA.

HAVANA, *October* 23, 1869.

Let it be observed.

CABALLERO DE RODAS.

No. 109.

Mr. Plumb to Mr. Davis.

No. 196.] HAVANA, *October* 26, 1869.

Another reform of some importance has been established here, in the publication on the 20th instant of a decree removing the restrictions which for some time have existed upon the formation of joint-stock companies for industrial and other purposes, and terminating after a short period the intervention which the government has heretofore had in such companies.

* * * * * * * * *

No. 110.

Mr. Plumb to Mr. Fish.

No. 183.] HAVANA, *October* 15, 1869.

* * * * * * * * *

Shortly after the insurrection commenced last year, the insurgents occupied the town of Bayamo, a place of two thousand three hundred whites, two thousand eight hundred free blacks, and nine hundred slaves, and subsequently destroyed it.

They also temporarily occupied the town of Holguin, a place of two thousand nine hundred whites, one thousand four hundred free blacks, and five hundred and sixty slaves.

Since then the only places that have been mentioned as in their possession are Sibamcá, a small village or hamlet in the district of Puerto Principe, and Guaimaro, another village stated to have five hundred inhabitants.

No. 111.

Mr. Plumb to Mr. Davis.

No. 207.] HAVANA, *November* 2, 1869.

In my dispatch No. 183, of the 15th ultimo, I stated that the only towns on this island that have recently been reported as in possession of the insurgents were Sibamcá, a small village or hamlet in the district of Puerto Principe, and Guaimaro, another village stated to have five hundred inhabitants.

It now appears that both of these places have been destroyed.

Having seen in the papers here a statement to that effect, I have made inquiry through both private and official channels, and the assertions appear to be confirmed.

No. 112.

Mr. Plumb to Mr. Davis.

No. 208.] HAVANA, *November* 2, 1869.

On the 30th ultimo I received from Mr. Hall, United States consul at Matanzas, a letter, in which he states as follows:

"Inclosed I send you a slip that was probably printed in New York. Comments upon it are unnecessary. Evidently the leaders of the insurrection, despairing of getting up a rising of the whites in this part of the island, have commenced tampering with the negroes. The consequences, if the plan should succeed, will be fearful for the blacks. The slip I send you was received per mail by a resident here. He gave me this one, and destroyed the others."

* * * * * * * * *

Such means as are indicated by this incendiary document are simply those of destruction.

No desirable state of affairs on this island, no change for the better in its institutions, can be brought about through the adoption of such measures.

The elements that will remain will be far more likely to make the island a desert than to successfully establish a free republic.

[Translation.]

The negroes are the same as the whites. The whites are not slaves, nor do they work for the negroes. The negroes, therefore, should not be slaves, nor work for the whites. The Cubans wish that the negroes should be free. The Spaniards wish that the negroes should continue to be slaves. The Cubans are fighting against the Spaniards. The negroes who have any shame should go and fight along with the Cubans. The Spaniards want to kill the Cubans so that the negroes never can be free. The negroes are not fools; they have a great heart, and they will fight along with the Cubans. When the Cubans who are fighting pass where the negroes are, then the negroes should go with them, in order to be free. When the Cubans who are fighting are far from the negroes, then the negroes should run away and should go with the Cubans; but before they go they should burn the estates. If in the estates there were not slaves, and they gave the negroes their money for their work, the estates would be good, for they help the poor people to live; but in the estates the negroes have nothing more than the lash, and all the money is kept by the master to give to the Spaniards. If the estates are not burnt, the crop will be made, and the money of the crop will go to the Spaniards, and then the Spaniards will send a great many soldiers, with guns and cannons, to kill the Cubans, and the negroes will remain slaves forever. The time to fight has come. It is better to be in the mountains fighting along with the Cubans, so that everybody—the negroes the same as the whites—shall be free, than to be working as slaves. *Vive la libertad!* Fire to the estates, and everybody to the mountains to fight against the Spaniards.

LA JUNTA LIBERTADORA DE COLOR,
Press of the Negro Laborante.

HAVANA, *October* 1, 1869.

No. 113.

Mr. Plumb to Mr. Davis.

No. 211.] HAVANA, *November* 4, 1869.

In the Official Gazette of this city of yesterday there is published, by order of the Captain General, what purports to be an order issued by the insurgent General Cavada, commanding in the vicinity of Cienfuegos, addressed to a subordinate insurgent officer, under date of the 5th ultimo.

In this order, stated to have been found among documents taken from the insurgents, after acknowledging the receipt of a communication from the officer referred to, reporting that "in conformity with instructions of the superior government" he had destroyed a certain sugar estate, Cavada proceeds to order him without delay to destroy a certain other estate called "Marsillan," and then gives a list of various estates which he directs him to destroy as early as possible.

"The estates," he adds, "belonging to Cubans, whose conduct with reference to our cause does not merit chastisement, are to be left until the time, should it arrive, when their destruction becomes a peremptory necessity."

The Captain General, in publishing this document, states that he does so in order that the public may be informed of the plans and intentions of those who call themselves saviors of the interests of this island, and in order that the owners of the estates mentioned may take such measures as may be necessary, in addition to the aid that will be given to them by the forces of the government, to impede, as they are now doing, the destruction of this class of property.

In the same edition of the Gazette there is published what purports to be another document, taken from the insurgents in the department of the four cities, in which, by order of the same insurgent General Cavada, instructions are given for the selection of persons who, as soon as the cane-fields are in proper condition, are to endeavor to effect their total destruction. This at certain seasons of the year, say by the month of January next, can be easily accomplished by setting them on fire, if there are persons so evilly disposed.

In the publication of this document it is stated that, in consequence of the same, the Captain General has directed that from that date, the 3d instant, all incendiaries who may be apprehended, whatever their number may be, shall be immediately shot.

Should the desperate course of warfare that appears to have been adopted by the insurgent leaders be persisted in, and the general destruction of the cane-fields be attempted, the exasperation that will ensue may lead to a fearful loss of life on this island.

No. 114.

Gen. Sickles to Mr. Fish.

No. 31.] MADRID, *November* 3, 1869.

* * * * * * * * *

The commission organized to prepare and report for the consideration of the Cortes a plan of administrative reform for the island of Porto Rico, of which I advised you in my dispatch No. 19, has been dissolved.

The Marquis de la Esperanza, one of the deputies of Porto Rico, and a member of the board, informed the secretary of this legation, Colonel Hay, that the commission was unable to agree upon any plan. The disagreement between the government and the provincial members included among others the questions of slavery, tariff, and taxation. The decree dissolving the commission, which appeared recently in the Gazette, assigns as the reason for the measure, that the time limited for the sittings of the board has expired. I shall inform you of whatever else may transpire on this subject. It is probable the matter will soon be brought up in the Cortes by the deputies from Porto Rico.

* * * * * * * * *

No. 115.

Gen. Sickles to Mr. Fish.

No. 33.] MADRID, *November* 14, 1869.

* * * * * * * * *

The colonial minister declared on the 8th instant in the Cortes that the government would not bring forward any measure of reform for Cuba until the last hostile band was dispersed, and the insurgents had lost all hope. You will perhaps find some interest in a comparison of that view of Mr. Becerra with his expressions on the 6th of October, and I inclose reports of his remarks on both of these occasions.

* * * * * * * * *

[Translation.]

THE COLONIAL MINISTER.

OCTOBER 6, 1869.

GENTLEMEN: Our transmarine provinces have a right to reforms which are in harmony with the constitution which Spain has framed, and the government is resolved to make in them such (reforms) as may be necessary.

It is possible that a colony may have, at a given time, more liberty than its metropolis; possibly it may have less. The government will examine this matter with liberal judgment, not suffering itself to be misled by dangerous ideals, but grappling resolutely with all problems, social, political, and administrative.

Nor does it become Spain to carry on a retaliatory warfare, and the government will adopt the necessary measures to cause the suppression of the insurrection in Cuba to proceed in accordance with the forms of regular warfare, according proper treatment to the wounded, to prisoners, and to those who surrender, relying upon the good faith of Spain, without interfering with the action of the courts, in the case of common crimes which may have been committed.

It has been said that the cause of the insurrection was our bad colonial system, which does not comply with the demands of the age.

This may be partially true; but it is also true that under this pretext an attempt is made to attack the integrity of our territory. Very well; we will let it be understood that determined as Spain is to initiate the reforms which are demanded by the enlightment of the present century in America, she is equally determined to sacrifice her last man, her last cent, and her last cartridge, sooner than allow her honor to suffer any detriment. If fate shall be adverse to us, history will say: "Here lie the Spaniards, who, sooner than stain their honor, preferred to die like brave men." At this very time we are giving proofs of our purpose, by sending our soldiers to Cuba and Porto Rico, to prove to the world that our domestic contentions will not prevent us from employing all necessary means to conquer our enemies, and that the nation of Lepanto knows how to fight to-day as well as then.

THE COLONIAL MINISTER.

NOVEMBER 9, 1869.

In due time the deputies of Cuba will come here, and with us will decide what best comports with the honor of Spain, and the welfare of those provinces which, distant as they are, have no less right to the reforms which civilization claims.

But Spain is in the position of a man of honor, who does not yield what is asked of him by an armed adversary. The first thing is to conquer; if possible, bloodlessly; but if this be impossible, the right of force and the force of right will decide. (Tokens of approbation.)

No. 116.

General Sickles to Mr. Fish.

No. 35.] MADRID, *November* 25, 1869.

The minister of the colonies yesterday evening read to the Cortes the project of reforms for Porto Rico, about which there has been so much discussion and conjecture during the past month. I inclose the report which is contained in the journals of this morning.

* * * * * * * *

[Translation.]

The minister of ultramar occupied the rostrum and read the following plan of a law:

ARTICLE 1. The island of San Juan de Puerto Rico, which forms a part of the national territory, is considered as a province of the monarchy, with the same rights and conditions as those of the Peninsula, saving the modifications which may be established by law with regard to its government.

ART. 2. The Spanish constitution, promulgated by the Constituent Cortes, June 1, 1869, shall henceforth extend to the island of San Juan de Puerto Rico, with the following alterations and additions:

Article 8, paragraph 2, shall be thus modified:

"When the writ lacks this requisite, or when the grounds on which it was based are judiciously declared illegal or notoriously insufficient, the person who shall have been arrested, or whose arrest shall not have been approved within the time specified in article 4, or whose dwelling shall have been forcibly entered with a search warrant, or whose correspondence shall have been intercepted, shall have the right to bring a suit against the judge who gave the writ for damages proportionate to the injury caused, but never for less than one thousand dollars."

Article 18 shall read as follows:

"No Spaniard residing in Porto Rico, who is in the full enjoyment of his civil rights, and who is able to read and write, shall be deprived of the privilege of voting at the elections for senators, deputies to the Cortes, provincial deputies, and members of municipal boards."

Article 17, first paragraph, shall read:

"No Spaniard residing in Porto Rico shall be deprived," &c.

Addition to the first paragraph:

"All public discussion by any of the means specified in the preceding paragraph, which may tend to promulgate ideas touching a separation of the island of Porto Rico from the mother country, or designed to impair the integrity of the Spanish territory, is prohibited. Likewise, so long as the state of slavery shall exist, all public discussion with regard to it is prohibited."

To article 19 shall be added:

"Notwithstanding the provisions of the preceding paragraph, the superior governor of Porto Rico, giving ear to the authorities, in the form prescribed by law, may, on his own responsibility, order the dissolution of any association whose object or whose measures may compromise the safety of the State, reporting to the government by telegraph, if possible, or by the first opportunity, whether offered by a national or foreign vessel.

"The government, all things being considered, will obtain from the Cortes the passage of the law referred to in the preceding paragraph, or will otherwise revoke the measure adopted by the superior governor of Porto Rico."

Article 21 shall read thus:

"The privilege of holding worship in public or private, in any form, is guaranteed to all inhabitants of Porto Rico without any restriction save the universal rules of morality and law."

Article 24 shall read as follows:

"Any Spaniard may establish and maintain educational institutions without previous license, save the inspection of the proper authority, on grounds of hygiene and morality, and regarding the special prohibitions laid down in article 17 for the maintenance of the national integrity."

Article 31, paragraph 3, shall thus be modified:

"But in neither law can any guarantee be suspended other than those given in the first paragraph of this article, nor can the government be authorized to banish Spaniards from the kingdom."

Addition, at the end of the article:

"In case of invasion of the territory, or under circumstances which he may deem grave, the superior governor, giving ear to the authorities in the form prescribed by law, may, on his own responsibility, suspend the guarantees mentioned in paragraph 1 of this article, reporting the fact immediately to the government by telegraph, if possible, or, if not, by the first vessel, national or foreign. If the supreme government, on due consideration, shall think it necessary to prolong the suspension of guarantees, it shall ask of the Cortes a law to this effect; otherwise, it shall order the suspension of guarantees in the island of Porto Rico to cease."

Article 37 shall receive the following addition:

"The legislative powers of the provincial deputation of Porto Rico shall be fixed by law, always without prejudice to the supreme right of the Cortes of the nation."

Article 60, paragraph 5, shall be modified:

"To this effect the electoral body of each municipal district shall elect a number of arbitrators equal to the sixth part of the number of members who are to constitute the municipal board."

Article 99, paragraph 5, shall receive the following addition:

"Definition of their powers and duties with regard to taxes, so that provincial and municipal functionaries may never be brought into opposition to the tributary system, and that they may in no case fail to grant and vote the means necessary for the services and expenditures made incumbent upon them by law."

Article 100, paragraph 2, is rescinded.

Article 108 is rescinded.

The following additions shall be made provisionally:

"The rights laid down in the present constitution shall not be applicable to persons in a state of slavery while this exists, but they shall become so applicable as said persons gain their liberty by any of the means established by law; they shall then enjoy all the rights guaranteed by this constitution to the Spanish inhabitants of Porto Rico."

ART. 3. As soon as the Cortes shall have voted upon and sanctioned the present law, the government shall see that the constitution be published, with the alterations and additions which it shall have undergone, in order to become applicable to the island of San Juan de Puerto Rico.

The Minister of Ultramar,
MANUEL BECERRA.

MADRID, *November* 18, 1869.

It was announced that this plan would go to the sections for the appointment of the committee which is to report upon it.

No. 117.

Gen. Sickles to Mr. Fish.

[Telegram.]

MADRID, *November* 28, 1869.

Am authorized by minister of colonies to inform you that government measures for Porto Rico will include local self-government, free press, public schools, impartial suffrage, gradual but speedy abolition of slavery, civil and political rights without distinction of color, domiciled foreigners to vote for town officers after six months' residence, and for members of provisional council after one year, and that these reforms will in good faith be executed in Cuba when hostilities cease, and deputies are chosen in compliance with Article 108 of Spanish constitution.

No. 118.

Gen. Sickles to Mr. Fish.

[Telegram.]

MADRID, *December* 3, 1869.

*   *   *   *   *   *

Foreign secretary * * * wished me to assure you that Spain now desires the most friendly relations with all the American republics, and intends in her colonial policy to begin immediately the most liberal reforms.

No. 119.

Mr. Lowrey to Mr. Fish.

WASHINGTON, *December* 15, 1869.

SIR: As requested by the President, I called upon the Attorney General immediately after my interview with the President and yourself on the afternoon of the 13th instant, and again with Mr. Evarts on the morning of the 14th. At the last interview he stated very clearly the purpose of the government, and declared that the affidavits presented by me were not regarded as furnishing evidence so good as is already in your possession, and that they would be disregarded. This being the case, I have withdrawn the letters and exhibits, they being private property, and, according to my understanding with the President, I now send you the affidavits for such use as you may choose to make of them. They are those of Miguel de Aldama, J. M. Mestre, Mr. Cavoda, William C. Tinker, F. B. Coppinger, Enrique Loring, and F. X. Cisneros. The persons whose affidavits are submitted are ready and willing to come here for examination orally if you desire. Mr. Tinker, as I informed you, was in the ante-room during the conference, and I hoped he might have been called in, as I proposed, to be heard. He will remain at the Arlington House for a few days ready to respond to any call and be further examined in any way you may require.

Very respectfully, your obedient servant,

GROSVENOR P. LOWREY,
78 Broadway, New York.

Hon. HAMILTON FISH,
Secretary of State.

No. 120.

The Attorney General (Mr. Hoar) to Mr. Fish.

ATTORNEY GENERAL'S OFFICE,
December 16, 1869.

SIR: In compliance with your oral request, I send you, in writing, my opinion upon the question whether it is proper for the United States to cause a libel to be filed, under the third section of the statute of April 20, 1818, entitled "An act in addition to the 'Act for the punishment of certain crimes against the United States,' and to repeal the acts therein mentioned," against the gunboats building in New York for the Spanish government, on the ground that they are procured to be fitted out and armed with intent that they shall be employed in the service of Spain, a foreign state, with intent to cruise or commit hostilities against the subjects, citizens, or property of a "colony, district, or people" with whom the United States are at peace, namely, a "colony, district, or people" claiming to be the *republic of Cuba.*

The statute of 1818 is sometimes spoken of as the *neutrality act*, and undoubtedly its principal object is to secure the performance of the duty of the United States, under the law of nations, as a neutral nation in respect to foreign powers; but it is an act to punish certain offenses against the United States by fines, imprisonment, and forfeitures, and the act itself defines the precise nature of those offenses.

The United States have not recognized the independent national existence of the Island of Cuba, nor any part thereof, and no sufficient reason has yet been shown to justify such a recognition. In the view of the government of the United States, as a matter of fact, which must govern our conduct as a nation, the Island of Cuba is a territory under the government of Spain, and belonging to that nation. If ever the time shall come when it shall seem fitting to the political department of the government of the United States to recognize Cuba as an independent government, entitled to admission into the family of nations, or, without recognizing its independence, to find that an organized government, capable of carrying on war and to be held responsible to other nations for the manner in which it carries it on, exists in that island, it will be the duty of that department to declare and act upon those facts; but before such a state of things is found to exist, it is not, in my opinion, competent for a court to undertake to settle those questions.

The judicial tribunals must follow and conform to the political action of the government, in regard to the existence of foreign states and our relations to them; and it would, in my opinion, be inconsistent with the honor and dignity of the United States to submit to a court, and allow to be declared and acted upon, in such an indirect manner, rights and duties toward a foreign nation which the government is not prepared distinctly and upon its own responsibility to avow and maintain.

It has been brought to my notice, as to yours, by persons who profess to represent the Cuban insurgents, that libels have already been filed in the courts of the United States, under the statute of 1818, to procure the condemnation of vessels, on the ground that they were being fitted out and armed with intent to be employed in the service of a "colony, district, or people," namely, the "colony, district, or people" of Cuba, with intent to cruise and commit hostilities against the subjects of Spain, a nation with whom we are at peace; and it is urged that this involves what is claimed to be the converse of the proposition, that as we assert in those libels that Cuba is a "colony, district, or people" capable of committing hostilities against Spain, the law equally applies to an armament procured or fitted out by Spain for the purpose of hostilities against Cuba, and that the executive government by filing those libels has virtually recognized the "colony, district, or people" of Cuba as belligerents.

This argument seems to me to involve an erroneous legal notion, and to be based upon the idea that the statute of 1818, being an act to protect and enforce the neutrality laws of the United States, cannot be applied except where there are independent parties to a contest entitled to equal rights. But this, I think, is an opinion wholly unsound. Undoubtedly the ordinary application of the statute is to cases where the United States intends to maintain its neutrality in wars between two other nations, or where both parties to a contest have been recognized as belligerents—that is, as having a sufficiently organized political existence to enable them to carry on war. But the statute is not confined in its terms, nor, as it seems to me, in its scope and proper effect, to such cases. Under it any persons who are insurgents, or engaged in what would be regarded under our law as levying war against the sovereign power of the nation, however few in number, and occupying however small a territory, might procure the fitting out and arming of vessels with intent to cruise or commit hostilities against a nation with which we are at peace, and with intent that they should be employed in the service of a "colony, district, or people" not waging a recognized war. The statute would apply to the case of an armament prepared in anticipation of an insurrection or revolt in some district or colony which it was intended to excite, and before any hostilities existed.

But, on the other hand, when a nation with which we are at peace, or the recognized government thereof, undertakes to procure armed vessels for the purpose of enforcing its own recognized authority within its own dominions, although there may be evidence satisfactory to show that they will aid the government in the suppression of insurrection or rebellion, in a legal view this does not involve a design to commit hostilities against anybody. If the illicit distillers of any section of the United States combine together to resist by force the collection of the revenue, and arm themselves for this purpose, with the intent to set at defiance permanently and by force the laws of the United States, they may be levying war against the government; but when the government sends its officers to disperse or arrest the offenders, although it may find it necessary to employ military force in aid of its authority, it certainly cannot be considered as committing hostilities against the territory over which such operations extend.

The question of belligerency between organized communities is a question of fact, and may be one of the gravest facts upon which a nation is called to decide and act. The concession of belligerent rights to a "colony, district, or people" in a state of insurrection or revolution necessarily involves serious restrictions upon the ordinary rights of the people of this country to carry on branches of manufacture and trade which are unrestricted in time of peace. To prevent our mechanics and merchants from building ships of war and selling them in the markets of the world, is an interference with their private rights which can only be justified on the ground of a paramount duty in our international relations; and however much we may sympathize with the efforts of any portion of the people of another country to resist what they consider oppression, or to achieve independence, our duties are necessarily dependent upon the actual progress which they have made in reaching these objects.

This subject, as you are well aware, is one to which long and careful consideration has been applied, and the result, which I have thus briefly stated, and which might receive much fuller statement and illustration, is that upon which the administration have acted. I trust that I have made my view of the law intelligible, and have the honor to be,

Very respectfully,

E. R. HOAR,
Attorney General.

Hon. HAMILTON FISH,
Secretary of State.

No. 121.

AFFIDAVITS SUBMITTED TO THE ATTORNEY GENERAL BY MR. GROSVENOR P. LOWREY AND MR. WILLIAM M. EVARTS, COUNSEL FOR THE CUBANS, TO ESTABLISH THE EXISTENCE OF A STATE OF WAR AND OF AN INDEPENDENT GOVERNMENT IN CUBA.

Considering it is of the utmost importance for the best service of the state, and having the firm determination that the rebellion already quelled by the force of arms in the interior part of the island may not receive from outside any kind of resources that may serve to make it live longer with great harm to property, to industry, and to commerce, and in use of the supreme and discretional faculties of which I have been invested by the supreme government of the nation, I decree—

Only article: All ships that may be captured in Spanish waters or in free seas near the island, with cargo of men, arms, and ammunition, or effects which may in some way serve to promote or swell the insurrection in this province, whatever may be his port of sailing and destination, after his papers and roll may be examined, will, in fact, be considered as enemies of the integrity of our territory and treated as pirates in conformity with the navy rules.

All men found in them, whatever their number may be, will be immediately shot.

DENUNGO DULCE.

HAVANA, *March* 24, 1869.

On this date I have considered convenient to decree the closing of all the ports and landing places of the central and western departments where there may not exist custom-houses, not only to coastwise commerce, but also to ocean navigation. It will be the duty of the commanders of men-of-war to make known this measure to the captains or masters of the ships they may find sailing in direction to any one of said ports, with the object that they may sail to the place nearest to their destination, where a custom-house may be found, and that is published that it may be generally known.

LERSUNDI.

NOVEMBER 9, 1869.

CARLOS MANUEL DE CÉSPEDES, PRESIDENT OF THE REPUBLIC OF CUBA.

In use of the power and authority which I exercise, and of the ratification of the said power by the House of Representatives on the 22d of April, 1869, and taking into consideration that it is very important for the cause of the independence and freedom of the nation to constitute a special mission near the government of the republic of the United States, with all powers to secure the triumph of the holy cause which the sons of the said island are maintaining to emancipate themselves from the ominous domination of Spain, and considering that citizen José Morales Lemus fully possesses all the requirements to fulfill so delicate a mission, I name and ratify him especial envoy and minister plenipotentiary of the republic of Cuba, near the government of the United States, which commission he will exercise with full power, which I grant to him in the name of the nation I represent, authorizing him to exercise all the faculties due in all civilized nations to diplomatic agents and chargés d'affaires, and especially to urge near the said government of the United States of America the recognition of the independence of the Island of Cuba, and all moral and material help for the prosecution of the war.

Given at Berrocal this 31st day of May, 1889, in the second year of the independence of Cuba.

[SEAL]

CARLOS MANUEL DE CÉSPEDES,
President of the Republic.

RAMON CÉSPEDES,
Secretary of Foreign Affairs.

Affidavit of Miguel de Aldama.

CITY AND COUNTY OF NEW YORK, *ss:*

MIGUEL DE ALDAMA, being duly sworn, says: I am a native of the Island of Cuba, and have for the most part of my life resided in the city of Havana, but am at present resident in the city of New York, and am president of the Cuban Junta in that city. That said Junta is the financial and business agent in the United States of the government of the republic of Cuba, and in a considerable degree manages and controls all the business and affairs of the people of the Island of Cuba who yield allegiance to said republic. As president of the Junta it is my duty to receive official communications from the government of the republic, and to know, and I do know, the actual state and condition from time to time of the revolution and its forces in Cuba. I have read the affidavits of William C. Tinker, Enrique Loinaz, of Mr. Coppenger and Mr. Cisneros, and I know those affidavits to be strictly true so far as they relate to the organization of the government, the general condition of the country, the administration of the laws, the sentiments of the people, and all the circumstances of the republican government, and I believe them to be true in every other respect concerning those matters of which I have no personal knowledge. The gentlemen above named are persons of good repute and standing in the island of Cuba, and their statements are entitled to the utmost credit.

Late on Thursday evening I caused a telegraphic message to be sent to the President of the United States, asking him to hold the thirty Spanish gunboats until I could address to him proofs which would satisfy him that the government of Cuba is a *de facto* government, sufficiently established to be entitled, if not to recognition, to a fair administration in its favor of the neutrality laws, and that it is actually carrying on a war in the international sense of that term, and maintaining itself against its enemy successfully. I received an indirect intimation from a friend in Washington, late on Friday, that my communication would be received up to Monday, December 13. I make this explanation because, having had only Friday evening and Saturday to gather the witnesses, and compare their statements, and examine my correspondence bearing upon the subject, and select and arrange such documents and translations thereof as are material, it seems necessary to excuse the hasty and probably imperfect manner in which the work has, within that short time, been accomplished. Mr. Loinaz is the last person who, so far as I know and believe, has arrived from the republican district of the Island of Cuba, and before his arrival Messrs. Cisneros and Tinker were the last persons. The accounts given by them in their affidavits are strictly true according to the accounts rendered by them, as a performance of their duty to this junta, concerning the state of things in Cuba, and is in strict accordance with all other advices received from the government of the republic. The subsequent advices have been by sailing vessels and the mail, by indirect routes, and come down to a period as late as about the 15th of November. The last communication was from General Cavada, and contains the captured Spanish letters which have been published in the newspapers. I have no doubt whatever of the entire authenticity of these captured Spanish letters, and that they actually state the condition of things in the Cinco Villas district, of the Spanish troops.

These communications are submitted, and translations have been made of as many of them as time would permit, and further translations will be continued, if desired, so that all can be read in the English language. They do not disclose any falling off, nor do I believe there has been any falling off or retrogression in the revolution. On the contrary, I believe that it has constantly gained force, strength, and territory from the day of the outbreak in October, 1868. I also believe and declare as my solemn conviction that the almost entire Cuban people, without respect to age, rank, or circumstances, are engaged in this rebellion, urged thereto by a long course of oppression beyond all conception by any person who has not lived under a Spanish colonial government, and that they are fully determined to sacrifice everything rather than again submit to Spanish rule, and that, should the war be prolonged, the only result in the end must be that the dominion of the island will be wrested from the Spanish government, or that the entire property of the island will be destroyed. I know of my own knowledge that, as one of its first acts, the government of the Cuban republic, composed largely of persons who owned slaves, declared the emancipation of all slaves, and that that action has met with the universal approval of all adherents of the republic. I was the owner, before October, 1868, of about 2,000 slaves. I now regard these slaves as all free, and as my equals in every political privilege and right in the Island of Cuba. All of my slaves, however, unfortunately for them, lived on plantations within the Spanish lines, and have been confiscated as property, and are still held in slavery without my consent and against my wish. I only mention my case, because my desires and purposes concerning these slaves are the same as those of every other Cuban owner of slaves who is loyal to the revolution. I know by public and private information that the republic of Cuba has been recognized as an independent nation by the republic of Peru, and that it has, according to diplomatic form, been recognized as a lawful belligerent by the republics of Chili and Bolivia and Mexico; also, that it has sent diplomatic representatives to France, England, Peru, Bolivia, Venezuela, and Mexico, and that Mr. José Morales Lemus is its duly accredited diplomatic representative to the government of the United States; and I herewith attach a translated copy of his commission, which is in due and usual form. Mr. Morales Lemus is at present ill at his house in Brooklyn, and is therefore unable to participate in this representation. I know that the republic of Cuba owns five ships, which have been purchased with a view of forming a navy, and that the President has issued commissions to officers to command those vessels, and that he has also issued letters of marque and reprisal. I also know, by having seen the proclamation of the Captain General, that the ports mentioned by Mr. Loinaz in his affidavit have been closed by his decree to neutral commerce, they having before such decree been open to commerce with other nations on the same terms as all other Spanish ports. I attach hereto a translated copy of the decree. I know by public information that Spanish cruisers have claimed and have exercised the right upon the high seas to visit and search neutral vessels, instances of which are mentioned in the President's late annual message. This power is claimed to be exercised under a decree of the Captain General, dated March 24, 1869, a translated copy of which is hereto annexed. I know that two vessels have been seized in the United States and libeled by the government thereof, namely, the Catharine Whiting, at New York, and the Cuba, at Wilmington, for condemnation, on the ground that they had been fitted out and armed within the limits of the United States with intent to cruise and commit hostilities in the service of the republic of Cuba, against the foreign state of Spain, and those two vessels are now held and being prosecuted upon that ground, and that various persons, including Mr. Morales Lemus, have been indicted in the southern district of New York for hiring and enlisting men to enter the service of a certain foreign people, to wit, a portion of the people of the Island of Cuba. I know that it is impossible for any person, not a Cuban, visiting Havana, or any of the ports or towns in the possession of Spaniards, to obtain reliable information concerning the revolution. In most cases the Spaniards themselves are not able to obtain it, being unable with their utmost force to penetrate into the country held by the patriots. But the Cubans in those places possessing such information never dared to impart it to any person not well known to them, for fear of persecution and death by the Spanish soldiery.

I left Havana in May last. I was well acquainted with the general condition of affairs in the island at that time, and I know that there were not less than 30,000 regular Spanish troops in the island, besides about 30,000 Spanish volunteers. I have been informed, and believe, that General Prim declared, at a session of the Spanish Cortes, but a short time since, that he had sent 40,000 troops and fourteen men-of-war to the island, and notwithstanding the presence of this large army, I know, from my own authentic correspondence, that the territory from time to time brought within the scope of the revolution has not, nor has any part of it, been taken again, and that the lines of the revolutionary territory have been gradually extended until they now include nearly two-thirds of the entire island, and about one-half the population. The Spanish troops are armed with the most modern and efficient arms, such as repeating rifles, and the Cuban troops have no better arms than the common Springfield musket, or Enfield rifle. According to my best information and belief, the Cuban army now consists of about 40,000 men, armed, more or less, and there remain nearly 80,000 more men duly enrolled, and ready to take the field as soon as they can be armed with any weapon. The disposition of these troops has been resolved upon by the military authorities in full view of the special circumstances of the country, of the danger of risking great battles against experienced soldiery, armed as the Spanish soldiers are, by soldiers gathered from all occupations, and so indifferently armed as the Cubans are. It is deemed by them better policy to exhaust the enemy, all of whose provisions and supplies have to be brought from abroad, and constantly to improve the efficiency of our own troops by drill, discipline, and military supplies, as we can obtain them. Notwithstanding this, many combats have taken place, and been officially reported to the junta, in which the Cubans have gained important advantages, and inflicted very severe loss upon the Spaniards. I have read in an official report of the Captain General to the government in Spain that the Spanish army had lost fourteen thousand troops this year in battle and by sickness. These combats have all been conducted according to the customs and usages of war, by organized and enrolled men, under military discipline and command, and all subject to the order of a commander-in-chief, who is himself subject to the control of the civil government, in the same manner as the General of the army of the United States is subject to the President and Congress.

I am acquainted with the coasts of the Island of Cuba, and I know that the vessels known as the Spanish gunboats are adapted to be used on these coasts for the purpose of cruising and committing hostilities against the citizens, subjects, and property of the republic of Cuba, and of the people and the district controlled by it, of which republic Manuel Cespedes is the duly elected President, and a true copy of the constitution of which, publicly promulgated, is submitted and attached to the affidavit of Mr. Tinker.

The republic of Cuba has adopted a flag, and all its military operations are identified by, and conducted under, this flag, as the symbol of its power and claim to national existence. I am informed from the island, and believe, that the republican troops are under good discipline. The army is composed of farmers and respectable country people and the emancipated blacks, and all their operations are under military control and the usages of war, and there is almost an entire absence of robbery or disorder within the lines of the republican forces. Within these lines no authority is acknowledged by the people but that of the republic; and no laws are or can be executed but those of the republic; and all the civil relations of the people are regulated and controlled by these laws through courts and officers created by the republic.

I have personal knowledge of the fact that Captain General Dulce sent two commissions, under a flag of truce, to General Cespedes, then the president and general-in-chief of the republic, to negotiate for a cessation of hostilities. These commissions were composed, the first of three persons, the second of two; and they did pass under a flag of truce through the line of the republican forces, and held communication with General Cespedes.

My information concerning the matters of which I have spoken is derived from numerous sources, so various that I cannot in this short time particularize them, but they are all, in a certain degree, official and creditable, and are such as I rely upon in the performance of the duties of my office, and the belief which I have expressed above is solemnly entertained by me without doubt of its correctness in every particular.

MIGUEL DE ALDAMA.

Subscribed and sworn to before me this eleventh day of December, 1869.

CHARLES HARRIS PHELPS,
Notary Public, County of New York.

HAVANA, *July* 9, 1869.

It being of the utmost importance for the extermination of the bands of rebels which, till now, have been able to maintain themselves only with exterior aid, to exercise the utmost care and vigilance on the coasts of this island, adjacent keys and Spanish sea, with the object of giving a vigorous impulse to the prosecution, and with the idea of dispelling all doubts that may present to our cruisers about the exact meaning of the decrees of this superior government of 9th November, 1868, and 18th and 26th February, and 24th March, of 1869, I have determined to join and explain in this all the above dispositions, and in use of the faculties of which I am invested by the supreme government of the nation, I decree hereby:

ARTICLE 1. All the ports of the north coast from Cay Bay of Cadiz to Punta de Main, and in the south coast from Punta de Main to Cienfuegos, will remain closed for all commerce of importation and exportation, and for all ships, not only of coastwise navigation, but also of ocean navigation, with exception of Sagua, Carbarien, Nuevitas, Gibara, Baracoa, Guantanamo, Santiago de Cuba, Manzanillo, Santa Cruz, Zara, Casilda o Trinidad, and Cienfuegos, places in which there are custom-houses. All those ships which will try to enter in closed ports or communicate with the shore will be pursued, and in case of capture will be punished as infractors of the law.

ART. 2. Ships with cargoes of gunpowder, arms, and military supplies will be tried according to the same laws.

ART. 3. The transportation of men in the service of the rebellion being much more important than that of contraband of war, will be considered as an act completely hostile, and in consequence the ship and crew will be tried as enemies.

ART. 4. If the men to which the above article refers are armed, that will be considered as a *de facto* proof of their intentions, and they will be tried as pirates, and the crew of the ship also.

ART. 5. All ships armed in war or not, that may be captured sailing under an unknown flag, will also, according to law, be considered and tried as pirates.

ART. 6. Cruisers in the free seas contiguous to the island will limitate their action on ships denounced, or on those whose bearings may appear suspicious, to the right consigned in the treaties between Spain and the United States in 1795, and Great Britain, 1835, and those made afterward with other nations, and if, in the exercise of these rights, they happen to find ships acknowledged as enemies of the integrity of the territory, they will take them to port for the consequent legal investigation and trial.

CABALLERO DE RODAS.

Affidavit of I. M. Mestre.

CITY AND COUNTY OF NEW YORK, *ss:*

I. M. MESTRE, being duly sworn, says: I am a native of the island of Cuba; a lawyer by profession. For several years, until the beginning of the present year, I was the professor of jurisprudence in the University of Havana. I am now the secretary of the Cuban Junta in New York, and reside at No. 135 West Twenty-first street, in that city. As such secretary it is my duty to be informed from time to time, as communication is practicable, of the actual state of the revolution in Cuba, and all the circumstances connected with the struggle now going on there. I have read the affidavits of Aldama, Tinker, Cesineros, Loinaz, and Coppenger, and the statements therein concerning the resources and operations of the revolutionary party, their organization and administration of civil government, the sentiments and purposes of the people, the closing of ports by the Captain General, are true, within my own knowledge, as derived from my own observation and official communications received by the junta. I concur in Mr. Aldama's statement, that, according to all the information in the possession of the junta, the revolution has constantly gained strength and ground, and has never lost any of either from the first uprising in October, 1868. It is my solemn belief, and I know that that belief is concurred in by the junta, and by all persons who are in the way of receiving any information from that part of the island controlled by the republic, that the revolution is stronger to-day than ever before, and in a fair way to achieve independence and the liberty of all persons, according to the twenth-fourth article of its constitution adopted on the 10th day of April, 1869, as follows:

"XXIV. All the inhabitants of the republic of Cuba are absolutely free."

At the time of the late revolution in Spain, it was the desire of a large part of the people of Cuba to participate in the blessings of liberty which the Spanish people claimed for themselves, and for this purpose a number of prominent persons, some of whom were officials, solicited an audience with the Captain General, at his palace in Havana, in order respectfully to petition for the granting of certain rights, without which they believed it impossible to restrain a popular outbreak. Their appeal, which was made with the hope of saving bloodshed, was insolently received and repelled, and all hope that Cuba would benefit by the revolution forbidden to them. I was present as one of this deputation, and the account of that interview, hereto annexed, is correct.

Communications with and from the government of the republic are necessarily unfrequent and irregular. But it is well known, however, that there is no serious difficulty in making a port in Cuba in which free communication can be had with the revolutionary government; the only real difficulty consisting in departing from or coming to adjacent neutral ports.

I attach hereto a true copy of a proclamation by the Captain General, issued July 9, 1869, containing the blockade of domestic ports against neutral countries, which was first decreed by the proclamation attached to Mr. Adams's affidavit.

I. M. MESTRE.

Subscribed and sworn to before me this 11th day of December, 1869.

CHARLES HARRIS PHELPS,
Notary Public, County of New York.

Memorandum of the incidents of a meeting held at General Lersundi's palace, of several respectable and worthy citizens of Havana, on the 24th of October, 1868.

The telegraphic news of revolutionary movements in Spain was naturally sympathized with by a majority of the people in Cuba, whose sentiments are decidedly liberal; and the principles there proclaimed deeply agitated the public mind, inspiring the wish to participate in similar advantages. The desire was evident to obtain a guarantee, an assurance or a direct promise, that the island was not to be cut off as before from the national progress, nor its inhabitants despoiled of the rights of Spanish citizens, much less be left under the imputation of being obdurate partisans of the fallen dynasty. The desired promise not being made, nor the guarantee obtained, fears were entertained as to the policy contemplated, and many suspected that Cubans would not be allowed the exercise of the rights acknowledged for the rest of the nation; and not a few imagined that in the incipient stage of the revolution a decree might be received from the metropolis ordering the sudden abolition of slavery, thereby imperiling the social existence of the country. It is proper to add that this last idea was artfully suggested by the enemies of free institutions, with a view to preserve the *regime* of Isabel in these distant regions.

Notwithstanding the efforts made to keep order and peace, the masses were excited, and a rising took place far away from the capital, the leaders yet invoking in their war cry, "Spain, Cuba, and Freedom!"

Thus, expectancy, anxious doubts, and alarming fears produced an extraordinary and indescribable situation, while the impatient could not be restrained and would claim what they feared would be denied; the over cautious, little pleased with the glorious revolution of Spain, were a subject of annoyance to the former, who in them saw a powerful obstacle to their aspirations. Addresses were therefore made by one party to maintain *statu quo*, while the other rose in arms, the last resort of oppressed nations. Hence originated the thought of allowing a certain expansion by frank adherence to the principles of the provisional government of Madrid.

* * * * * * * * * * *

On Friday, 23d October, Messieurs Rato, Zuleta, Pelligero, Fernandez Bramosio, Mestre, and other aldermen, were discussing the subject in an extra official and friendly manner in the recess-room of the city council of Havana. It was generally granted that meetings of citizens should be authorized by the government to soothe public anxiety, quell disturbances, and discuss the slavery question; a few hours later invitations were received to a meeting at the Captain General's palace. The gentlemen mentioned at the bottom of this memorandum, and others whose names are not remembered, appeared on the 24th October at the palace, and were shown into the private apartment of Lersundi, who, in a tone of evident displeasure, said he had no idea the meeting was to be so large, but since it was so, they could pass into the parlor, where there would be room for all. Once there, he said he had been told that several residents desired to address him; he had agreed to hear them, and though not expecting so many, the number only added to the honor and pleasure with which he ought to hear them.

These remarks were calculated to embarrass the invited party, who had come to hear the suggestions of the government rather than to initiate the subject themselves, and a profound silence followed. This being noticed by Lersundi, he required Rato, who had been one of those proposing the invitation, to state the object of the meeting.

Señor Rato said that in the grave circumstances the island was going through several persons had wished to express to the Captain General sentiments of adhesion and personal respect. Lersundi seemed disposed then to hear others.

Señor Mestre then spoke. He said that his individuality was of little account, and that he should rather be the last than the first to speak, but the remarks of Senor Rato forced him to precede gentlemen with better right to take part in the conference; he would speak in perfect frankness, because there are moments when all should be frankly told; he had conversed with Senor Rato and others, to the purpose that it was expedient to authorize or tolerate meetings for the discussion of public matters interesting to all, and therefore he thought it incumbent on him to make certain explanations; he said the serious events happening in Spain had produced excitement and trouble easy to understand; the government in power having proclaimed the most advanced political creed, every Spaniard, no matter in what part of the world he found himself, should feel he was entitled to the enjoyment of the acknowledged rights of the revolution, therefore the inhabitants of Cuba could but believe that they would be extended to this province as an integral part of the nation. He would ask what should be done? We should doubtless adopt an open and decidedly liberal course in harmony with the established and legal *régime* of the peninsula. He said that the meetings he had referred to were expedient as well as to give greater scope to the press in order to furnish public sentiment with safety valves; that when these were closed the expansion would burst through clandestine issues, the danger of which it was needless to explain. He enjoined to take care that no disunion should ever exist between the property holders and the advocates of advanced freedom; that the latter should never notice disagreement between these two elements, which would cause great mischief. By the means he proposed, a proper expansion of feeling within reasonable bounds would be harmless, and important changes would be accomplished with no danger; he said the most liberal policy should be held as the most conservative. This was the motive for asking meetings. He thought it calculated to prevent present as well as future evils. At these meetings honest and patriotic men would investigate the serious points now pending, would infuse a spirit of unity, and carry to the furthest ends of the province hope and a feeling of security in the future, and thereby exercise a salutary influence all around.

Señor Modet* said he adhered to all the remarks of Senor Mestre. He said that as a member of the Cortes he had advocated the extension of political rights to the inhabitants of Cuba and Porto Rico. In his opinion the country would become quiet if the legitimate hope were in any way expressed that this province would be assimilated to those of Spain, that the liberties gloriously conquered would be enjoyed here, since it was known from reliable accounts that a provisional government existed in Madrid accepted by all the provinces, although temporary in its character. He said that by such means union, tranquillity, confidence, and order among the inhabitants of Cuba would be established. Should a doubt arise as to the proper course, he proposed the home government to be consulted by telegraph.

The Captain General then suspended the conference, saying he had understood that some residents desired to offer him their support, and found the contrary that they had come only to show mistrust, to censure his acts and address him charges to which he would briefly refer. It had been insinuated that the revolution had acknowledged certain rights to all Spaniards—that persons having constituted a provisional government at Madrid desired to make those rights extensive to this island; that some one was in the way between the mother country and this province, and that such party was him-

*This gentleman, a native of Spain, and colonel of engineers, was sent to Spain by Lersundi, in consequence of this speech; he returned under Dulce, and has now been sent back, frightened away by the volunteers.

self. For his part he had received no direct communications from that government, not even by telegraph, excepting one from the new minister of the colonies, which had been published entire by his order. What else could he do in favor of the island in the fulfillment of his duty than overlook his own personal views and sympathies? He would obey orders that might arrive from the Madrid government, the government, he added, of the Duke de La Torre, the government of General Serrano. He was determined to resign his command when the time came, handing over the island in the condition he had received it. But he would in no way express adhesion, as would be intimated by the gentlemen who had spoken, because his loyalty rose as high as the throne of God. He said the remarks of Senor Mestre were analogous to those made by the insurgents of Yara in arms, whose conduct he seemed to excuse; he said that such had been the commencement of insurrections in the Spanish countries now republics in America. He discussed these topics at large, and stating that the government counted on means adequate to suppress and punish the rebels and agitators, he remarked that the answer he had thought proper to give Messrs. Mestre and Modet being ended, he would close the conference, which ought by no means to be held longer.

Señor Modet asked to be allowed to speak, and was refused.

The vehemence of gesture, tone of voice, and unexpected severity of Lersundi, naturally left a most disagreeable impression on all present. They began to retire with evident discontent, when Señor Morales Lemus told the Captain General how much he regretted that his excellency should have interpreted as accusations the suggestions made with the best intentions; the general insisted on the impropriety of the meetings asked for, saying it would be more useful if the newspaper, El Pais,* should pointedly and energetically condemn the movement of the insurgents, or if two commissioners were sent to obtain their surrender. His experience taught him that no convictions were ever gained by debating. Sometimes, he added, as it were casually, it is unquestionable that timely severity produced the best results; the sacrifice of a few lives at a proper moment will save from greater and more painful losses.

Those yet remaining at the palace departed after this effusion, and thus ended a scene, initiated under favorable auspices, which might have exercised a beneficial influence on the destinies of Cuba. This new page of its history needs no comment.

NAMES OF THOSE KNOWN TO HAVE BEEN PRESENT.

Conde Canongo,
Apolinar Rato,
Manuel de Armas,
Conde San Ignacio,
José Morales Lemus,
Julian Zulueta,
Antonio Fernandez Bramosio,
Francisco Ibanez,
Pedro Martin Rivero,
Eduardo Alonso Colmenares,
Conde Pozos-Dulces,
José Suarez Argudin,
José Manuel Mestre,
Juan Modet,
Gonzalo Jorrin,
Ramon Herrera,
Marques Aguas-Claras,
José Villasante,
José M. Morales Cerro,
Nicolas Martinez Valdivieso,
Domingo Guillermo Arozarena,
José Ruiz de Leon,
Juan Poey,
Nicanor Troncoso,
Miguel Antonio Herrera,
Hilario Cisneros,
Juan Ariza,
Antonio Gonzalez Mendoza,
Francisco Duran Cuervo,
Adolfo Munoz,
Sabino Ojero,
Francisco Acosta,
José Pelligero de Lama,
Enrique Farres,
José Antonio Echeverria,
Pedro Sotolongo,
José Caraza.
Antonio Mora.

Affidavit of Emilio F. Cavado.

[The affidavit of Emilio F. Cavado is omitted at the suggestion of Mr. G. P. Lowrey, for satisfactory reasons stated by him.]

Affidavit of William C. Tinker.

CITY AND COUNTY OF NEW YORK, *ss.*:

WILLIAM CLARENCE TINKER, being duly sworn, doth depose and say: I am a native of the city of New York, and have lived in Cuba from the year 1852 up to April, 1869. I am extensively acquainted with the Island of Cuba and the people there, both the Spaniards and the native Cubans. I am related by marriage to Spaniards holding official positions; one brother-in-law of mine is colonel of engineers in the Spanish army, and another a commander in the navy. I was educated in a military

* El Pais, organ of the Cubans.

school at the city of Lippstadt, in Westphalia, and have some acquaintance with military affairs. In April last, I was forced to leave the city of Havana, on account of my well-known sympathy with the Cuban revolution, my house having been three times violently searched, and myself fired upon in the streets seven times in one evening. The circumstances of this outrage to me, personally, are stated in the correspondence of the then consul general of the United States, which I suppose is on file in the State Department. On the 14th day of May last, I landed at Nuevas Grandes, from the steamer Salvador, together with one hundred and fifty men, and from that time until the second day of August I was in the Island of Cuba, within the district thereof which is controlled by the insurgent government. During this time I had frequent and continuous meetings with the various officers of the republic, and had ample opportunity to see the men under arms, the military disposition of forces, the civil departments of government, and all the operations, civil and military, of the government of the republic of Cuba. Upon landing, I took eight men and went forward into the country; I had proceeded about twelve miles when I came to the first encampment of Cuban troops, at San Martin. There were about eighty men there, under command of a captain; they were armed and uniformed; those men were placed there to act as a *posse comitatus*, or guard to the civil court, which was then in session at that place, the judge, M. C. Juan Salvador, being appointed, as I was then informed, and afterward learned to be true, by the supreme court of the republic of Cuba, according to the provisions of the constitution and the laws enacted by Congress. These men were, upon my representation, sent down to the coast to assist in landing the cargo; and I proceeded on and found several encampments of men, about the same size, all uniformed and armed, and in direct communication one with the other, by couriers. On arriving at Guaimaro, which is about thirty-six miles from the coast, I found that the capital had been removed the day before, to Berrocal, six miles from Guaimaro. When I arrived, the inhabitants of Guaimaro were in the streets, singing revolutionary songs, and setting fire to their own houses, it having been decided by the republican government to burn the town, as, in case it should be taken by the Spaniards, it afforded an advantageous shelter and strategical point for them. I followed on to Berrocal, where I found the President, the Congress, and the principal officers of the civil and executive government. I found that the constitution had been adopted. It had not at that time been printed, and a copy was made for me in writing, by order of the President, which copy is hereto annexed, marked A. The translation annexed is a true translation. I found there many persons, officers of the government, with whom I had been previously acquainted, and I had facilities of learning all that had been done. I found the government completely organized—the various officers performing the duties and functions belonging to their offices. There were the departments of war, of finance, of the interior, and department of public instruction. The Congress was then in session; I attended several of its sessions; it was proceeding according to the rules by which deliberative bodies are usually governed. It was presided over by a Cuban, who had formerly been a Spanish nobleman, but who had yielded his rank, under the constitution. He was a person of large wealth; his title was Marquis St. Lucia. The Congress had enacted laws, and while I was there I heard debates upon matters relating to laws which were under consideration, and in my presence several enactments were voted upon and became laws. I remember a question of the distribution and separation of civil and military power being discussed in Congress. A general, whose name I have forgotten, had claimed to exercise certain civil powers, and his right to do so was disputed in the Congress; and I remember, particularly, the speech of one member, M. Mendoza, formerly an editor of the Siglo, in Havana, who maintained that from the very beginning of the government in Cuba it was necessary that we should avoid the error of the Spanish government, and separate distinctly civil from military power. The discussion was very full; and finally an act was passed, clearly defining the power of the military and civil officers. I was not present, but I know, by common report, that the Congress had passed, also, an act making civil marriages lawful, all marriages, before, having been necessary to be made before a priest.

While I was there, there was an issue by the government, of paper money. I, myself, put the stamp of the government upon the first series of notes, by direction of the President and secretary of the treasury. This money was similar to American money, and by it the Cuban republic promised to pay to the bearer certain sums named thereon. I afterward had occasion to use this money, and saw it used. It was freely received by all at par, and change given back in gold or silver, as the case might be. The civil administration of justice was going on while I was there, but I did not attend any of the sessions of the courts. A man under my command was accused, before the civil court, of having stolen some property from a farm-house, and, upon complaint of the owner, a warrant was issued for him, and certain civil officers, corresponding to constables in this country, came to my camp and demanded the man, exhibiting the warrant and a letter from the judge, in which he notified me that one of my men had been accused of an offense against the civil law. I rendered the man up and he was taken to answer the charge. I have still with me the letter of the judge, a correct translation of which is annexed, marked B. During the time I was in the island, I visited a considerable number of the encampments of the republican army, situated between Puerto Principe and Santiago de Cuba. I found, in the district which I visited, about twelve thousand men under arms, of which one-half were thoroughly armed with Springfield, Enfield, and various other kinds of muskets, and the other half imperfectly armed, but all carrying the *machete*, which is a long sword. I found that all the people in this district were apparently engaged in the revolution, and yielding obedience to the republican government. The entire country, with the exception of garrison towns, was in the possession, almost undisputed, of the revolutionists. I found that the slaves had all been liberated within this district. They were as free as any white citizens, to choose what they would do, or where they would go. Large numbers of them were in the army, and proved to be very good soldiers. I talked with numbers of them. They understood that they were free, and that their freedom had been given to them by the republic of Cuba and their former masters, and they understood that their freedom had resulted in some way from the emancipation of slaves in the United States. They had pictures of Abraham Lincoln, and spoke of him familiarly as the *emancipador*, or emancipator. I have seen them fight, under the command of white officers and under the command of black officers, and one black man, named Cintra, particularly distinguished himself in the action at La Cruz and Aurora. These were two battles at which I was present. The forces on the Cuban side at La Cruz were about eight hundred. It was fought in July. There were actually engaged about three hundred Cubans, against one hundred and fifty Spanish, who were intrenched in a position of their own choosing. The Spanish lost their commander, their second in command, and several others killed and wounded. On that day we lost none, having attacked them while they were moving from one part of their intrenched position to another. At Aurora there were about five hundred Cubans actually engaged against the Spanish, whose number I am unable to judge of, fortified in a stone building, with out-houses of stone made into block-houses. I should think there were one hundred men. We succeeded in capturing a neighboring encampment, and a large quantity of war material and stores, and afterward destroyed the encampment. I heard the day afterward that the Spanish lost about twenty men. Our loss was seven killed and twelve wounded. In each of these engagements the Cubans made the attack and gained their object. They were conducted under the immediate command of Generals Jordan, Marmol, and Gomez. The troops were maneuvered and fought under their respective captains, majors, and colonels.

I was acquainted with General Dicente Garcia, commanding the department of Las Tunas, who informed me, (and I believe it to be true,) that he had exchanged a flag of truce with the commander of Las Tunas, for the purpose of exchanging Spanish officers captured in a battle fought a few days previously, for Cubans, in possession of the Spanish, and for his wife and children, who were in the town. He was unable to negotiate the exchange, and it did not take place. I was at the battle of Las Calabayas and several others. All these military operations were conducted under the supreme control of one man, who was the commander-in-chief, and whose name is Manuel Quesada. He had been a military officer in Mexico, fighting against Maximilian, and is a Cuban by birth. I found several persons there as officers who had seen military service in the army of the United States and in England. In traveling through the country, I carried with me two passports, which commanded all persons to allow me to pass. One was issued by the President, and the other by the commander-in-chief. They commanded all persons to respect me, and to assist me, and whenever I showed them they were universally obeyed. I had frequent occasion to use them. On leaving the country, I was only able to get out by means of the passports. At the time I left, the revolution was in successful operation, and had lost nothing from the time it had begun, but had continually gained, and was then gaining both territory and force. It needed nothing to be perfectly successful, in my opinion, to the entire exclusion of the Spanish rule from the island, but arms and ammunition. In the interior, I traveled with perfect safety, carrying a large amount of money for government use. The people who could not be armed were about their ordinary avocation, but were all included in some military company or organization, and were ready to be called upon whenever arms should arrive. The number in the army was only limited by the amount of arms. I found the people exceedingly enthusiastic, apparently everywhere devoted to the government of the republic, and I was everywhere entertained hospitably by them, it being understood I was in the service of the republic. I conversed freely with all classes of persons concerning the future of the republic of Cuba, and I found that almost unanimously they looked to the United States for recognition as soon as it could be given, and after that, to annexation. It was their expressed hope, and a part of the plan of the revolution, as understood by the people at large. A petition for annexation was, as I understood, adopted by the Congress and approved by the secretary of state, and forwarded to the Department of State at Washington. The people were depending very largely for the final success of the republican government in Cuba upon the friendship and support of the people of the United States, and the wish most frequently expressed was, that they should be permitted to become a part of this country. It was common for officers of the government to wear upon their hats the stars and stripes on one side, and on the other the Cuban cockade. To my knowledge, a very great number of the officers of the government were persons who had been educated in the United States, who were well acquainted with their institutions, and who had been for years anxiously desiring to bring about this revolution and obtain annexation. They were well acquainted with the American form of government, and avowed that they had inaugurated this revolution to obtain such a government for Cuba.

Soon after I arrived there the capital was permanently located near Sibanicu, at a place to which the government had removed, because they found there ample buildings and accommodations for all the departments of government. Sibanicu is the general name of the locality. From that place there is direct communication by high roads with several parts of the island, and it is on the main road from Puerto Principe to Santiago de Cuba, both of which places were in the hands of the Spaniards. Sibanicu is only forty-eight miles from Puerto Principe, on a good road. The country about it is all open and cultivated. There was but a small military force there; the main forces being thrown further out. There are certain lines of defense which had been assumed before I arrived, and which were maintained up to the time of my leaving, and which, from late reports, I know to be still held. These lines of defense were, from Nuevitas on the north to Puerto Principe, a distance of about eighty-five miles, and from Puerto Principe to Santa Cruz on the south. There is also a line of communication which has been held uninterruptedly from the beginning, from Puerto Principe to Ciago de Avila. Uninterrupted communication is kept up along the different roads leading to the Five City district. That line is about one hundred and eighty miles long from Puerto Principe westward. The military encampments were all in communication with each other by couriers and a regular system of communications. Postal arrangements had been perfected by the republican government throughout all the region controlled by it, which is about two-thirds of the whole island, and I myself sent and received communications through this post. There was no difficulty in communicating by post anywhere through that part of the island. I left the island on the 2d of August. I have received communications from the island up to within about ten days ago, and I believe that the revolution has been in no way retarded since that time, except from scarcity of powder and arms, and that it has continually gained in numbers and territory. There was a government printing office at the capital, and two papers were published there.

I annex hereto a paper which contains a copy of the constitution and the debates in Congress, which is marked Exhibit C. I also annex a proclamation (marked Exhibit D) abolishing slavery, issued by the government of the republic before the adoption of the constitution. I also annex hereto two proclamations (marked Exhibits E and F) issued by the President of the republic, to the people. Bulletins of war were issued from time to time for the information of the people. There were numerous ports to which the Cubans had access at any time, and in which they received such supplies as had succeeded in getting away from the United States, Jamaica, and other places; but they made no efforts to hold those ports, because they had not the means of resisting the artillery of ships, and it was their policy to go from port to port, so as not to attract the attention of Spanish cruisers. They relied upon the signals of their cordons of sentinels to inform them when it was necessary to concentrate upon any one point for the purpose of receiving arms or ammunition. I am not aware of any function or power ordinarily exercised by a government for which provision was not made, or which was not exercised, within the district controlled by the republican government, so far as there was any call or occasion for such exercise. The republican government had all the paraphernalia, accompaniments, and incidents of a regularly organized government. The President executed the laws simply, and did not interfere in military matters. The commander-in-chief had entire control of the armies, and did not in any way interfere with the civil administration. The general division of powers and duties was very similar to (and copied after) that in the government of the United States, and was strictly observed so far as was compatible with a state of war. A stranger coming into the district lying south of a line drawn from Nuevitas to Puerto Principe and Santa Cruz, excepting within the walls of four or five garrisoned towns, would have, in my opinion, no reason to suppose that any other government prevailed, or had ever prevailed, there than the government of the republic of Cuba. The people were engaged about their ordinary avocations, and no government was spoken of or admitted except the government of the republic of Cuba, and no laws were or could be enforced there, unless by the aid of overwhelming military force, except those of the republic. The part of the country of which I have spoken is principally devoted to grazing, but is in a very considerable degree cultivated, only about one-sixth of it being wild land; and throughout that district every right of private persons was provided for and protected solely by the laws and power of the republic. There were certain special enactments intended to do away with abuses of power which had been common on the part of the Spanish soldiery before the revolution. These special enactments of which I speak instructed the people as to their rights, and advised them, in case of any infringement of those rights by the military, to apply immediately to the nearest court. These enactments were posted in different places for the information of the people, and particularly in the court-rooms.

I know that the Cuban Republic has also issued letters of marque and reprisal, and commissions for the Cuban navy. I have seen several of such commissions, and I know also that the officers in command in Cuba were acting under commissions issued by the war department. I saw several of their commissions, and the officers exercised command and control according to the rank mentioned in their commissions. Rank was acknowledged according to established military usage. To my knowledge, the republic of Cuba has purchased a number of vessels, with the view of constituting a navy.

WILLIAM C. TINKER.

Sworn and subscribed before me this eleventh day of December, 1869.

CHARLES HARRIS PHELPS,
Notary Public, County of New York.

Affidavit of Francis Coppinger.

STATE OF NEW YORK, *City and County of New York, ss:*

FRANCIS COPPINGER, being duly sworn, says: I am a native of Cuba, born at Havana, and have lived there all my life, until about the beginning of this year, when I came to New York, by order of the President of the republic of Cuba. I reside at present at the St. George Hotel, corner of 20th street and Broadway, New York.

In May last I returned to Cuba, and engaged in the military service of the Cuban government. I was at first in active service, in command of a company, with the rank of lieutenant; and, as such, between May and August, took part in several battles and skirmishes; of the former the three most important were those at Ramon, Cuaba, and Calabazas, in each of which the Cuban force engaged numbered from five hundred to seven hundred men. I was afterward attached to the staff of General Peralta, with the rank of captain. Each state of the Cuban territory had been divided into military districts, each under command of a general, and General Peralta was such general in command of the military district of Holquin, in the State of Oriente.

It was the duty of the staff officers to carry on communication between their general and the next superior military authority, and I was thus engaged, while on staff duty, in carrying dispatches and instructions between General Peralta and General Jordan, who was, at that time, in command of the whole State of Oriente. The organization of the Cuban army, and all departments of the military service were, at the time to which I refer, similar in all the States to that in Oriente.

While I was in the island I traveled from Holquin to Las Tunas, through the center of the island, a distance of about one hundred and fifty miles. In all this territory I found the civil department of the revolutionary government, the State governments, the prefectures, the constabulary or civil police, the postal service, and all the ordinary civil administration fully organized, and in regular and systematic operation. The military occupation of the country was complete, and all the separate camps and bodies of soldiers of the Cuban army, however separated from each other, were all parts of one military system, and all under commands, subordinate, in different grades, to the commander-in-chief, who received his authority immediately from the Congress.

I would like to add, that when I was in the island the former slaves were all free, having been made so by virtue of that clause of the Cuban constitution which secures freedom to all inhabitants of the State. The negroes were enrolled in the Cuban army, and were armed, equipped, and uniformed, like the Cubans, and held in equal respect in the service. There were, in my company of sixty men, several negroes, who had been slaves up to the time of their emancipation by the Cuban government.

As to the celebration of marriages in that part of the island which was controlled by the revolutionary party, it came under my notice that marriage was no longer regarded by the Cubans as a sacrament, nor was the ceremony performed, as it had always been under the Spanish dominion, by the priesthood exclusively; but, by virtue of the constitution, it was regarded as a civil contract, and the rite was performed by civil officers. I attended, myself, the celebration of such a marriage according to the new Cuban laws.

Deponent further says, that he has heard read the depositions of William C. Tinker and Enrique Loynaz, and that the statements contained in them, respectively, as to the civil and military affairs of the Cuban government, and their administration, coincide with deponent's own experience and knowledge on those subjects, and that the statements made by said Tinker and Loynaz in regard to them are true.

F. COPPINGER.

Sworn and subscribed before me this eleventh day of December, 1869.

ARCHIBALD F. CUSHMAN,
Notary Public in and for City and County of New York.

Affidavit of Enrique Loinaz.

CITY AND COUNTY OF NEW YORK, *ss:*

ENRIQUE LOINAZ, being duly sworn, says: I am a native of Puerto Principe, in the Island of Cuba. I joined the revolution in Cuba on the 25th of December, 1868. I left the Island of Cuba on the 8th of September last, and am now remaining here under orders from the President. For some time I commanded a company of volunteers in the republican army, and afterward was promoted to the staff of Manuel Quesada, and held, and now hold, the rank of major. I have participated in about twelve actions of considerable importance, besides many skirmishes. The largest number of men which I have ever known to be engaged on the Cuban side was at the battle of Las Tunas, at which I was present, and which took place at the town of Las Tunas, about the 16th or 17th of August last—I do not remember which. In that battle there were four brigades, of one hundred and seventy-five men each, engaged, besides thirty, the escort of the general-in-chief, and forty men of the President's escort. The President was present at the battle. The Cubans attacked the Spanish forces, consisting of about six hundred line troops and two hundred volunteers, who were intrenched in the center of the town, in the plaza. The combat lasted from four o'clock in the morning until three o'clock in the afternoon. The Cubans drove the Spaniards into their intrenchments in the church, a building in the square, and held them there, sacking the town and capturing the medicines, clothing, some guns, military stores, and other things. The attack was made for the purpose of rescuing families of Cubans that were perishing in the town, and these families being removed, the Cubans retired. We captured fourteen standards or battle flags. Our loss was forty dead and eighty-five wounded. I do not know the Spanish loss, but it was reported by a captain, whom we captured, to be about two hundred. This battle, and all the others in which I have participated, were conducted under military orders and under the control and management of officers of different rank, each yielding obedience to the other, and the troops engaged were disciplined troops, who had been trained and accustomed to military movements, and who were held, in all their operations, in strict military discipline. They are never permitted to engage, and have never engaged, in any fighting except under military orders, discipline, and subject to the plans of the commander-in-chief. At the time I left, the government of the republic held exclusive control of all the Island of Cuba lying south of a line drawn from Nuevitas, on the Atlantic coast, to Puerto Principe, and thence to Santa Cruz, on the Caribbean Sea, except a few garrison towns and encampments along the railroad established from Nuevitas to Puerto Principe. All the rest of the country, which is mostly an open, cultivated, inhabited country, was exclusively occupied or controlled by the republican government, and no Spanish laws were, or could be enforced, except by the presence of overwhelming military force. The laws of the republic were voluntarily obeyed by the people, or executed by simple civil force, such as by constables or prefects. Throughout this district complete postal arrangements were established by the republic, and regular service of mails kept up by its officers. Post offices were established at villages and farm-houses on the public high roads. The Spaniards were under great difficulties to hold their position in the garrison towns, and we were constantly occupied in attacking their convoys, and many combats ensued in this way, and we were able to capture, and did capture, frequently, their convoys and appropriated their material of war. This was particularly the case as to the town of Las Tunas. The town of Las Tunas was an important station for them, was situated about thirty-six miles from the north coast, and connected by three high roads with three forts, only about thirty-six miles distant. I have often heard it estimated, and believe it to be true, that since the breaking out of the revolution the Spaniards have lost over two thousand men in maintaining this communication, and have frequently lost their convoys. These circumstances have come to my knowledge in the performance of my duties as staff officer. The Spaniards have never been able to penetrate the surrounding country from these towns more then two or three miles. They have never made the attempt, except in one or two cases, when they have been driven back. The people in the country are all loyal to the republic, and immediately give information of any movement among the Spanish troops. The negroes in that district have all been freed. They understand that they are free, and it is so understood by all persons, and they are given by the constitution and the laws all the rights and privileges of citizenship that are given to white persons. Even in addressing them the former owners of slaves address them by their names as citizen so-and-so.

At the time I left Cuba the revolution had been constantly gaining, and had never lost anything, either in force or in territory. The army was increasing in numbers as fast as they could be supplied, and persons, who, at the beginning, had been wavering and doubtful, were giving their adhesion to the government of the republic. I have not seen or heard anything since leaving there to induce me to suppose that the revolution is in any less forward condition than when I left, but on the contrary, I believe that it is able to hold its own for a long time without any more succor, and that, with a few more arms and with sufficient ammunition, the Spanish authorities could be entirely driven from the island by the forces now here. We need nothing from outside the island except arms and munitions. I know from my experience that the Cubans, almost without exception, are for the republic. On the other hand, native Spaniards on the island are almost without exception against the republic. The lines of defense which were held, and, according to my information, are still held by the republican forces, were taken up by them about February last, and have been maintained uninterruptedly ever since. I have read the affidavit of Mr. William C. Tinker, who is known to me, and who was with me in Cuba. The facts stated by him concerning the condition of the country, the action of the government, the administration of the law, and the amount of forces are true, within my own knowledge. In the entire island there are over thirty thousand men in the republican army. In the central department, with which I had more immediate connection, there were over ten thousand, organized and under discipline. Of these, three thousand were armed with all sorts of guns, carbines, muskets, and rifles; the others were all armed with the machete, a long sword, and frequently went into action with only this weapon. Of the fire-arms in that department, about one-third had been captured from the Spaniards. There are about eighty thousand men remaining, ready to take arms as soon as arms can be procured. I was commanding the siege of Nuevitas, in January last. During that siege, I received and entertained a flag of truce from the Spaniards, and twice after that, having occasion, I sent flags of truce to them, which were received and entertained. The communication sent by me was from General Quesada to the governor of Nuevitas, and the communication was replied to by him. The flag of truce which they sent to me accompanied three commissioners who were appointed by the Spanish authorities to communicate with the Cuban committee, which, at that time, had charge of the Cuban affairs, that being before the election of Congress. These commissioners were given a safe-conduct, and passed on through our lines to communicate with our committee. One of the communications under flag of truce by General Quesada, sent by me, related to an exchange of prisoners, which exchange was finally refused by the Spaniards. By proclamation of the Captain General, issued in January last, six large ports, which were formerly ports of entry, have been closed to commerce, and all intercourse with those ports forbidden. The civil government has made arrangements, which are now in operation, by which the local constabulary and prefects of each county are charged with the distribution of rations to the families of persons who are in the field and the persons who are discharged and unable to support themselves. This distribution of rations takes place extensively and constantly, and is sufficient for the wants of the people. The inhabitants are perfectly united in support of the revolution, and seem willing to devote, and have devoted, their entire time and property to its success, without any complaint or objection, and, in my opinion, it would be impossible to find a population more united and determined than is this population in its determination to throw off Spanish tyranny. The commander-in-chief has been named by Congress, and is under the same control by the President as are generals of armies of the United States. The troops are all organized into companies, battalions, and brigades, and are not permitted to go upon any roving expeditions, or to separate themselves in any way from their commands; and property captured by them is always turned over to the commander of the district, for the republic.

ENRIQUE LOINAZ.

Subscribed and sworn to before me this 11th day of December, 1869.

CHARLES HARRIS PHELPS,
Notary Public, County of New York.

Affidavit of Francis Xavier Cisneros.

CITY AND COUNTY OF NEW YORK, *ss:*

FRANCIS XAVIER CISNEROS, being duly sworn, says: I am a native of Cuba, having been born at Santiago de Cuba, and for the greater part of the last fifteen years, and until recently, have been a resident of Havana. I was by profession a civil engineer in that city. I am living for the present in the city of New

York, at No. 254 West Twenty-fourth street. In May, of this year, I left New York for Cuba, and arrived there about the eleventh day of that month. Upon my arrival I communicated with the republican general, in command of the district, General Peralta, and then with the commander-in-chief, General Quesada, and then went to the seat of government, at Sibanicu, and communicated there with the secretaries of the Cuban government, whom I found in the active administration of the business of their several departments. From that time up to the first of August I was constantly traveling in the island, and especially traversed that part of it which lies between Santo Espiritu, about the central portion of the island, and Santiago de Cuba, near the eastern extremity, a distance of about three hundred and fifty miles. I made this journey at the instance of the government of Cuba, for the purpose of inspecting the condition of affairs under the government, and the progress of the revolution. This I was instructed to do, in order to make a report of my observations to the Cuban Junta, at New York. This district to which I have referred is only a portion of the territory which is occupied and controlled by the revolutionists, and which is more than two-thirds of the area of the island. This republican territory is bounded by lines extending from Santiago de Cuba, on the Caribbean Sea, near the eastern part of the island, to Baracoa, on the Atlantic Ocean; from Baracoa to Sagua la Grande, along the northern coast; thence across the island to the Bay of Broa, on the Caribbean Sea; and thence along the southern coast to Santiago de Cuba. The total extent of the island is about thirty-six thousand square miles, of which the republican territory, just described, embraces about twenty-four thousand square miles. This territory includes some wild tracts, but for the most part is open, cultivated country. It embraces some of the considerable cities of the island—say nine or ten—which were then in the possession of the Spaniards; but a larger number—say twenty or thirty—of the considerable towns, with numerous smaller villages and all the open country to which I have referred, were occupied and controlled by the republicans. The occupation of these large towns by the Spaniards compelled them to withdraw large bodies from their fighting force for garrison duty. This district, also extending to the sea, on both the northern and southern sides of the island, embraces many ports to which the Cubans had free access; but having as yet no means of fortifying those places, they had made no attempt to hold exclusive possession of them. Within this district, between May and August, I visited almost all the military encampments of the revolutionists, about thirty in number. At some of the camps there were as many as two thousand men, and at none less than two hundred and fifty. To the best of my judgment and belief, there were in all those camps, in May, about fifteen thousand well-armed soldiers; and in August, when I left the island, there were, I should think, about twenty thousand. The Cuban forces were encamped around most of the principal towns occupied by the Spaniards, and prevented communication by the Spaniards between those towns. Besides the force of regular soldiers in camp, the entire male population throughout the district I have described was organized as a volunteer military force, but, being without arms, could not be brought into actual military service.

The Cuban republic was divided into four States, and each of those States was subdivided into districts, each district being placed under the command of a general, appointed by the government. Each of these generals had control of all the forces in his district, subject to the commander-in-chief; so that all the forces of the revolutionists were under the supreme command of General Qnesada, the general-in-chief who was appointed by the Cuban Congress.

During my stay in the island there were frequent conflicts between the Cuban and the Spanish forces, in many of which I participated; in the most important of those in which I took part, which took place on the 18th of June, at Calabazas, the Cuban forces numbered about seven hundred. The Spaniards had attacked, but were repelled, and retreated. A few days before, a fight had taken place, in which, as I was then informed, and believe, the Cubans numbered fifteen hundred. Many other combats took place with various results. The condition of the country was one of constant fighting between considerable forces, and, on the part of the Cubans, all of the battles were conducted under the control of the commander-in-chief.

At the time of my visit to the island, the Cuban revolutionary party had already adopted a constitution embodying a republican form of government, guaranteeing the liberty of the press, of religion, and education, and abolishing slavery; it had also a completely organized government, represented by a President and Congress, and secretaries of state, war, treasury, and interior, and other officers and bodies. The Congress was composed of eighteen delegates, elected by the people from all parts of the island; it was, at the time to which I refer, in session, and I attended many of its meetings. The elections for governors of the States took place during my stay on the island, and were participated in by all the inhabitants of the district described by me, except of the towns garrisoned by the Spaniards.

The capital of the republican government was at Sibanicu, a town situated in the interior, in an open plain, on the great central highway of the island, and approached by good roads from all directions.

The island had then also been divided by the Congress into four States, namely, Oriente, Camaguay, Las Villas, Occidente; governors of each of these States had been elected by their inhabitants, and they had assumed and were administering their offices. The government had also established and maintained regular postal service throughout all its territory; had created courts and appointed judges and sheriffs or prefects; the local judges had opened and were holding their courts; the supreme court of the state was not yet convened; the court administered laws which had been enacted by the Cuban Congress, and which were universally recognized and enforced throughout the territory of the Cuban government which I have described.

F. J. CISNEROS.

Sworn and subscribed before me this 11th day of December, 1869.

CHARLES HARRIS PHELPS,
Notary Public, County of New York.

III.—CORRESPONDENCE BETWEEN THE DEPARTMENT OF STATE AND CONSULAR REPRESENTATIVES IN CUBA.

No. 122.

*Mr. La Reintrie to Mr. Seward.**

No. 105.] HAVANA, *October* 17, 1868.

SIR: Rumors are prevalent in this city, to which many attach credit, that the telegraph wires beyond Puerto Principe have been cut, and the insurgents (progressive party of Cuba) are rising in various parts of the island, with the view of asserting their independence from the mother country.

It is even said that movements are now on foot on this end of the island to proclaim the independence of Cuba, and the friends of liberty would rejoice to see the United States come to their aid in some shape.

The Catalans in Cuba are opposed to slavery, and it is expected they will unite with the native Cubans and negroes in declaring themselves free.

The arrival of the next mail steamer from Spain, expected on or about the 25th of this month, is looked to with great anxiety, and the reticence of the Captain General on the subject of the political situation in Spain is a cause of great discontent among the people.

I have understood, to-day, that the fortifications around and about this city are being strengthened and put in fighting condition.

Several domiciliary visits were made last night, and the houses of persons suspected of republican proclivities were searched by the police; among those so visited was Mr. Posada, a naturalized citizen of the United States.

In view of this probably approaching crisis, it would be well to have a squadron here.

Her Britannic Majesty's ship Favorite, with a strong battery, arrived here three days ago, and salutes were interchanged between her and the city.

As I have so little time to run about I give you the news as it is brought to me at the office.

---

* These dispatches (122, 123, and 124) precede the correspondence sent to the Senate December 20, 1869.

No. 123.

Mr. La Reintrie to Mr. Seward.

No. 107.] HAVANA, *October* 24, 1868.

* * * * *

Since my dispatches treating upon the political situation of this city and island, the excitement has been steadily increasing in all directions, and consequently the most active and stringent measures have been adopted by the Captain General to suppress any movement of a revolutionary character.

The national guard has been called out, say some five thousand men, to preserve order, while the regulars are sent out in various directions to put down the insurgents.

The authorities here inform us *officially* that the revolt in Manzanillo, Tunas, Gibara, and Zarra has been put down, while the opposition claim to have defeated the government troops; but the fact that more troops have been sent to the support of the government forces would suggest that the insurgents are still in arms.

It is said that the revolutionary forces now amount to four thousand men of all arms in the district embracing the towns above mentioned.

On Monday, the 19th instant, I called on General Lersundi to ascertain, if possible, the truth. His replies to me generally tended to assure me that he was amply prepared to face all opposition, from whatever quarter it might come. I suggested the propriety of my telegraphing to the Secretary of State for a naval force for the protection of our citizens and interests in this quarter. He assured me that he deemed it unnecessary, and would give me notice whenever the emergency arose to warrant my telegraphing to Washington.

He desired to know of me whether any filibuster expeditions were likely to come from the United States. I replied that I believed it was not likely; but certainly not with the consent of our government—that he might rely upon. He expressed himself highly gratified, and alluded to his sending Santa Anna off as a proof of his good faith in preventing like organizations. On the termination of our interview he informed me that his object and desire was "to preserve to Spain the Island of Cuba"—"Conservar la Ysla de Cuba para la España."

Yesterday, 23d instant, rumors were thick throughout the city of an intended rising of the republicans and negroes in this city for a general massacre and pillage. The excitement consequent almost paralyzed all commercial transactions.

A run was made upon the Banco Español, and their notes to-day are at a discount of some three per cent.

Numerous arrests have been made, among them some naturalized citizens of the United States, but as they have not called upon me for redress or protection, I shall await their complaints before taking any action.

In view of the situation, and deeming it critical, I request the presence of a strong naval force.

I inclose the programme of the republican committee of Havana, printed, I think, at Matanzas, and the extra of the "Diario de la Marina" of yesterday, which will give you additional information respecting the political views of the two parties now contending for political supremacy in Cuba.

At Bayamo the government troops have been defeated, and the city of Puerto Principe is said to have pronounced and risen against its authorities.

It is also probable that a declaration of the independence of Cuba from Spain may be issued from Puerto Principe. The people of the interior will accept nothing short of entire separation from Spain, and if their movement be successful they will proclaim either their independence as a separate state or annexation to the United States. Should a government *de facto* be established there, I should like to have instructions how to act in that case. Perhaps instructions may be also given to the commanding naval officer sent here, to consult and act in harmony and conjunction with me in the emergency indicated.

No. 124.

Mr. La Reintrie to Mr. Seward.

No. 119.] HAVANA, *December* 14, 1868.

I have only time to inclose to you a copy of a letter I have this moment received from Mr. Gibbs, the United States consular agent at Nuevitas, which gives you the latest news from that quarter.

UNITED STATES CONSULAR AGENCY,
Nuevitas, December 11, 1868.

DEAR SIR: Your very esteemed favor of 2d instant duly received.

I notice that you have asked for a squadron, and hope it will soon arrive, as American interests want it badly. As I understand, Spanish gunboats have boarded American vessels and searched them, to the eastward of this island, when they were out of sight of land. The gunboat Africa has been employed in this service for some time, and arrived here on the 8th. I was also informed that an American schooner from St. Thomas, bound to Baracoa, was hove-to, and the said gunboat sent aboard a boat's crew and took possession of her, overhauling papers and cargo, and after detaining her some time let her pass on her voyage. This has come indirectly to me from persons on board.

I have tried by all possible means to get true information of the affairs around here, but it is difficult.

Since I wrote on the 3d the troops of Valmaseda have remained at San Miguel; from all that I can find out by different channels of information, his loss of killed and wounded on his march from Puerto Principe amounts to one hundred and fifty men; he brought here in the afternoon of the 3d, per gunboat, about forty wounded, most part from waist upward; several have died since their arrival here, and more are expected to die.

By all accounts the insurgents on the 1st instant fought with desperation, and harassed the troops from ten in the forenoon until night. I cannot find out anything about the losses of the insurgents, but from all sides that I can learn I infer that they were few. To persons who have passed through their lines they positively state that in the attack of the 28th ultimo there was only one killed and four wounded, and that the attacking party were only sixty. They stated that they buried about forty of the troops.

Some three or four days ago two young men, insurgents, were shot in Principe, names Padillo and Barroso, about seventeen and eighteen years of age. They were taken prisoners on entering the town, and there was found on their persons a pass or safe conduct, signed by one of the chiefs or commanders of the insurgents, that they might go to Principe and return. Great efforts were made by all classes in town to save their lives, but useless.

I greatly fear that this department will be laid waste and devastated. I am informed on good authority that Valmaseda destroyed everything on his march twelve miles before he entered San Miguel. He burned two sugar estates, the Isabel and La Union, and a small one, El Destino; fences were destroyed and cut down, and all kind of live stock shot and left to rot on the road.

After he took possession of San Miguel it appears that a corporal of a guard was treacherously shot, and the infuriated soldiers sacked the town, with the exception of three houses. Yesterday forty negroes from plantation St. Linus, about twelve miles from here, came in and presented themselves to the government of this town, stating that their master wanted them to take arms, and they refused. This I know to be untrue, as I am well acquainted with the owners and know that they have nothing to do with this insurrection, one of them having last October purchased over thirty thousand dollars' worth of machinery in the United States, and sent it here for his estate.

Here a deadly hatred exists between the Spaniards and Cubans that is growing stronger day by day. There is no half way, no room for compromise; ninety-five out of every hundred of the natives are heart and soul in the rebellion, if not bodily. I don't care how neutral a man may be, how loyal he may be, how his interests may incline him to peace, the very fact of his being a native-born is enough in the eyes of the bigoted Spaniard to make him an enemy; and it can be plainly seen, as they are impotent to cope with the rebellion, they are determined to ruin the island and leave it withered and destroyed.

If this thing spreads it must have a great effect to the injury of the United States. I suppose Cuban produce pays over twenty-five millions of dollars into the United States treasury yearly, for imports. American merchants must have some millions advanced to planters on this island; I know one house in Brooklyn which has advanced alone in this district nearly one hundred and fifty thousand dollars.

Up to the 1st of December the insurgents held all the country in every direction, excepting the cities and seaports. No outrages were committed; every thing and person were respected; only demands were made on planters and cattle farms for beef for their maintenance. The field hands were not molested, but on account of Valmaseda's behavior and actions, attacking the estates and carrying off the negroes, all is changed. Three days ago two farm-houses, some three or four miles from here, belonging to Spaniards, were burnt and destroyed, and all their stock carried off by the insurgents. To the south of this, on the night of the 9th, a large light was seen, and it is supposed some other estate or farm was destroyed. Guamaja, a small town to the westward of this some twenty-five miles, was taken possession of by the insurgents. A small force of troops and sailors were dispersed, two killed, two wounded, and nine prisoners; the rest escaped in a boat belonging to the government.

From officers who have been with the troops between Mariti and Las Tunas I learn that they have to be in large bodies to convey the provisions, and are continually harassed by guerillas.

I am very sorry to report as yet I have not had the great pleasure of seeing an American man-of-war in this harbor this year.

Yours, respectfully,

RICHARD GIBBS,
United States Consular Agent.

H. R. DE LA REINTRIE, Esq.,
Vice-Consul General, Havana, Cuba.

A true and correct copy of the original.

LA REINTRIE.

HAVANA, *December* 14, 1868.

No. 125.

Mr. de La Reintrie to Mr. Seward.

No. 130.] HAVANA, *January* 29, 1869.

The inclosed copies and translations of a correspondence between this consulate general and the Captain General of this island, under date of the 25th instant, will bring to you the sad news of the murder of Mr. Samuel Alexander Cohner, a citizen of the United States, and, so far as I can learn, a native of the State of New York. He was also at one time an employé in the navy of the United States.

Although I have not been thus far enabled to ascertain the name of the assassin, it is generally thought that he met his death at the hands of some one of the volunteers, recently organized in this city with the view of maintaining the public peace and order by General Lersundi.

These volunteers are displeased with the new system inaugurated here by General Dulce, and for the past two weeks had roamed about the city at will, and without their officers, uttering threats of vengeance against all Cubans and foreigners who did not agree with them in political opinions.

As the nights set in their demonstrations were more open, hailing and stopping all passers, with bayónet to their breasts, and compelling them to cry out "Viva España." The freedom of the press having been granted by General Dulce, it extended to the theaters where new local and other piquant plays were presented to the public.

This occurred particularly at the Villanueva Theater in this city, where, on Thursday, 21st instant, the performance was of a very liberal character, and elicited repeated bursts of applause from the audience. I was myself present, with my family, by invitation of the manager, and the entire play passed off without any incident to mar the pleasures of the evening. The next day, Friday, 22d instant, reports of the character of the performance spread in every direction, and a very large concourse of pleasure seekers attended. In the mean time a large body of the volunteers, without orders to that effect, gathered in the vicinity of the theater, and, as the applause arose from the audience, surrounded the building and commenced firing upon the assembled audience.

The military governor and chief of police, after great exertions, and aided by a few of the troops which were still under their control, succeeded finally in preventing the infuriated and riotous volunteers from firing the building, a perfect tinder-box; and after ordering them to their quarters, the audience were enabled to return to their houses. The result, seven killed and many others wounded.

The next day, Saturday, the 23d instant, General Dulce issued a brief address severely condemning the conduct of the volunteers, but in such vague terms that it would be difficult to say whether he meant the actors and audience, or the riotous volunteers. He may possibly have desired to address both. This, however, seemed to have no effect upon the volunteers, and on Sunday morning, 24th instant, it was publicly said they would attack the Louvre, the largest public café and restaurant in this city, kept by a Spaniard (native of Spain) universally esteemed as a good citizen by all classes. Accordingly the volunteers of the fifth and sixth battalions, and of others, on Sunday night collected around the Louvre, and, as it is said, a shot from a revolver was fired upon them from the roof of said building; whether true or not I have no means of ascertaining. This was about 9 p. m., and in less than *thirty seconds* after the firing of this shot the volunteers began shooting into the building and upon the persons there present; also, at all passers-by and in the vicinity of the Louvre. Mr. Cohner was killed at the corner of Consulado and San Miguel streets, full six hundred yards in a *diagonal direction* from the Louvre, which occupies one of the corners of the large block of buildings erected near and fronting the prado or main public park of this city.

It is clear to me that he could not have been shot by any of those immediately engaged in the assault upon the Louvre, as the distance was great and the intervening walls and masonry would naturally forbid such a presumption.

This being the case, and the firing by volunteers upon Mr. Tinker, in the same street where Mr. Cohner's dead body was found, leads to the inevitable conclusion that he met his death at the hands of a portion of said volunteers; and further, as the owner himself, Mr. Payret, of the Louvre, has informed me he was forewarned full 12 hours, and by several of his friends, previous to the attack upon his premises, I must also conclude that the outrage was a premeditated one on the part of these lawless volunteers, and that they were posted around and about the block with the purpose and intent to attack all persons attempting to evade their murderous designs. In this connection it must also be borne in mind that the Louvre is resorted to by both Cubans and foreigners, and of the most respectable classes. Fortunately, and at the time, and the public notoriety given to the intended attack, kept many from resorting to the Louvre that evening. The result of this brutal act of vandalism is the cold-blooded murder of Mr. Cohner, an American citizen, both peaceful and respectable, a photographer by profession and in which he had acquired a competent fortune, and of seven other persons, including also many others severely wounded; of the latter two are Prussians.

Having accomplished their fiendish act of brutality and vandalism, the cry was raised of death to the Aldamas, and the crowd of soldiers and others aiding them made for the palatial mansion of Mr. Miguel Delmonte y Aldama, a gentleman of large wealth in this city, who in September, 1868, forswore his allegiance to the Queen of Spain, and made his declaratien of intention to become a citizen of the United States before the superior court of common pleas of the city and State of New York. Fortunately, both for Mr. Aldama and his family, he, having had previous notice of an intended attack upon his elegant premises, had gone to the country; otherwise they would have all been murdered. The mob of soldiers, however, found ingress to his mansion, and committed every species of vandalism possible to imagine.

I myself visited some twelve of his rooms yesterday and can speak of my own knowledge.

These rooms were completely ransacked, valuable jewelry stolen, furniture destroyed, shots fired into the ceilings, &c., objects of *vertû* carried off or destroyed, wine cellars and pantries broken open, and of which these villains amply partook.

Finally, the torch was applied, but the fear of self-destruction and the instinct of preservation induced some of their least inebriated comrades to extinguish it.

This was not enough to satisfy their fury and madness. A young negress, 13 years of age, was forcibly violated, and a middle-aged Irish woman also shared the same fate.

After four hours of riotous, brutal, and inhuman conduct, the chief of police made his appearance, and with some of the civil police, more through persuasion than force, induced them to leave the building. The result has been the loss to Mr. Aldama of some $30,000, to say nothing of the destruction of pictures and other objects of *vertû*, impossible to replace. General Dulce himself has visited Mr. Aldama's premises, at his request, to see the damage and injury perpetrated, and has expressed his deep condemnation of the outrage. I beg herewith to inclose a protest addressed to me by citizens of the United States, both natives and naturalized, in which you will find their just complaints fully set forth.

I must here remark that, previous to its receipt, on the 26th, I had already addressed my remonstrance to the Captain General.

Of his reply you will yourself be enabled to judge. In my opinion it does not come up to the demand.

He seems to treat the murder of Mr. Cohner as an accidental affair. Such is not my opinion.

It is an open outrage to our country, which must receive ample and full reparation.

I have hitherto applied for a naval force for the protection of citizens of the United States and their interests. I have received your answer and that of the Secretary of the Navy. I now, through you, would appeal directly to the Congress of the United States at Washington and in session, and say to them that "at this time the lives and property of citizens of the United States are not safe here."

The proof is in that large numbers of persons, of both sexes, are fleeing hence for safety elsewhere. The landing nightly of marines and seamen from the Spanish naval squadron here to guard the city amply attests, also, the fact that General Dulce cannot rely upon the volunteers to protect himself and the people of Havana.

I would most earnestly recommend that when a force does come here for the purpose of rendering protection to our people and their interests its commanders receive instructions, at their discretion and sound judgment, to use that force effectively, and give them the protection which the law of nations guarantees to them.

This is the beginning of these outrages, and you may rely upon it that the end is not yet, and until Cuba shall be free.

I leave to your able hands the case of Mr. Cohner, as my position as a vice-consul general of the United States does not permit me to pursue it further for the present, and until your further instructions shall have been received. The reply of General Dulce is by no means satisfactory to me, and I could well have answered it. The fact is, however, that he has not sufficient force within his immediate reach to compel the disarming of these volunteers, and he is compelled to temporize.

The threat has openly been made that Dulce must be forcibly removed from office, and Lieutenant Genaro Solorzano, of the first battalion of volunteers, a native of Vizcaya, is now in prison under suspicion of attempting the life of General Dulce.

The inclosed extras of the 25th, 26th, and 27th instant will give you the accounts which are furnished by the press of the city touching these occurrences.

Referring again to the attack on Mr. Aldama's house, I desire your instructions as to how far in his case (as he is in a transitory state) I can extend to him the protection which would inure to a *naturalized* citizen of the United States.

He left the United States with the intention of returning after closing his business affairs here, and under the advice of Messrs. Evarts, Choate & Co., eminent lawyers of the city of New York.

No. 126.

Mr. Phillips to Mr. Fish.

[Extract.]

UNITED STATES CONSULATE,
Santiago de Cuba, January 3, 1870.

* * * * * * * * *

The political state of affairs at this consular district is in a most deplorable condition. The assassination at Bayamo of the citizens sent from this city by order of Count Valmaseda, which fact I have already communicated to the department, was nothing more than what is daily perpetrated. It is well known that Valmaseda aspires to the position of Captain General of the island, and in order to increase his popularity among the blood-craving Catalans, who are operating in his behalf, both in this island and in Spain, gives imperative orders to make this a war of extermination, and we daily learn of peaceful citizens residing in the country assassinated by the mobilized Spanish troops. These orders are probably carried to an extreme, from the fact that those commanding such troops are constantly supplying some Catalan produce dealers of this city, and whose object is to suck the country and forward to their agents such portions of the crop as may fall into their hands. The planters are persecuted to such a degree as to be compelled to flee from their estates, whose crops are immediately sequestered and appropriated to private purposes.

Very little credit can be placed upon the Spanish press, being a government organ, which maintains that the insurrection is finished in this department, which is far from the truth. The insurrection continues in full force, and frequent encounters take place, as is seen by the frequent arrivals of wounded Spanish soldiers. The Cubans, being better armed and disciplined than formerly, in many cases take the offensive, and, having had their ranks increased by desertion from the Spanish army, are becoming bold and fight well. Much sickness prevails among the newly arrived Spanish troops, who find it impossible to endure the climate. It is estimated that fifty per cent. of the Spanish volunteers from sickness are put *hors du combat;* the hospitals are full to overflowing. Much anxiety has been felt by the Cubans respecting the position of our government in the Cuba question, and I am inclined to believe, unless some action is taken upon the matter, the insurrection will continue for a long time, as it is impossible for any force that Spain can send to exterminate the rebel force, owing to the climate and topography of the country, while both contending parties destroy every vestige of agriculture. It is generally known and admitted by the liberal minded Spanish officers, who do not conceal the fact, that it is impossible to suppress the insurrection, and the only inducement offered for the continuance of the same is that the commanding officers are filling their pockets at the expense of the country.

The above is the actual state of the country, founded upon a long residence and thorough knowledge of the people and country.

The health of the city continues in an abnormal condition; small-pox, endemic fevers, and misery to an alarming extent prevail.

* * * * * *

No. 127.

Mr. Hall to Mr. Davis.

JANUARY 31, 1870.

The accompanying is a slip from the New York Sun of October 5th ultimo, containing a statement in regard to the murder of one Robert Wells at Cienfuegos. The statement appearing to be based upon evidence, I thought it my duty to make inquiry in regard to its truth, and with that view I transmitted it to Mr. Morris, the United States consular agent at Cienfuegos. To-day I have received the following reply:

> I have received your official note to me of 20th ultimo; it has not been answered in course, owing to my illness.
>
> * * * * * * *
>
> The paragraph in the slip you sent me, relating to Mr. Robert Wells, is pure invention; no such person was ever known here. I return the slip as requested.

[From the New York Sun, October 5, 1869.]

THE REVOLUTION IN CUBA—THE UNITED STATES EXCHANGING DIPLOMATIC NOTES—MEANTIME THE SPANIARDS WANTONLY MURDERING CITIZENS OF THE UNITED STATES—NO CESSATION OF SPANISH ATROCITIES IN CUBA—HOW LONG, OH, HOW LONG?

[Correspondence of the Sun.]

HAVANA, *September* 25.

The situation in Cuba becomes more and more painful to contemplate. Each month ends with its new lists of infamous, more than semi-barbarous deeds at Spanish hands. No little interest is evinced by our sugar dealers regarding the next crop. What do the insurrectionists propose to do with the ripening cane? is now the question. They have already disabled some three hundred engines of so many sugar cane mills, and rendered useless for this year as many steam boilers. I have heard sugar merchants say within the last few days that if the revolution could not be suppressed by December 1, only a one-third crop could be gathered. The amount on hand in the five large sugar warehouses of this city is 192,500 boxes, against 237,000 this time last year.

FORTIFYING THE RIVERS.

Count Valmaseda, since he received absolute command in the Eastern department, has ordered that the Rio Salado, at its junction with Rio Canto, be fortified with earthworks and cannon. Also, he orders that Rio Canto be fortified at its mouth on the coast. It is the largest river on the island. Valmaseda also has directed that Gibara, Puerto Padre, Nuevitas, and Trinidad be doubly fortified by additional lines of earthworks. The rumors recently received of piratical vessels, and the frequent mention made of the Hornet, have awakened the Spaniards to a sense of threatening dangers. One vessel, well manned and armed, and commanded by a brave, wise commander, would be able to well nigh ruin the coast trade of Cuba, and interrupt the arrival and departure of Spanish mail steamers.

ANOTHER AMERICAN ASSASSINATED.

How easily Americans are murdered in foreign lands and their assassinators escape punishment or even reproof, has been exemplified so frequently that it seems useless even to chronicle their death. Not many weeks ago Mr. Robert Wells, a citizen of the United States, and of late years a foreman in a Jersey City machine shop, came to Cuba to arrange the settlement of his father's estate or property, left him at his death. From this city he went to Cienfuegos, where his father left some unsettled accounts. Himself and two friends were walking by the Spanish barracks one evening about three weeks since, when the sentinel on duty called his "*Quien vive*"—who comes there—in a smothered tone. Neither he nor his friends hearing the call, they walked on. The sentinal, enraged at having no response, rushed upon the three gentlemen and gave Mr. Wells a bayonet thrust, from which he died three days afterward. His brother-in-law arrived here day before yesterday from New York, expecting to carry his body back. His family reside in Lawrence Street, Brooklyn. Nothing to be done, we find on making inquiry at the consul-general's office. The great United States does nothing but exchange consular notes when an American is murdered in a foreign land. How different with the Britons! When young Ferguson was arrested at Manzanillo, the English consul there chartered and sent a sailing vessel to Nassau to inform the British commander there that a British subject was in danger. The result was that two British men-of-war were sent to Manzanillo to take Ferguson, either peaceably or forcibly. He was taken away. When the Spanish commander there hesitated to surrender him, the commander of the English frigate sent him word he must do so or he would bombard the city.

No. 128.

Mr. Hall to Mr. Davis.

No. 47.] HAVANA, *February* 5, 1870.

I am unable for want of time to give the department a full account of the events that have transpired here and at Matanzas during the past week, and since the news of the assassination of the editor of a paper of this city at Key West.

There have been popular demonstrations in many places, growing out of the affair at Key West on the 31st ultimo. At Matanzas these demonstrations culminated in a riot, in which, fortunately, no lives were lost. On the 2d instant a person by the name of Dr. Vicente Dawney, or Dauni, was shot in an affray with some volunteers at a coffee-house in the city. It is stated that he attempted to give his own version of the assassination, reflecting upon the conduct of the deceased Castañon. He arrived in the same steamer that brought the remains.

It is also said that Dauni was a citizen of the United States, although a native of this island; but I have not yet been able to obtain any positive evidence of the fact. The affair is now undergoing judicial investigation, the result of which will be communicated to me by the political secretary, to whom I have applied for information.

It is possible that there may be, as there have been on other occasions, efforts made to create the impression that the lives of American citizens are in jeopardy here. In my judgment, they are as well protected here at present as any other class; in fact, I do not remember that, at any time, there has been less evidence of jealousy or prejudice toward them, and it is to be hoped that nothing will occur to disturb the existing harmony.

By the earliest opportunity I shall communicate further to the department in reference to the affair at Key West.

No. 129.

Mr. Hall to Mr. Davis.

No. 52.] HAVANA, *February* 9, 1870.

Following upon the news received here of the disastrous retreat of General Puello from Guaimaro, which, with the elation of the Cubans, perhaps foolishly manifested, caused much excitement and bad feeling among the lowest and worst class of Peninsulares, was announced on the 31st ultimo by the cable that Don Gonzalo Castañon, editor of the Voz de Cuba, of this city, had been assassinated at Key West.

The news was communicated by several dispatches, among them one to the office of that paper, which was immediately published in the form of a handbill, and circulated all over the city. An impression was created that he had died a martyr, and all the excitable passions of the class referred to were directly appealed to.

On the 2d instant the funeral of the deceased Castañon was celebrated with great pomp, during which, and up to the 5th instant, everything had passed off much more quietly than was expected, and it was confidently hoped that order would continue.

But it would seem that in permitting and encouraging the demonstrations that have been made over the remains of the deceased Castañon, the authorities have unconsciously caused an excitement that they cannot control. They promise protection to all, native as well as foreign, and their earnest desire and anxiety to comply cannot be doubted; but their inability to protect the lives of peaceable inhabitants, or to punish the atrocities that are being daily committed, is evident.

It is probable that the present excitement will quiet down; but a similar one, with like results, may at any time be aroused by events that cannot be foreseen, and which the authorities will be found equally powerless to prevent.

At present there are none of our vessels of war in any of these ports, and, in view of the facts above recited, I beg leave to repeat the suggestion made in my No. 50 of the 7th instant, as the presence of national vessels may be needed for the purpose of offering a refuge to our citizens in the event of popular outbreaks, against which, as I before stated, there appears to be little security.

No. 130.

Mr. Hall to Mr. Davis.

No. 53.] HAVANA, *February* 11, 1870.

I have the honor to inclose herewith a copy of an interesting communication addressed to me from Matanzas, narrating the recent occurrences at that place, referred to in my despatch No. 47, of 5th instant.

MATANZAS, *February* 7, 1870.

I beg leave to report the following facts in connection with the disturbance which occurred in this city on the night of the 1st instant:

The killing of Don Gonzalo Castañon in Key West was known here, through the Havana papers, received on the morning of Tuesday the 1st instant, and naturally caused profound indignation. It was the topic of excited conversation during the day, and threats were uttered against many prominent Cubans. Nothing occurred, however, to disturb the public order, and the day passed without any incidents of importance.

At about six or seven o'clock in the evening the second battalion of volunteers, which had been occupying and protecting the Aldama estates for the past month, returned to the city, having been relieved by the third battalion. As usual, they were paraded through some of the principal streets, and were then dispersed to their respective houses. There was no demonstration beyond the accustomed "Vivas" to Spain, the Captain General, and the volunteers, and they separated in perfect order and quiet.

Notwithstanding the apparent tranquillity, a plan had been formed in the morning, so it is now said, to take from the jail during the night certain Cuban prisoners, who were held there under charges of having concealed weapons on their estates, and to put them to death in revenge for the murder of Castañon. I am convinced that if such a plan existed it was known to very few volunteers, as the subsequent results indicated a want of system and order in carrying out their intentions.

In the first part of the night nothing unusual occurred, and very few had any apprehensions of trouble or disturbance. The streets and plaza were frequented, and private houses, stores, and public buildings open, indicating either perfect ignorance or a sense of security.

At about 11½ o'clock the trumpets of the different battalions were heard, and afterward drums were beaten, and the calls sounded through the streets requiring the volunteers to come out and assemble. Nearly all did so.

The companies were formed at the usual places of rendezvous, and were then marched to the Plaza de Armas, where the battalions were formed. By 12½ o'clock almost the entire volunteer force of the city was under arms, and assembled in the plaza in front of the palace. Each company was commanded by its officers, and the battalions by their chiefs, so that the crowd had the semblance of organization, though there was no apparent uniformity of wish or purpose. It was evidently a demonstration set on foot by a few evil-disposed persons, and the majority of the volunteers had come out merely in answer to the call, and without knowing the object of their being brought together.

Assembled in front of the palace loud cries were at once raised, "Death to traitors," "Death to the prisoners," "To the jail," and similar cheers and violent shouts. The governor came down and met them in the portico of the palace, asking what they wanted and what they meant by such a disorderly proceeding and such violent language. One or two of the boldest came out then and told him openly, that they had come to demand the prisoners who were in jail, to shoot in revenge for the death of Castañon. He replied firmly that they could not have them; that the prisoners were charged with a crime against the state, that they would be tried by the proper tribunal, and if found guilty would be put to death; if innocent would be released. To this they replied with vile abuse directed against the governor and against their field and line officers, all of the former and most of the latter endeavoring to restrain the men and induce them to desist from their purpose.

The real commotion commenced at this time, and the rioters became frantic in their shouts and cries for vengeance, and in their vituperation and scandalous abuse of their officers; some twenty or thirty shots were fired into the air and threats were freely made against some prominent Cubans of the place. Maddened by the refusal by the governor to give up the prisoners, they sent ten men to the jail to force a way in, and subsequently sent some twenty more. These fellows presented themselves at the gate and demanded the keys, which were refused. The guards were turned out under arms and were ready to resist an entrance, which the rioters seemed determined to force, when the governor rode up with his staff and succeeded in allaying the excitement, sending the men back to the plaza.

This want of success still further influenced the volunteers, but they seemed to content themselves with seditious cries, and with hurling insults at their officers. Many shots were fired, some at private houses. Two balls entered the house of D. Ramon Binfau, breaking the stained glass over the windows, and the houses of D. Pablo Maria Gracia and D. Benigno Gener were fired into.

On the return of the governor from the jail he again harangued the assembled crowd, stating in plain terms that they were guilty of criminal disorder; that if Spain should ever lose the island of Cuba, it would be due to their excesses; that many of the disturbances that had occurred had been promoted by them, and that instead of a support to the government they were a continual source of anxiety from their unrestrained, lawless tendencies. Meantime, while these matters were going on at the plaza, the battalion of marines, two companies, were forming at the wharf, and the governor galloped down and addressed them a short speech, asking if they were disposed to assist him in the maintenance of order. A unanimous cry of "yes" was the response, and he at once marched them up to the plaza and formed them in line in front of the palace.

By this time the disorder had somewhat abated; the day was dawning, and an order was issued for a general review at eight a. m., in the Plaza de Vigia. The efforts of the officers began to have effect; the peaceable volunteers found that they were the victims of a lawless plot of the violent ones; and these latter saw themselves baffled in their schemes and had no other recourse but to yield.

The review was held, and the governor made an energetic and decided speech to the volunteers, repeating the substance of his previous remarks, and stating further that he intended chastising with the utmost rigor of the law the promoters and ringleaders of the riot, and called on the peaceable men to come forward and disclose to him the authors of the scandal.

During the above affair there were but sixty veteran soldiers in the place. These were in the barracks, and were kept under arms during the night, an extra supply of ammunition being issued and decided orders given for any emergency.

The conduct of the governor during the affair is deserving of high praise, and his determination and courage cannot be too highly eulogized.

After the review the troops dispersed and the trouble for the time ended.

In pursuance of his promise to seek out and punish the instigators of the riot, the governor on Friday night last arrested and placed in the Castillo de San Severino six individuals, who were especially prominent in the affair. On Sunday morning these men were carried, tied or in hand-cuffs, to Havana, and, I am told, were shipped to Spain by the steamer which sailed on that day.

This last proceeding has excited almost as much commotion as the previous one, except that in this instance the indignation is against the governor and the officers of police who executed the order. Last night rumors were rife that another demonstration was to take place, but the governor, apprized of the fact, called together the commanding officers of the volunteers and warned them against any disorderly proceeding, stating further that he had given orders that the battalion Napoles, now in Colon, should be ready to move, that a train was prepared for them, and that in three hours after the first symptoms of the trouble they would be under arms in the city of Matanzas.

The night passed without disturbance.

P. S.—The town is full of rumors. The volunteers are terribly excited against the governor and Ibañez, the chief of police. They say that to-night Ibañez is to be ousted; also, they say that the Napoles battalion will arrive in town to-night; also, that the six men who were arrested are coming back, and that they are to be feted; also, that they want to oust the governor; also, that a large number of telegraphic dispatches have passed to-day between the governor and the Captain General; also, that three men were killed in Havana to-day; also, that a number of Cubans have been killed in Key West, in an attempt to rescue the prisoners detained for the murder of Castañon.

And lastly, brings the news from Havana that they are talking of inviting Rodas to resign.

MATANZAS, *February* 8, 1870.

The volunteers last night at nine o'clock informally, and not in uniform, assembled in front of the palace, and required that the chief of police tender his resignation. He did so and it was, of course, accepted. There was no row, no violence nor trouble. Last night the governor had a double guard posted at the palace, and though the turn to do guard duty there fell to the first battalion, it was given to the marines. This excited a little comment, but nothing occurred. No veteran troops have arrived here. To-day the weather is stormy, but all else is quiet.

www.ingramcontent.com/pod-product-compliance
Lightning Source LLC
LaVergne TN
LVHW011219110826
845150LV00006B/1470

* 9 7 8 1 4 2 5 5 1 6 4 2 0 *